WHEN THE MEDIUM WAS THE MISSION

NORTH AMERICAN RELIGIONS

Series Editors: Tracy Fessenden (Religious Studies, Arizona State University), Laura Levitt (Religious Studies, Temple University), and David Harrington Watt (History, Haverford College)

In recent years a cadre of industrious, imaginative, and theoretically sophisticated scholars of religion have focused their attention on North America. As a result the field is far more subtle, expansive, and interdisciplinary than it was just two decades ago. The North American Religions series builds on this transformative momentum. Books in the series move among the discourses of ethnography, cultural analysis, and historical study to shed new light on a wide range of religious experiences, practices, and institutions. They explore topics such as lived religion, popular religious movements, religion and social power, religion and cultural reproduction, and the relationship between secular and religious institutions and practices. The series focuses primarily, but not exclusively, on religion in the United States in the twentieth and twenty-first centuries.

Books in the Series:

Ava Chamberlain, *The Notorious Elizabeth Tuttle: Marriage, Murder, and Madness in the Family of Jonathan Edwards*

Terry Rey and Alex Stepick, *Crossing the Water and Keeping the Faith: Haitian Religion in Miami*

Jodi Eichler-Levine, *Suffer the Little Children: Uses of the Past in Jewish and African American Children's Literature*

Isaac Weiner, *Religion Out Loud: Religious Sound, Public Space, and American Pluralism*

Hillary Kaell, *Walking Where Jesus Walked: American Christians and Holy Land Pilgrimage*

Brett Hendrickson, *Border Medicine: A Transcultural History of Mexican American Curanderismo*

Annie Blazer, *Playing for God: Evangelical Women and the Unintended Consequences of Sports Ministry*

Elizabeth Pérez, *Religion in the Kitchen: Cooking, Talking, and the Making of Black Atlantic Traditions*

When the Medium Was the Mission

The Atlantic Telegraph and the Religious Origins
of Network Culture

Jenna Supp-Montgomerie

NEW YORK UNIVERSITY PRESS
New York

NEW YORK UNIVERSITY PRESS
New York
www.nyupress.org

References to Internet websites (URLs) were accurate at the time of writing. Neither the author nor New York University Press is responsible for URLs that may have expired or changed since the manuscript was prepared.

Cataloging-in-Publication data is available from the publisher.

Library of Congress Cataloging-in-Publication Data
Names: Supp-Montgomerie, Jenna, author.
Title: When the medium was the mission : the Atlantic telegraph and the religious origins of network culture / Jenna Supp-Montgomerie.
Description: New York : New York University Press, 2021. | Series: North American religions | Includes bibliographical references and index.
Identifiers: LCCN 2020015034 | ISBN 9781479801480 (cloth) | ISBN 9781479801497 (paperback) | ISBN 9781479801503 (ebook) | ISBN 9781479801527 (ebook)
Subjects: LCSH: Church and mass media—History. | Protestantism. | Atlantic Telegraph Company (Limited)
Classification: LCC BV652.95 .S87 2021 | DDC 261.5/209—dc23
LC record available at https://lccn.loc.gov/2020015034

New York University Press books are printed on acid-free paper, and their binding materials are chosen for strength and durability. We strive to use environmentally responsible suppliers and materials to the greatest extent possible in publishing our books.

Manufactured in the United States of America

10 9 8 7 6 5 4 3 2 1

Also available as an ebook

This book is for my mother, Katrin Tiitsman, whose life and love are sure signs of the wonders that have come across the Atlantic and whose deep courage is a constant reminder that fracture and fullness are not opposed.

And this book is for David Supp-Montgomerie, my steady miracle, who has made impossible dreams for what life could be come true.

CONTENTS

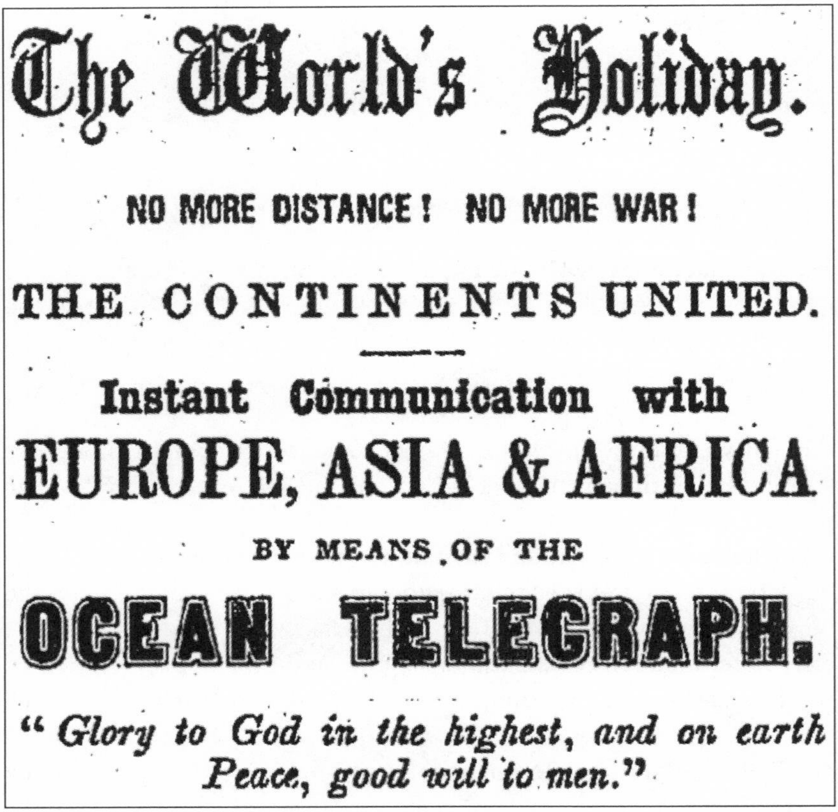

The World's Holiday.

NO MORE DISTANCE! NO MORE WAR!

THE CONTINENTS UNITED.

Instant Communication with

EUROPE, ASIA & AFRICA

BY MEANS OF THE

OCEAN TELEGRAPH.

"Glory to God in the highest, and on earth Peace, good will to men."

Figure P.1. "The World's Holiday," *Circular*, August 12, 1858. (ProQuest American Periodical Series)

PREFACE

This book investigates the way religion has shaped media, engendering grand hopes of worldwide unity, and its legacy in obscuring the important activity of disconnection, without which networks could not operate. It brings insights from religious studies and media studies to bear on how we understand networks and their imagined promise of connection. Early in the life of this project, I set out to make sense of what I understood as media studies' peculiar disciplinary obsession with the telegraph. (Beware the siren song of the telegraph—it will capture the least suspecting.) I turned to historical newspapers hoping that by making sense of why the telegraph felt exciting when it emerged as a new technology, I could make sense of why this obsolete technology appeared to be so exciting to scholars now. I came across a strange headline about the Atlantic Telegraph Cable of 1858 that enthusiastically announced in robust capitals, "The World's Holiday. NO MORE DISTANCE! NO MORE WAR! . . . *Glory to God in the Highest.*"[1]

This struck me as odd for many reasons. First, it seemed a rather wild celebration of media infrastructure. How quaint, even laughably optimistic. A world's holiday for a telegraph line? I could not imagine even a local celebration for a new highway or an internet cable. And, yet, at the same time this seemed eerily like the declarations about the internet in the mid-oughts as a new technology that would topple dictatorships, eradicate poverty, equalize the world, and finally and truly realize free speech on a global scale. This utterly nineteenth-century moment was uncomfortably like but not quite like today. Celebratory US Americans in the nineteenth century shared a set of beliefs in network media we still value but were attentive to materiality in ways we are not. We are convinced by the promises of "cloud" computing and ubiquitous, ethereal cell access such that I often feel compelled to show pictures of subterranean internet cables to convince colleagues that all of our communication is not simply bounding about in the air.

Second, these declarations of the new global village were grounded in a religious discourse that I would not expect to see coupled to technology. So many myths of secularism—the opposition of science and religion, the retreat of religion once mediated publics emerged, the death of divinity in the face of globalization—wilt in this unabashed alignment of Christianity and telegraphy. Stranger still, it turned out that this headline of planetary proportions was issued by a small newspaper from a religious experiment in communal living that was a necessarily local venture. Among the many distinctive practices of the Oneida Community, the most famous and most scandalous was the "complex marriage" of all of the women to all of the men and vice versa (there were about three hundred members in the community's heyday). Their determined rejection of monogamy required a large mansion house with multiple single bedrooms and a large common room where they hashed out the complications that necessarily arose. So why were they so fascinated by telegraphy as a *global* project? And, given that they were so profoundly different from the world around them, a fact they reveled in, how did they become so like the rest of the country in this one particular way: the effusive celebration of the Atlantic Telegraph Cable of 1858?

Third, the cable subject to these hyperbolic celebrations fell apart in less than one month. And, as it turns out, cabled networks fail all the time. The vast majority of telegraph lines in the nineteenth century did not work; fracture was part of the network. And yet networks continue to be imagined as *connective* media, so much so that we have trouble thinking of networks in terms of the disconnection they actually rely on. Consider for a moment the way participation in digital networks depends on firewalls, passwords, out-of-office messages, and the delicate art of unfollowing. Historically speaking, networks would not exist without all the disconnection that went into their establishment. So why did US Americans then and why do US Americans now consider networks to be primarily, sometimes exclusively, connective?

Thus began a meandering research project that landed me in communal utopias and missionary outposts and, ultimately, under the sea. My hope is that the answers I have found in these diverse places will make a useful contribution to those who study religion, those who study media, and certainly those who study the way each is integral to the other. First and foremost, this book joins the robust conversation of the field of religion and media: its attention to the fundamental entanglement of religion and media aims to add a new perspective to canonical scholarship that has concerned itself with central questions of what happens when religions take up media or appear in mediated forms. I am concerned with the way religion has shaped media in its most material, infrastructural, and imaginative incarnations. This book also joins recent scholarship in American religions that pays particular attention to the mundane, material, and lived expressions of religion, particularly as a sustaining element of US public life. The diffusion of public Protestantism that emerged in the nineteenth century is, as this volume argues, one of the central techniques that have made networks meaningful to us today.

My orientation to the telegraph takes its cue from media theorist John Durham Peters (and his Canadian and German predecessors) to think of media "not only as the channels and institutions that propagate messages and symbols, but also as elemental techniques that organize time, space, and power."[2] The telegraph and certainly the faulty 1858 cable that preoccupies this book are not notable here for their ability to transmit messages. They are, rather, notable for making worlds out of fiction and having those worlds become persistent and durable even if resolutely impossible.

Introduction

The Divine Destiny of the Shrinking Planet

The first time in the United States that words publicly traveled faster than an animal and farther than a line of sight was attributed to God and sent from the chambers of the Supreme Court. This strange confluence of media, religion, and US nationhood lies at the foundation of global networks.

Samuel Morse, largely funded by the US government, success-fully sent the first public long-distance electric telegram in the United States in 1844 from Washington, DC, to Baltimore, Maryland.[1] It read, "What hath God wrought," and was answered in echo, "What hath God wrought." The first telegrams were more liturgy than information, more ritual than transmission of content. The circular conversation turned to greetings and the weather, but the religious communication that started it all reverberates in various ways through a network that has crept around the world, morphed from copper cable to fiber optics, and negotiated a dynamic set of cultural conditions that we might now refer to as globalization. Religious actors put telegraph technology in place around the world, religious language described this new mode of global communication, religious imaginaries governed what the worldwide telegraph network would become, and religious forms of communica-tion indelibly marked the idiomatic conventions of networks. Network culture has a surprisingly religious origin.

That liturgical echo of 1844 is harder to hear today in a country that celebrates the internet in an assumed secular frame. For many US Amer-icans, the advances of science and technology appear to have displaced the old influence of religion; the digital age seems to offer new ways of being human together that render divine intervention obsolete. In 1997, at the height of the first wave of the internet's popularization, MCI declared its ownership of the world's largest internet network in an ad that promised a space that had no race, no genders, no age, and no infirmities. "Utopia?" the ad asks. "No. The Internet."[2] Just a few years later, more than half of US households had internet access, and excitement reigned for the new releases of Facebook, YouTube, and Gmail. Riding high on this wave of techno-utopianism, Thomas Friedman's best seller *The World Is Flat: A Brief History of the Twenty-First Century* (2005) declared that the world we live in is "shrinking . . . from a size small to a size tiny and flattening the playing field at the same time," caused by "the creation of a global fiber-optic network that has made us all next-door neighbors."[3]

Despite the waves of violence that rocked the planet in the first years of the twenty-first century, belief in the internet's capacity to connect the world persisted. As part of a defense of file-sharing sites in 2010, the hacktivist collective Anonymous launched a series of internet attacks to shut down the website of the Recording Industry Association of America. A media kit released by Anonymous affiliated file sharing with a much broader sense of communitarian practice: "Anonymous is tired of corporate interests controlling the internet and silencing the people's rights to spread information, but more importantly, the right to SHARE with one another."[4] As this book demonstrates, however, there is nothing new about the myth that a shrinking planet and worldwide connection are the direct result of networks. Nor is there anything new about a vibrant imaginary of network connection that makes use of the regularity of disconnection (in the technology, by geography, from each other) to shape and sustain those very networks. One hundred fifty years before these exuberant claims, in far more overtly religious language, US Americans were enthusiastically celebrating a world they declared suddenly united by a much earlier network medium: the telegraph.

This book traces the shaping influence of religion—particularly US American Protestantism—on network culture through the story of the 1858 Atlantic Telegraph Cable. In the middle of the nineteenth century, this medium was emphatically the mission of a motley crew of US Americans: Protestant missionaries who hoped new technology would "civilize" non-Protestants, public figures who used the telegraph to establish an implicitly Christian national culture, utopianists who understood this new technology to herald the advent of global and divine accord, and all the many who passionately believed the cable would connect the world.[5]

People acting in the name of religion—from US Protestant missionaries to the Ottoman sultan—spread Morse's telegraph machine around the world and linked the telegraph to an emerging discourse of global unity. Christian tropes infused enthusiasm into fantastical public discourse about the telegraph's capacity to connect. New religious communities in the United States indelibly affiliated networks with promises of perfect harmony. And Protestant-inflected religious affect charged essentially meaningless signals with profound cultural significance. In all of these activities, religion—especially US Protestantism—forged an imaginary of networks as connective, so much so that we broadly define networks as systems of connection.[6]

This book tells the story of the establishment of the imaginary that networks connect and then traces the failures of networks to do just that. While religion shaped the fundamental promise of connection affiliated with networks, religion also participated in the disconnections that riddled telegraph technology, the many ways in which disconnection structured social life, the imperative of impossibility in utopian imaginaries, and the constitutive failures of communication. Religion thus helped to create the defining characteristic of network culture: an imaginary of connection paired with practices and technologies that rely on disconnection. Because of the power of this imaginary, fueled in no small part by the power of religion, disconnection both is utterly standard to network use and function and always appears as a scandal. While disconnection is integral to networks and our daily engagement with them, it seems to violate their fundamental purpose. In other words, network disconnections always appear problematic not because they disrupt networks (networks expect and even rely on them) but because they disrupt the religiously empowered myth that networks connect.

Just fourteen years after Morse's first public telegram, on August 5, 1858, the Atlantic Telegraph Cable was successfully laid across the ocean from the west coast of Ireland to Newfoundland.[7] Claims that this new medium for intercontinental communication would unite the world took the United States by storm. In a telegram sent on the cable, President James Buchanan declared that through the Atlantic telegraph "the nations of Christendom [would] spontaneously unite."[8] The American Board of Commissioners for Foreign Missions (ABCFM), the primary engine of nineteenth-century US American Christian mission activities,

Figure I.1. The Atlantic Telegraph Jubilee on September 1, 1858, New York. (The J. Paul Getty Museum, Los Angeles)

declared that the Atlantic telegraph clearly indicated God's support for its work to Christianize the globe, since it had brought Japan, China, and Africa "to our doors."[9] A headline in the newspaper of the Oneida Community, a new religious movement of Christian communists, proclaimed, "NO MORE DISTANCE! NO MORE WAR! THE CONTINENTS UNITED. Instant Communication with EUROPE, ASIA, & AFRICA BY MEANS OF THE OCEAN TELEGRAPH."[10] Across the young nation, US Americans extolled the cable that they claimed heralded a new shape to the world: wire-powered global Christian unity.

It may not be surprising to find such utopian declarations issued from the ABCFM, an organization dedicated to converting the world to Christianity, or from the Oneida Community, a utopian Christian community founded on the assertion that moral perfection was possible in the members' lifetime. But scores of US Americans marked the middle of the nineteenth century with impassioned celebrations of a shrinking planet. On September 1, 1858, cities across the young nation held "jubilees" for the Atlantic Telegraph Cable. A parade for Cyrus W. Field, the cable's mastermind, swept up Broadway to Forty-Second Street in New York City, while one hundred miles south the Honorable William D. Kelley, judge of the Philadelphia County Court of Common Pleas and a founder of the Republican Party, rose to give the oration at the

Philadelphia jubilee. "What is the event we celebrate?" he asked. "One which has made the whole earth vocal. . . . It has not destroyed or obliterated space; it has not dried up oceans: and yet it has brought the nations of the earth face to face, that they may enter into social converse."[11] The Atlantic cable, according to Kelley, was God's "last great blessing" given to the world to be accomplished by humankind at God's directive.[12] This nineteenth-century US form of globalization promised a planet unified by communication technology in terms strikingly similar to Friedman's later claim that fiber optics have flattened the world. But in this earlier context, before the narratives of secularism reigned, we find US religion more overtly hard at work offering imagery, vocabulary, structure, and power to the persistent myth that networks are media of connection.

These national celebrations of network media are uncanny for many reasons but particularly so because this mid-nineteenth-century excitement over a newly united global humanity diverged dramatically from the reality that most of these celebrants experienced: this America—despite its claims of nascent global peace—was embroiled in wars between Native Americans and the US Army; Kansas was in its third year of bloody conflict over slavery; the Civil War loomed; and colonial and anticolonial violence rocked the world.[13] God's last great blessing was falling short. In fact, as Justice Kelley closed his address at the Philadelphia jubilee and sat down amid "vociferous applause" (duly noted by the enthusiastic phonographer), the Atlantic cable itself was failing. While Cyrus Field was feasting at the banquet thrown to hail his radical success, he received one of the last messages that would pass over those oceanic wires, but it was too garbled to be deciphered. It was later discovered that the cable was riddled with faults, including manufacturing errors, breaks in the internal wire, unsuccessful splices, insulation degraded by time in storage, and leaks caused by the high voltage used to power messages across the Atlantic. That evening, twenty-three days after the first transatlantic telegraph message was received, the signal failed permanently. This first successful attempt at crossing the Atlantic with a medium for electric communication—lauded as an instrument of God, the unifier of humanity, and a guarantee for a lasting global peace—lasted for less than one month. Not until 1866, after Field had regained the faith of investors, after new cables were manufactured, and after the American Civil War had passed, was an Atlantic cable successfully laid again.

The connected, peaceful, vocal world that US Americans imagined in the middle of the nineteenth century was a fiction, but one with real and lasting effects. The shrinking telegraphic planet did not reflect the reality of new communication technology, nor did it portend newfound global political or religious agreement. Rather, it indicated an important, new, and persistent way of building, imagining, and inhabiting the world as connected by network media, even as that world faced acute failures of both network technologies and the attendant promises of unity. Networks were always first and foremost imaginaries, and imaginaries must not be understood as descriptions; as descriptions, network imaginaries failed a violent, disconnected world quite dramatically. Imaginaries are best understood, rather, as enactments. *Enact* bears the double meaning of "to perform" and "to make into law": these network imaginaries were performed in ways that instituted particular forms of social and material life. Similar to how laws are enacted, this imaginary instituted a world through acts of declaration, and similar to how plays are enacted, this imaginary functioned through performances of it. Media historian Lisa Gitelman's study of the phonograph illustrates the ways in which "extrinsic" forces retroactively appear as "intrinsic technological logic."[14] Likewise, the very factors that we now understand as the affordances of networks were built through religion, politics, and matter and only later understood to be inherent to network media.

Once, when I was running headlong into a protracted research project on images of Jesus Christ in US cinema, a wise mentor told me that if you are looking for religion in the United States, every guy with his arms outstretched appears to be crucified. There is a danger to studies that simply notice appearances of religion, because religion appears to be everywhere in the United States. Sometimes those are legitimate appearances, and sometimes those are effects of religion's power to assimilate symbols, to turn every pair of perpendicular lines into a cross. In this case, however, the appearances of religion matter not simply for the fact of religion's presence (always a surprise in a culture invested in its own secularism) but because they can tell us something important about what religion is, what media are, how networks function, and how networks have participated in globalization. Rather than simply noticing religious motifs, this book delves into discursive and material culture to map the effects of diverse forms of highly contextual religion on the

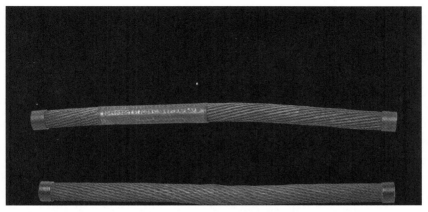

Figure I.2. Sample of the first transatlantic cable, manufactured by Glass, Elliot and Company, England, 1857–58. (The Science Museum Group)

technological, social, utopian, and communicative aspects of networks in the nineteenth century, taking each of these aspects as the topic of a chapter. This book does not offer a comprehensive narrative of network or religious history; by locating itself at the site of their entanglement, it refuses the bird's-eye view. Nor is it a story of the heroes of the telegraph (such as Cyrus Field and Samuel Morse) who traditionally feature at the heart of such studies; attending to the agency of public discourse, matter, religion, and affect rejects the idea that men with lofty intentions controlled what happened as networks took shape. This book articulates archival research, critical theory, and cultural history to offer a media archaeology of networks that corrects a long-standing myopia around religion.

The 1858 Atlantic Telegraph Cable, still disintegrating at the bottom of the ocean, is the anchor of this book. It may seem a strange choice to focus on a (quite literally) profound failure, especially given that the next major attempt in 1866 succeeded and transoceanic cables subsequently multiplied into the internet today, with 223 international underwater cable systems transmitting 99 percent of all digital data that cross the ocean.[15] A study of networks as connective media that emerge from a history of innovation and progress would be better served by beginning the story with later cables and their more durable inauguration of electric communication across the Atlantic. But this study is not a story of progress or victory. Dragging the 1858 cable into view with its rusting aura of divine destiny makes plain the complicated mix of grand success and tremendous failure that animate networks and the similarly ruptured forms of globalization in which they participate. The fundamental disconnections at the origins of cabled networks were not overcome by later developments in network technology; disconnections were for the most part simply better integrated into the functioning of networks and better obscured by increasingly adamant imaginaries of connection.

This book attends to religion at the origins of networks, particularly in the empowerment of an imaginary of connection in the face of perpetual disconnections. The intimacy of religion and media acts as a frame for a deeper dive into the central terms of this study: *religion*, *network*, and *disconnection*. Some definitional clarity around each will highlight why the relationship among them matters to all sorts of networks and their attendant forms of social life, then and now.

Religion as Media/Media as Religion

While networks have been studied as effects of technology, harbingers of globalization, and modes of social life, no description of network media is complete without attention to the role of religion. The entanglement of religion and media has been overlooked or misunderstood by those who assume that technology is merely instrumental, that religion is primarily about belief, and that religion and media only collide in terms of representations of religion in media or uses of media by religious people. But, as this book shows, religion and media were interacting in all sorts of material, cultural, and political ways that defied human intention, broke with traditions of dogma, and demonstrated that the dynamic relationships of religion and media matter—far outside the terms of representation or use—in ways that have marked the earth and shaped our inhabitation of it. The religious origins of network culture epitomize the assertion by founding scholar of religion and media Stewart Hoover that media and religion "occupy the same spaces, serve many of the same purposes, and invigorate the same practices."[16]

Understanding the vital role of religion as part of media infrastructure upends a common distinction between religion and media. As religion and media scholar Jeremy Stolow powerfully frames it in his now-canonical review essay about the field, *religion and media* is a pleonasm: religion is always mediated, and media is always religious.[17] There is no way to talk about or engage in religion without also talking about or engaging with media, whether stone tablets, voice, drum, burning bush, or book. If we take media to mean modes of communication, religion in any form entails media. Studies of religion *as* media, as Stolow terms it, have helped to orient our attention to the messy material lives of religion, to the frictions of religious communication, and to the ordinary ways in which religion is practiced.

According to Stolow, the inverse is also true: media are, by definition, religious. "Every medium necessarily participates in the realm of the transcendent, if nothing else than by its inability to be fully subject to the instrumental intentions of its users."[18] Less attention has been paid to this second half of his formulation—media as religion—and this study supplements that perspective. I take up Stolow's call for scholarship that starts with the unavoidable relationship of religion and media. Cabled networks came into being through religious actors, tropes, affects, imaginaries, and logics, and those religious affiliations durably shaped where networks were, how they worked, and what they became.

There can be no exhaustive account of all the elements that are active in or essential to any given network, or to any instance of religion, for that matter. These terms share a semantic territory for which attempts to create definitive boundaries always end in failure. Quite a pickle, then: the very terms I am using to explain what makes up this conjuncture are themselves just as slippery as the thing they compose. They share that, at least. And this: these are both terms that were birthed in particular conditions and imposed on processes and things retroactively in ways that brought the very elements they named into being, thereby embodying and establishing distinct cultural and material relationships. In that sense, they form what feminist theorist Karen Barad calls an entanglement: the dynamic set of relationships that brings the agencies it comprises into being.[19] Religion and network do not preexist this relationship and simply arrive into this particular assemblage; rather, any definitional identity that each term forges emerges only from its entanglement with the other. This is the argument at stake: networks and religion are inextricably bound up in each other, and their entanglement offers an essentially hidden role to the disconnections that network life relies on. Teasing each element out for a moment is an exercise poised at the verge of collapse. Taking up each of these elements—in ways that embrace that precarity, without any pretense at comprehensiveness—will help explain how they constitute each other.

Religion

While religious studies scholars have worked hard to shrug off the old definition of religion as a system of belief, the coupling of religion with belief or even systematicity in general (as embodied by institutions, moral codes, identities) has a tenacious hold on our imaginings of religious life. Religious studies scholar Winnifred Sullivan points to the powerfully persistent sense of religion as "private, voluntary, individual, textual, and believed," which is so deeply entrenched in its Protestant origins and simultaneously so diffusely present in US public life that it rarely reads as particularly Protestant.[20] Sullivan demotes the first letter of *protestantism* to signal its ubiquity in the United States.[21] The shaping of religion-in-general into a protestant form masks many of the most potent aspects of religion in the United States: the ways in which religion is public, compulsory, unintentional, material, and practiced in everyday life.

The religion at work in networks bears these characteristics, especially religion's relationship to media in its most material forms, the work religion does to shape and anchor US public culture, the persuasiveness of religion's most powerful fictions, and the many ways religion produces and sabotages communication. A broadened definition of religion to include not just institutions, identities, and beliefs but also matter, processes, logics, affect, and discourse allows us to trace the vitality of religion as part and parcel of network infrastructure and make sense of the strange ways in which religion helped to produce the pairing of myths of connection to processes of disconnection that is so necessary for networks to come into being.

This is not to say that religious beliefs and the ways in which religion made meaning in the nineteenth century did not matter to networks. Religion's function, psychoanalyst Jacques Lacan once declared, is to "find correspondences between everything and everything else."[22]

Taking his hyperbole with a much-needed grain of salt, we might say that one of religion's capacities is to create meaning in social life by forging complex webs of associations. Religion provides a storehouse of images, vocabularies, structures, and logics that objects take up. Because these resources carry the hefty weight of the emotional, material, and intellectual investment in religion as a body of meaning, they not only provide a set of meanings and attendant associations but also weight those meanings such that they become culturally significant. In the most obvious form, religion assimilates certain symbols so that their meaning is understood as primarily religious (a cross, a six-pointed star, etc.). Yet religion is also hard at work in other, less expected areas of life in the United States.

In the case of the transatlantic telegraph, a diverse community—from Protestant missionaries to civic leaders—spoke of the newly united world that electric speech would create in explicitly Christian terms. President Buchanan called the telegraph "an instrument destined by Divine Providence to diffuse religion, civilization, liberty, and law throughout the world."[23] Missionary documents described the telegraph as the "opportunity" that would finally allow missions to establish "a living Christianity everywhere."[24] These statements are not merely religious ways of speaking about the telegraph; the affective weight borne by this Christian vocabulary and imagery forged the affiliation of the telegraph with nascent forms of US identity as expansionist, dreams of global community as Christian, hopes for a very particular (Christian and US) future, and illusions of the divinely sanctioned power of perfect communication.

An account of religion as part of infrastructure extends beyond institutions and their demands—particularly systematic belief—and into the territory of everyday life. Religious people rarely act completely in accordance with the major doctrinal or ritual markers of any religion; they are tactical creatures who find creative paths through landscapes textured by plural religions.[25] Because religion is not decreed but lived, it is thus always somewhat fractured and incoherent. Even in its infrastructural manifestation, which one might think lends itself to logical grids, religion cannot be considered systematic. While there are strong patterns and habits of religious action at work in the origins of networks, there was rarely any true coherence. And the networks that religion helped produce likewise bear signs of their disjointed and uneven construction. Religious imaginaries defied experience, promising peace on the brink of war and ushering in an era of "unity" on the backs of those people who were adamantly excluded from so-called civilization. Electricity appeared to induce reverence for God while defying working understandings of natural law. The fact that Bible Communists practiced free love long before that slogan reappeared for hippies—in fact, long before women commonly showed their ankles—cannot be explained through any direct lines of cause and effect. Religion as infrastructure directs our attention to religion in its most chaotic appearances, grounding the vicissitudes of everyday life.

And religious *people* are not the only act in town. Taking infrastructural religion seriously also means taking the activity of nonhuman actors seriously: books, trees, symbols, bells, shofars, loudspeakers.[26] Religion in this case cannot be restricted to human activity. Once religion became embedded in networks, it took on a life in wires, electricity, and cables. The pathways of the cables were (and are) religious; they mapped places of colonial-religious importance and routes that mattered to colonial-religious actors, both those advocating for colonialism and those resisting it. All of the many material actants involved in religion, including humans, tended to do things in ways that embody what philosopher of science Bruno Latour names the "slight surprise of action," that propensity of action to exceed intention.[27] While US missionaries endorsed and spread certain technologies, those technologies acted without intention and had no regard for the structuring beliefs about them or the world around. For example, while Christian missionaries promoted Morse's telegraph in the Ottoman Empire to Christianize the land and Muslim officials there advocated for an Ottoman telegraph network as a way to cohere the empire under the sultan, the telegraph surprised both groups. In its ability to speed complaints to the government and its own attachments to other imaginaries of modernity, the telegraph network became a primary agent in the dissolution of the empire and the establishment of a secular nation-state.

In the United States, the wily nature of religion takes a very particular form because religion not only eludes systematic characterization but is embedded deep in the foundation of national culture in those diffuse and fractured ways. The old story of Western modernity goes like this:

once print afforded the emergence of public discourse, media, science, and technology elbowed out religion as a shaping cultural force. Yet it is often in the very media that frame modern public culture that we find religion most active. The now-classic formula of linking the European printing press to the emergence of modern publics takes the proliferating Bibles and tracts of the Reformation as necessary participants.[28] As scholar of US religion Tracy Fessenden amply demonstrates in her examination of *The New England Primer* in the colonial United States, the establishment of US English and literacy was profoundly intertwined with resolute efforts to build a distinctly US culture on the foundation of Protestantism.[29] Likewise, the establishment of a broad reading public in the antebellum United States owed much to the literary and publishing efforts of Protestant religious leaders and their various moral causes.[30] When secularism emerged as a viable name for US culture, it was already protestant in nature.

To be clear, as much as the story of US secularism is the story of a triumphant, if often hidden, protestantism, it is always also the story of all the many other religions at play. Colonial discourse was as much anti-Catholic as it was Protestant dogma, as much anti-indigenous as it was pro-white.[31] Thus, the story of (protestant) secularism is also necessarily the story of the wide religious diversity of the North Atlantic world. It includes the North African roots of Christianity (e.g., Augustine); the internally diverse Islam, Judaism, Yoruba, and many other often-unclassified religions that coexisted with and shaped Protestantism; and the many ways protestant secularism became what it did in complicated power-rich relationships with these colonial "others."[32] Protestantism in any form but especially the diffuse public form under study here was never just Protestantism in and of itself; it was always a fluxing, negotiated, diverse, power-ridden set of plural discourses, identities, relationships, and ways of life.

In many ways this book is about a quintessentially US phenomenon: the upstart nation building dreams of global community on a single frail line, assuming that utopian vision could overcome political fracture and material failure, believing that the investment of enthusiasm could make this cable the United States' entrance into the world at large despite the fact that the cable ran from Ireland to Newfoundland, and throwing mountains of money at a nearly impossible project that would ultimately

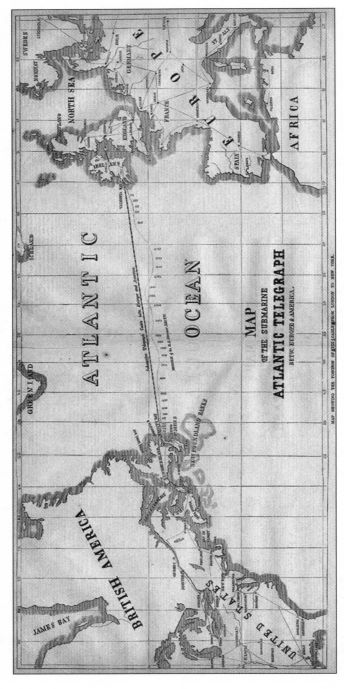

Figure I.3. "Map Showing the Position of the Cable from London to New York," *Frank Leslie's Illustrated Newspaper*, August 21, 1858. (Accessible Archives)

molder undersea. It was a US story of valiant effort to overcome impossibility with a heady combination of divine destiny, the momentum of progress, wild enthusiasm, and an adamant disregard for reality. But, at the same time, the idea of anything "quintessentially US" is itself a fantasy. The nascent country—like any country—never did anything coherently, and everything distinctive about it could be found elsewhere in other forms. The focus on the United States here brings certain elements into relief not as unique in the world but as a particular articulation that enabled religion and telegraphs—and ultimately networks as a whole—to do specific things for a specific group of people.

Janet R. Jakobsen and Ann Pellegrini's edited volume *Secularisms* makes this vividly clear: US protestant secularism is one secularism among many.[33] Rather than couching the nineteenth century in terms of the emergence of a mediated public sphere free of the influence of religion, it is a more useful periodization when regarded as the site of emergence for a particular relationship of religion and media. Under the condition of enthusiasm for scientific discovery and the surging creativity of religious movements in the wake of the Great Awakenings, religious ways of living and thinking were both deeply influential on burgeoning network media and increasingly buried under the very webs they wove. Thus, we have retained the strong sense of the universal value of networks articulated by Justice William Kelley at the laying of the 1858 Atlantic cable ("no event has occurred which is to work so large an influence upon nations and people, upon the social, political, commercial and economical relations of mankind—no event, the influence of which is to be so far-reaching, or so all-pervading") while adamantly forgetting that such universal imaginaries were written with Christian vocabulary and affective power ("To whom shall be ascribed the glory of this great event? Not unto us, not unto any man, not [unto] any nation of men, but unto the Great Omnipotent One").[34] Religion helped make networks what they were and what they were imagined to be in ways that are so ingrained that its influence has become nearly invisible today.

But, as with the religion that undergirds secularism, it is best not to confuse invisibility with powerlessness. The religious roots of media are deep, and the religious roots of scholarship on media are deeply shaping of what we understand communication to be. Many of the field-establishing scholars of media are only able to describe media as such or communication more broadly through religion: Harold Innis, Marshall McLuhan, Lewis Mumford, and Walter Ong all developed narratives of media informed by their preoccupations with religion; James Carey attributes both ritual and transmission communication to religious origins; Friedrich Kittler intersperses discussions of media theory with biblical exegesis; and John Durham Peters tells us that "communication is unthinkable apart from the task of establishing a peaceable kingdom in which each may dwell with the other."[35] In colloquial discourses of media, the deep influence of religion is buried under our assumptions that media are intrinsically secular, and the metaphors religion birthed are literalized in ways that obscure their influence, but religion remains powerfully entangled with media in general and networks in particular. To see it, we must turn to the nineteenth century, when the public nature of religion was more overt, religious actors more obvious, and the structure of the relationship of religion and media more available to us.

Religion in this volume thus describes the confluence of discourses, logics, institutions, identities, habits, practices, matter, and affect that was borne by and orbited social groups that instituted themselves through religious histories and traditions. These histories are significantly marked by protestantism and its development and dominance in the United States.

Network

At the advent of global telegraphy, US Americans articulated the public image of a world connected by communication cables in newspapers, religious communities, celebratory speeches, missionary reports, and telegrams. Other global imaginaries existed, such as the Britons' vision of their own sunlit empire, and there were certainly alternative ways of inhabiting cabled land, such as strategic cable sabotage by Sioux.[36] But the world connected by communication infrastructure was a dominant imaginary in the United States, and it remains so.

The mid-nineteenth century in the United States was, in many ways, the age of infrastructure. Enthusiasm for infrastructure was equated with enthusiasm for the United States that was being built through new modes of communication and transportation and for the relationships the United States might forge with the rest of the world. This was the era of the rise of railroads, telegraphy, and electric and gas lines for lighting. It was a time marked by the attempts to weave a nation together through the Civil War in which the grapevine telegraph, Underground Railroad, and electromagnetic telegraph were key participants. New mobility within the United States contributed to the establishment of towns on the moving frontier, which brought the politics of religion and infrastructure to the fore. The violent incursion into the homeland of indigenous peoples, over which the telegraph and railroad rode roughshod, led to the development of and resistance to the reservation system.[37] Modern industry and science, put to work building transportation and communication infrastructure, spurred "an information explosion."[38] This, along with the resultant effects of the movement of humans and their diseases around the world, catalyzed the establishment of systems of classification of all sorts, on which infrastructures ultimately depend.[39] Although these technologies and the social life that would be affiliated with them were not yet called networks, the mid-nineteenth century was a critical epoch in the establishment of networks and the popularization of a set of definitions for them. This book contends that this time preceding the colloquial use of *network* can tell us much about the meanings, practices, protocols, promises, and politics of networks by revealing the cultural labor that went into producing them.

A network is a form of technological and social life organized around multiple links among a set of nodes. In the most straightforward colloquial definition, a network is a system of connections. This book is largely an effort at redefinition, in order to foreground that such systems of connection have always also involved—and been sustained by—various forms of disconnection. That is, first and foremost, network is a *form*: a particular way of building, describing, and imagining an entity that attributes it with particular shapes, patterns, or structures.[40] We identify certain social and material processes with *connection* and imbue that attention to connection with the heavy affective weight *network* has accrued (in part, through religious power) as the dominant imaginary of communication since the nineteenth century. But what we call networks did not emerge naturally as such.

The term *network* became popularized in the nineteenth century. According to historian of science Laura Otis, engineers, neuroscientists, and novelists all used the metaphor of networks. Otis points to the convergence of experiments to animate dead frogs with jolts of electricity, the construction of multiply intersecting rail and telegraph lines, and the frame of social systems in George Eliot's *Middlemarch*, all of which were described as networks. That the dominant structure in these disparate disciplines was a network was not a result of the coincidental discoveries of electricity, telegraphy, neurology, and so forth. Rather, Otis argues, the power of network as a metaphor fueled these discoveries.[41] This is metaphor's clout; metaphors draw disparate ideas together in powerful constellations that organize discursive fields.[42] Neuroscientists and engineers recognized electricity as the agent for both neural systems and telegraphy. The material form of the telegraph emerged from the analogy with nerves, and emergent understandings of nerves were profoundly shaped by the telegraph system. *Network* pulled aspects of each field together in its capacious embrace and, in so doing, shaped not only the way such systems were described but also how they were understood and built.

Otis's study offers an important correction to the illusion that networks were birthed in nature and simply translated to technology. Networks are not the natural—let alone the only—way to imagine or create social life, technological systems, or media more broadly; the network is one aesthetic of communication among many.[43] Presuming that networks are an empirical reality or that sociality, technology, or media can emerge only in networked form imposes a significant set of demands on the relationships or structures we imagine as networks and masks the vital activity that falls outside common understandings of networks.

The idea of the network infused nerves, social life, electricity, and communication with key articulated promises, and above all the promise of connection reigned. In a reflection on the mid-nineteenth century in the *Chicago Daily Press*, reprinted in the *Lake Superior Miner*, the author marveled at the recent progress in the United States: "Who knew that thousands of miles of railroads would now be spread like network over all these States; from the Atlantic to the Mississippi—that by the magic wand of the telegraph, the extremes of our country would be brought into instantaneous communication—that California and Australia were to increase so immensely and opportunely, the circulating medium of the world?"[44] The network of railroads, the magic wand of the telegraph, and the circulating medium of the world here paralleled each other as connectors marked by their incomprehensible power to unite. Through the shared territory of metaphor, discourse, and practice, *network* organized a vital convergence in social life: excitement over scientific, social, and technological innovation was excitement for the network, and excitement for the network was excitement for the promise of connection as a mode of communicative relationship.

Dystopianism regularly arises alongside new technologies, and this was certainly true for later network media such as electric lights, telephones, and the internet.[45] However, the Atlantic telegraph fell at an interesting conjuncture after the concerns that arose with early industrialization and before the concerns that marked the networks that spread at the end of the century. In both cases, these anxieties were largely framed by the nostalgic idea that new media would force a separation from a peaceful pre-industrial past. An article on the telegraph published on the cusp of the twentieth century, titled "An Aid to Nervousness," warned of this danger for people who previously had "their horizon bound by the surrounding hills": "With the advent of the railroad came a shock to their nervous system, and when to this was added the telegraph wire, alarming them with the accumulated disasters and crimes of a whole world, they were no longer the bucolic citizens . . . which they had been before, but became nerve-wracked and distraut."[46] In fact, neurologist George. M. Beard considered the telegraph (alongside the even more harrowing "mental activity of women") one of the primary causes of a rise in nervousness.[47] In addition, a minor discourse arose around telegraphy also in the later part of the nineteenth century that the stinginess of telegraphese would ruin the English language.[48]

Yet, in the middle of the nineteenth century, new network media were largely met with optimism. The majority of worries about telegraphs in general and ocean telegraphs in particular were simply that they might not work. Secondary were legitimate concerns about the risk of fire from telegraph wires and injury from telegraph poles, both of which did occur. There was rarely, however, suspicion that telegraphy would cause any fundamental disfigurement to life as people knew it. The one exception was a lone letter to the editor of the *New York Times*. The author was unimpressed with the enthusiastic celebrations ("popular demonstrations amount to very little in my eyes"), skeptical that Buchanan's insistence on the cable's political neutrality would make a difference ("for I have read some little of history and I know the ease with which England has always cleared all obstructions in her path"), and, above all, insistent that "the Atlantic Telegraph can neither rescue a man from sin nor transport him to heaven."[49] This sentiment, however, was an outlier. Most US Americans celebrated the telegraph as the realization of an essential human connectivity blessed by God.

This prevailing imaginary for networks as connective media was empowered by a particularly charged source in the nineteenth-century United States: the emerging forms of public Protestantism and their relatively new heightened affect. Fervent discourse about the divinity of network media abounded in formally religious settings, from Protestant sermons to utopian newspapers. But assertions of networks' divinity also appeared in various forms of public discourse suffused with Christian tropes and marked by particularly protestant enthusiasms. Increasingly mainstream Protestant involvement in the production of an imaginary for networks was almost universally oriented to their connective capacities and abilities to produce new forms of globalism, while other religious attention to telegraphs, such as that from Reform Jews or Mormons, for example, focused much more on the ways networks produced new forms of localism. The invention of global connection as the defining element of networks may not have been solely a Protestant invention, but it emerged at the site of the powerful entanglement of protestantism and US public culture and was fueled by the affective charge of that live intersection.

Disconnection

As communication is increasingly imagined in terms of networks, connection has come to serve as the primary (and occasionally exclusive) way to imagine communicative relationships, both technological and social, intimate and general. In networks, disconnections, no matter how common, always come as a surprise and are met with dismay. My signal dropped! The Wi-Fi is out! The phone went dead! The train is stopped! The cable broke on the ocean floor! We are well aware that disconnections are inevitable, regular, and even desired (consider for a moment the passwords and firewalls that protect access to your financial information, email, or embarrassing text messages), but they always appear as inexplicable upsets. The question at the heart of this book is this: Given the regularity of disconnection in networks, why does disconnection always appear as a scandal?

The network metaphor takes its particular power from the conversion of consistent experiences of disconnection into abstract systems of exclusive connection.[50] Connection has become affiliated with a wide swath of terms; community, transportation, communication, romance, and globalization are all understood as modes of connection at various scales and through various modes. A joke published in *Harper's Weekly* after the 1866 Atlantic cable succeeded played on just these semantic affiliations: "Shall we call [the Atlantic cable's mastermind] Mr. Field an aristocrat because he is so very proud of his '*connections*'?"[51] Missionaries claimed that the telegraph erased distance such that all of humankind could hear each other's heartthrobs, public figures in the United States claimed the telegraph would render the country a neighborhood and unite the world under the banner of Christianity, and new religious actors across the United States understood the telegraph network to forge a new proximity to God or, at least, the dead.[52]

We are living in a long cultural era that prioritizes connection as a kind of communicative salvation. Today, connection remains the dominant description for relationships of all kinds and appears to be the necessary gateway to a better future: networking is the path to professional success, the hive mind is the new intelligence, and all of our social ills— from poverty to racism to war—could be solved if we would only connect to each other. Connection has become a mode of relationship marked by celebratory promises of proximity, intimacy, mutual influence, and community, set against anxieties about distance, detachment, and isolation. Even in contemporary scholarly environments, connection often reigns supreme: Bruno Latour's landmark text *Reassembling the Social* presents an important radical departure from understanding society as a stable ontological form and instead avers that the social could more productively be understood as "associations" and "a type of connection."[53] The expansive linguistic influence of connection is part of its muscle. It has become almost impossible to think about social and technological life outside of connection; it has overwhelmed other possibilities with a determining power.[54] This is only more true for networks, which seem to offer the ultimate form of connection: the connections of connections.

The central limit of network as a metaphor when so beholden to connection is that, while it can account for new social and technological affiliations, it cannot account for disconnection or how disconnection can engender new knowledge and forms of social life.[55] The network compels us to render social and technological life legible *only* through connection without providing a means to make sense of the many ways that sociality and technology arise through broken lines and miscommunications. Social worlds are just as shaped by breakups as by partnerships. The infrastructure of the telegraph was as much about the places it linked as the places it excluded, just as much about working cables as the miles of fractured lines. Disconnection gets a bad rap. Some breakups are good, some enmities important, some withdrawals useful, some unplugging necessary. There are important things to undo; there are disconnections we should not overcome. But, more important, our feting of connection misses the fact that technological and social life is indelibly constituted by connection *and* disconnection. If we frame connection as salvific, we cannot account for how disconnection helps create forms of life and death. We need a vocabulary for relationships that does not dismiss fragmentation as simply a social ill. Fracture is also a constitutive element in our becoming.

A notable exception to the emphasis on connection lies at the heart of network theory. Manuel Castells's field-defining volume *The Rise of the Network Society* (1996) locates fragmentation and exclusion as primary effects of networks. This aspect of his analysis has been overshadowed in part by his own optimism for networks' capacities to promote collective action. According to Castells, the end of the twentieth century marked a significant shift as new information technologies shaped social life. The rise of network society was marked by changes in space and time, both of which are now structured according to the flows of information and capital made possible by networks. This change has been met by a concomitant rise of religious fundamentalism: "It is significant that fundamentalism, whether Islamic or Christian, has spread, and will spread, throughout the world at the historical moment when global networks of wealth and power connect nodal points and valued individuals throughout the planet, while disconnecting, and excluding, large segments of societies, regions, and even entire countries."[56] A primary effect of networks has been the disconnection of some in a context of the "highly uneven" expansion of the new network economy.[57] Castells understands disconnection to be a result of networks, one that could be presumably overcome through network connectivity. This book demonstrates that disconnection is integral to networks; disconnection is required for networks to come into being.

This is of course only more true when we consider large infrastructural networks. As Stephen Graham and Nigel Thrift, whose research examines the politics of urban space, remind us, "All infrastructural systems are prone to error and neglect and breakage and failure, whether as a result of erosion or decay or vandalism or even sabotage."[58] For Graham and Thrift, "The problem with contemporary social theory is that it has predominantly theorized connection and assembly. But there are good reasons to think that, in the overall scheme of things, disconnection and disassembly are just as important in that they resist entities' means of enacting themselves: failure is key."[59] This volume argues something slightly different in respect to networks: disconnection does not resist networks' self-enactment; it enables it. Networks are just as constituted by disconnection as by connection. However, disconnection resists the religious imaginaries that have profoundly shaped what we understand networks to be and do. And this scandal of imagination takes place despite the fact that disconnection is integral to networks and an obvious aspect of how we use them.

Notwithstanding descriptions of networks as the ultimate connective media, networks use disconnection; they need it. Cabled network media came into being tethered to a series of promises about the possibilities for technology, social life, the future, and communication. They were understood—even before they worked—as a brand-new technology that would create social unity in a flawless future through instantaneous, ubiquitous, frictionless communication. They were understood as connective and divine. And yet the story of network media is riddled with *dis*connections—from the ruptures of the cables to the violence of the religiocolonial practices that built them to their utter failures to do the very things they seemed to promise. By 1861, a total of 11,364 miles of cable had been laid, of which just over 3,000 miles were working.[60] In other words, 74 percent of the world's first cabled network was broken; *most* of the network was disconnected. Broken cables, social fracture, impossible dreams, and miscommunication constituted networks—where they were, how they worked, who could use them, what they meant, and what they could convey. Both connection and disconnection are central to the function of networks in technological and social terms. For the telegraph, this is apparent in its most basic function: in order to communicate through Morse code, one must connect and disconnect the circuit to signal dots, dashes, and the critical space between them.

This is an effort at wresting disconnection from a teleological narrative of technology. Teleology always favors success; it trades in salvation such that each failure is just a misstep toward progress, each fracture has happened for a reason. But an antiteleological orientation can see an event outside of any narrative coherence and look instead to incoherence, fracture, and breakdown as moments that matter.[61] They matter not because they are illegible to discourses of progress—teleology has an infinite capacity for recuperating failure—but because they open the possibility of rendering discourses of progress illegible themselves. This is critically important in the politically charged connections and disconnections of networks. A story of network success misses the destruction in innovation's wake. For example, as demand surged for gutta-percha, the material used to insulate submarine cables, the forests of the Malay Peninsula were decimated.[62] For the 1858 cable, 242 tons of gutta-percha were used. By 1896, a staggering 5,403 tons of gutta-percha had been used for Atlantic telegraphy.[63] Such a story also persistently obscures the generative nature of disconnection for network function and development. The mundane luxury of using our phones as we move about is made possible by our phones' capacity to disconnect from distant or overloaded cell towers to more proximate or more efficient ones. Innovation has not overcome disconnections; it has allowed us to connect by disconnecting.

This book hopes not to glorify failure. There is no renegade antihero here, valiantly thwarting systems in inverted triumph. In fact, despite months of celebratory discussion of immanent success, most public discussion of the 1858 cable was rather subdued in addressing its failure. Despite the failure's grandeur, it was never rendered spectacular. The US publics I examine here, for the most part, looked away. There is only the quiet possibility that tracing these particular events of disconnection can illuminate the dark lines of fracture that structure networks.

This book examines an expansive set of affiliated terms as important to and influenced by disconnection: *failures* of technological apparatuses and of the imaginaries attached to them; social *fragmentation*; the *fracture* and *rupture* of cables, empires, and nations; technological *breakage* and communicative *breakdown*; the *impossibility* of imaginaries of global unity; and the *gaps* that persist between subjects and their futures. This wide linguistic territory illuminates the diverse roles of disconnection in network infrastructure and the ways religion helped to produce and obscure them.

Entangled Infrastructures

The diverse elements that combined to allow the telegraph to function—everything from cables to code—compose an infrastructure. Infrastructures are, in the simplest sense, built systems that sit below. Cables, wires, pipes, and tubes are buried in the ground to usher electricity, data, water, waste, trains, and people from place to place. Infrastructures also sit below in the sense that they undergird societies, organizing the processes that define a group of people in a particular time and place. It is in this latter *logistical* role that infrastructures matter, according to Peters.[64] Infrastructures, like highways or time zones, are frameworks that structure space and time, make both legible to us, and organize the possibilities for existence within them. Infrastructures locate us; we negotiate and inhabit the material, symbolic, and imaginative worlds they help to produce. To claim that religion plays an infrastructural role in networks is to point to the undergirding, organizing, and highly material framework of religion through which networks came into being.

To be familiar with the infrastructure of a given society is a marker of cultural membership, as any confused subway rider fumbling at a kiosk knows. Paul Edwards tells us that "belonging to a given culture means, in part, having fluency in its infrastructures. This is almost exactly like having fluency in a language: a pragmatic knowing-how, rather than an intellectual knowing-that."[65] He goes so far as to say that Western modernity itself is defined by its reliance on infrastructure, that infrastructures and modernity co-construct each other.[66] Infrastructures participated in exciting new capacities for Western moderns, but they mattered much more for the abstract senses of time, space, and cultural belonging they helped produce. This was certainly the principle that motivated Protestant missionaries to spread telegraphy around the world: to have the telegraph in place was to be civilized, and to be civilized was to be Christian. Fluency in each entangled one in the whole.

The trick with infrastructures is that precisely because of the foundational cultural work they are involved in, what counts as infrastructure can be wildly expansive. A telegraph cable without a telegraph operator is just a spasmodic electrical line. An operator without electricity is mute. A submarine cable without insulation connects nothing at all. Sharks, crocodiles, squirrels, or a pair of clippers could (and did!) sabotage a telegraph or fiber-optic line.[67] Infrastructures include sweeping systems and small pulses, broad maps and minor interfaces. They entail diverse technologies and engagements with all sorts of human and nonhuman actors at a wide span of scale. Edwards encourages attention to the micro, meso, and macro aspects of infrastructure.[68] Cultivating analyses that move nimbly among these scales allows us to consider the multiform influence of infrastructure on life, whether the power of an electrical pulse sent across the ocean or the new forms of nationhood that got wrapped up in telegraphy. Myopic insistence on greatness for infrastructures obscures the importance of intimacy and interface in infrastructural living. As scholar of gender and sexuality Ara Wilson tells us, intimacy works on every scale.[69] Try parsing out intimacy from large infrastructure the next time you share something secret—from a deep desire to a Social Security number—online.

Any form that extends beyond the capacities of immediate experience (and even those that appear to fit neatly within what we can perceive) requires imagination to make sense of the unwieldy. Infrastructures are thus as much imagination as plumbing. Global network infrastructures require imagination for all parts: the global, the network, and the infrastructures.[70] None of these elements is a given or natural entity. Rather, we live in a particular world that requires our interpretive activity and is shaped by a constellation of symbols, meanings, and affect. In other words, any world we live in is a particular kind of social imaginary.[71] According to the scholar of rhetoric and public culture Dilip Gaonkar, a social imaginary is "an enabling but not fully explicable symbolic matrix within which a people imagine and act as world-making collective agents."[72]

Indeed, imaginaries comprise symbolic structures, ideology, and discourse, but the concept of imaginaries affords the opportunity for a better understanding of the diversity of agencies and activities that produce and negotiate symbolic structures, ideology, and discourse in ways that never achieve stasis. Because imaginaries are lived, they are material practices with material effects and are built of ideas, images, and symbols as well as practices, habits, and things. Social imaginaries contend with the possibilities and limits of these elements and are structured and sustained in dynamic form by matter and affect. The imaginary of a networked globe was built with material elements of modern US life and organized by the investment of energy—what mattered, how, and to whom—that animated what it meant to be modern and US American.[73]

Peters situates communication between the desire for absolute communion and the "pathos of breakdown."[74] Networks, a dominant form in which we have imagined communication since the nineteenth century, manifest this same split. We attribute connection to the web of wires while regularly lamenting lost signals. Networks live in the space between the promise of connection and the ubiquity of disconnection, between communion and breakdown. Peters attributes the "dualism of 'communication'—at once bridge and chasm"—to the rise of new technologies in a context enthralled by Spiritualism, a wildly popular nineteenth-century religious movement that involved speaking to the dead.[75] That origin—so vital to the telegraph—has rippled through networks since.

This book takes an infrastructural approach to network media. Infrastructural media studies orients attention to media as cultural techniques that shape what forms of subjectivity, social life, material life, and discourse are possible.[76] Media are not considered here in their capacities to act as vehicles for information, entertainment, messages, or data so much as in their capacities to determine what counts as information, entertainment, messages, and data and what sorts of subjects and relationships are made intelligible by these forms of communication. More important, infrastructure's emphasis on materiality also foregrounds world-making in its most concrete iterations. What sort of globe came into being through this early global cabled network? Who could inhabit it? And how? This book joins recent media scholarship with infrastructural orientations, such as work by Lisa Parks, John Durham Peters, and

Nicole Starosielski, as well as interdisciplinary scholarship on infrastructure from Geoffrey Bowker, Paul Edwards, and Susan Leigh Star.[77]

The infrastructural approach in this volume takes up the foundational move of media theory to look at media beyond their content in ways attuned to Karen Barad's insistence that matter is discursive *and* discourse is material. Thus, this book understands media as an essentially ambiguous set of practices and agencies that refuses to decide between text and technology, between content and mode. The telegraph is discursively produced only insofar as discourse—that which determines what modes of existence are intelligible—is always already material; and the telegraph is material only insofar as that matter comes into being through discourse. The network infrastructures that are the subject of this volume are built structures of communication, and thus the matter and discourse that networks comprise are inextricable from each other. Raymond Williams took Marshall McLuhan to task for his nonchalant collapse of media and technology and the technological determinism that resulted.[78] Here, I also refuse a clear distinction between media and technology but do so to attend to the materiality of media and the immateriality of technology.

The concept of technology, which emerged in the late nineteenth century, had to stand in for a vast matrix of elements: machines (like the telegraph) but also expertise (like Morse code), infrastructure (like telegraph cables), a culture of travel and communication, the conventions and schedules and habits of practice that made these machines viable, the raw materials with which they were built, and the carnivorous colonialism that determinately pushed these machines around the globe.[79] The single machine that often serves to represent a technology is really an *arbitrarily* circumscribed part of an expansive system. Machines are faulty placeholders that unsuccessfully represent a grouping with few fixed edges. Take texting: What is the "technology" of texting? Is it the cell phone, itself a strange mix of wires, chips, metals, plastics, and electrical charges? Is it the pinging of the cell phone to cell towers that goes on as you walk the streets? The codes that run the programs we use to text? Or the cultural habit of rendering speech in inexplicable abbreviations? IDK. Technology, which at first seems so obviously material, is itself an intra-action of the material and the immaterial, wires and habits, electricity and imaginaries.[80]

The telegraph is not exempt from this omnivorous extension. It is a word whose fullness contains wires, lights, boats, candles, dots, dashes, competing patents, metals, wood, ink, paper, telegraphers, urgent messages, secret messages, trains, markets, love letters, money, sultans, missionaries, and no full stop. Even this book's limited anchor in the 1858 cable—just one of the early attempts at a transatlantic telegraph—becomes so filled with things, people, practices, energy, and dreams that it spills far beyond the confines of this text. This book is organized around the 1858 Atlantic cable, but to suss out the infrastructural religion in it, we must also spend some time with Ottoman telegraph wires, Bible Communists, US public nationalism, and British scoffing. All networks work this way, always reaching out.

Telling a story balanced on a wire entails some risk. My hope is not to load the telegraph with a determinism it cannot carry. This technology was one of many in a time of significant technological change. I never intend mention of the telegraph to be anything more than a failed figure imperfectly standing in for a host of things, people, practices, energy, and forces. Telegraphs themselves, already cacophonous mixes of matter and energy, did not single-handedly change the world, but they are good placeholders for the way the world was becoming at the time.

Chapter Summaries

The chapters take up the central promises of network imaginaries in turn—networks are (1) a new spectacular technology that will create (2) national and global unity, (3) a utopian present, and (4) perfect communication—and map the disconnection integral to each. While the theoretical orientations to these themes overlap, the chapters emphasize different bodies of theory to address materiality, publics, utopia, and communication, respectively.

Studies of Western modernity affiliate new technologies of communication with emerging forms of nationalism, from the printing press to the telegraph. Indeed, the meaning of the telegraph in the United States was distinctly *US* (as a comparison with British understandings of the telegraph will show), and the telegraph contributed in diverse ways to the establishment of the young nation before and through the Civil War. Yet this study starts abroad, with US missionaries in the Ottoman

Empire. Following historian Ian Tyrrell's argument that US cultural expansion shaped the nascent nation, particularly in the activities of moral reformers, this book situates the United States in a global context.[81] In one sense, the book moves from global to local, moving from international Christian mission to national culture in the United States to local utopian communities to the very texts of the telegrams sent on the 1858 cable. In another sense, however, the co-arising of global and local confounds the linearity of this formulation. At each setting, the book examines how local and global life were coming into being through the mutual constitution of religion and networks.

The first chapter takes up the promise of perfect technology and new materialist theories to clarify religion's role in the establishment of the global telegraph network. Among the primary agents for Samuel Morse and Alfred Vail's machine were Protestant missionaries who equated the adoption of new technology with a process of civilization that would lead to religious conversion. For many of these missionaries, urging the world toward Protestantism entailed also urging the world toward US technologies: the medium was the mission. The chapter traces the role of technology in US Protestant mission and the twisting story of telegraphy in the Ottoman Empire—a volatile mix of connection and disconnection as colonial interests, imperial goals, and diverse forms of resistance wove the network through the land and then used the network to take down the empire itself.

Chapter 2 explores the promise of social unity through networks by looking at the religious nationalism that emerged in the United States around the Atlantic telegraph. As US Americans tensely watched the struggle to transmit the world's first transatlantic telegram, a diverse community—from Protestant missionaries to civic leaders—spoke of the newly united world that electric speech would create in explicitly Christian and implicitly US terms. Public statements that claimed the telegraph as destined and blessed by God were not merely religious ways of speaking about the telegraph; the affective weight borne by this Christian vocabulary and imagery forged the affiliation of the telegraph with dreams of national coherence and global unity in particularly durable ways.

Public texts and speeches about the cable lauded its ability to unite the world while simultaneously revealing the difficulty of this telegraphic venture and how much closer the nation and the world were to con-flict than to peace.[82] While the telegraph significantly altered the way communication related to space and time and promoted the equation of communication with connection, it did not prove particularly use-ful in producing unity. Thus, the imaginary of connection at national and global scales was held together not by cables but by the investment of social energy. This chapter examines alternative imaginaries of tele-graphs that have lost cultural meaning to demonstrate that affect, not the technology itself, produced and sustained this network imaginary. It did so not despite the failures that besieged it but through them. The fragile cable of 1858 and the united "whole world" it was said to create point to the materiality and contingency inherent in the discursive and affective labor of making a public, a nation, and a world.

Chapter 3 addresses the potent US utopianism that greeted the Atlan-tic Telegraph Cable of 1858. US Americans articulated perfection to new telegraph technology with all the idealism utopia has come to connote but without the spatial or temporal inaccessibility that we traditionally associate with the "no-place" coined by Thomas More in his 1516 *Utopia*. In most formulations, utopia is set in a far-off land or distant future. Yet for many US Americans in the mid-nineteenth century, the moment the Atlantic Telegraph Cable was strung across the ocean and Morse code was sent pulsing beneath the waves, this technologically empowered utopian world began to arrive. With an anchoring focus on the Oneida Community, a small religious community that became obsessed with the telegraph's possibilities for unity among all people and with God, this chapter argues that in a US context utopia cannot be understood as a distant land or future event. Rather, the utopianism of this network imaginary demands a redefinition of utopia as proximate.

Chapter 4 explores the promises and failures of communication through an analysis of what was sent on the 1858 cable. It is a strange sort of content analysis, however, since most of the communication on the cable was mere signals before the cable was capable of transmitting code, and even much of the code the cable could ultimately transmit consisted of a single letter. The *V*—a Beethovenian dot-dot-dot-dash in Morse code—became the primary way to reestablish connection after failure.[83] These transmissions read more like babble than meaning, more like a stutter than speech. As such, they help to illustrate the constitutive disconnections that make communication possible and, in particular, highlight the telegraph's inauguration of a new form of language that neither represented things in the world nor referenced a system of meaning: the signal. This chapter turns to infrastructure as a supplement to structural and poststructural theories of communication and argues that the creative, affective force of religion made these essentially meaningless signals matter. Even before the Atlantic Telegraph Cable could transmit speech, it carried the hefty imaginary of a divinely sanctioned global unity.

The telegraph wove its way across the ocean at a time when religion's role in public life was commonplace. Since then, networks have become more vital to everyday life in easily perceptible ways, while religion is considered a less overt part of public culture in the United States. The epilogue proposes that the relationship of telegraphic networks to the networks that shape our world today is not causal or continuous but one of resonance, in which some elements are amplified and some are damped. The protestant dreams for the telegraph in the nineteenth century—particularly the promise of global unity, the celebration of unprecedented speed and ubiquity, and the fantasy of friction-free communication—reverberate in dreams for the internet and social media today. Cries that the internet makes us all neighbors amplify the electric pulse of the celebrations of the 1858 cable's capacity to unite the world in Christian community. And yet it is not a straight shot from then to now. Some elements have faded, particularly overt religious motifs in imaginaries of technology. But the original power of public protestantism in the first network imaginaries continues to resonate today in the primacy of connection.

A Broken World Woven of Wires and Dreams

This book encourages thinking of networks as one particular way of giving meaning to the technologies, practices, flows, gaps, structures, and people who participate in the world according to a specific set of limits and possibilities. The link between networks and connection is not a natural affiliation but one way of making networks meaningful. It has been a mode of meaning making that is profoundly pedagogical: it teaches us to value communication as a form of connection, to aim toward global unity, and to accept the terms of globalization's promise that the more we communicate, the more we will unify, and the more we unify, the more peace and prosperity there will be.[84] As the links forged by telegraphs and steam travel wove a web that would net the world, a mode of thought that prioritized connection itself came to prevail. This study denaturalizes this network logic in order to explore how miscommunication, disconnection, and, indeed, the failures of communication technology participated in generating and sustaining this way of thinking about and living in the world.

We must distance ourselves from the weight of inevitability that we have attached to the demands of networks and note the particular strangeness of a social form that posited itself as both the status quo and a utopian future. This network declared itself and deferred itself in the same breath, demanding that US Americans dream of it as their desired future because it was already a fact of their present. This double location in present and future and the double grounding in fact and desire established certain ways of living and forms of life as the only possible and the only desirable ones. This book endeavors to open such forms up to inquiry and contingency.

How did this particular way of imagining and inhabiting the world become so important, entrenched, and positively valued? How did certain forms of networked communication become tethered to ideas of unity? How did the speed of communication become affiliated with ideas of world peace? How did vast infrastructures become models of proximity, and proximity become a stand-in for agreement? These associations tell us a great deal about the contours of globalization and its demanding, pedagogical promises. They also allow us to locate the primary role played by religion in US culture, particularly if we think of religion as a means of making things meaningful. This book examines religious actors, practices, and discourses that emerge from both explicitly religious communities and the diffuse forms of theologically inflected public culture that emerged in the United States in the nineteenth century.

The last complete message was transmitted by the Atlantic cable on September 1, 1858. Despite desperate attempts that pushed through a few fragmented transmissions, the cable's signals died out completely on October 28, 1858.[85] Networks are geographically grand, are temporally enduring, and establish demanding standards for social membership, and yet they are themselves highly particular and contingent. While networks offer stability, universality, neutrality, and connection, they do so through constitutive dependency on instability, particularity, nonneutrality, and disconnection.

1

What's the Matter with Networks?

Spectacular Technology, US Mission, and Global Unity

The telegraph is beginning to spread its network of new life
over the land.
—The Reverend Judson Smith, "China and Christian Missions," *Missionary Herald*

US missionaries understood that in order to entice young evangelists
to foreign shores, convince the people there to convert to Christianity, and raise the massive funds needed to support these endeavors, a
little magic might be in order. In August 1847, a Protestant missionary named Cyrus Hamlin held such magic in his hands. He stood in
the summer palace of the Ottoman sultan Abdülmecid I (1839–61) and
carefully unwrapped a vital emblem of the emphatic spread of US Protestantism. It was not a cross. It was not a Bible. Rather, Hamlin and his
compatriots slowly removed the covering from Samuel Morse's electromagnetic telegraph.[1]

Hamlin's presence before the Ottoman sultan appears, at first glance,
to be the setup for a joke: a missionary, a translator, and a chemist walk
into a palace. The turn of events that led Hamlin, a missionary for the
American Board of Commissioners for Foreign Missions, John Porter
Brown, dragoman at the US legation (an interpreter and guide for the
US diplomatic office), and John Lawrence Smith, a US chemist employed as a geologist by the Turkish government, to find themselves
together doing Morse's legwork to sell his machine to the Ottoman
Empire reflects the strange confluence of cultural investments in new
technology that swelled through the nineteenth century. In a world enchanted by the possibilities of global communication, Morse's machine
seemed to promise the realization of *everything*, from industry to international relations to God's kingdom on earth. It was a fortuitous node

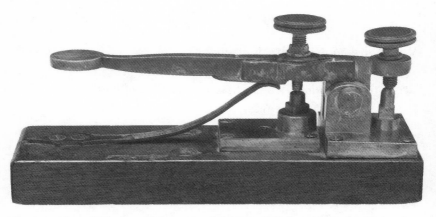

Figure 1.1. Morse-Vail telegraph key, 1844. (Division of Work and Industry, National Museum of American History, Smithsonian Institution)

in the world's first cabled network and a crystallization of an odd assemblage of technology, religion, and capitalism often given the shorthand "civilization."[2]

Missionaries were primary agents of the circulation of "civilization" and took as a central task the production of modern subjects adept at the protocols of the capitalist nation-state.[3] Much missionary attention to technological change in the nineteenth century celebrates innovation—of networks in particular—as a vital new resource in an effort to convert the world. The speed of new media like telegraphy, the reach of new transportation modes in steam and rail, and the promise of wide dissemination made possible by print seemed to multiply what missionaries could accomplish. This was an age of *faster* and *more*. As one missionary of the ABCFM claimed, "The missionary in the printing-office can do more to make Christ known among the people than ten men could do faithfully preaching daily in the streets and bazaars of the city."[4]

These missionaries did not simply employ these gadgets as the incidental conduits of a Christian message. That interpretation relies on a theory of media as transmitters of content. But media in mission were far more diverse in their capacities and, as such, far more powerful, especially as missionaries considered them: the shining, electrical, steam-churning power that made such speed and reach possible was taken itself to be godly. New media were, for these missionaries, performances of power, marvelous material evidence of God's work on earth, and enactments of the very culture they were thought to usher in. Hamlin was certain that "the general progress of civilization, the railroad, the steamboat, the telegraph, the expansion of commerce, the increase of travel, have all united in softening the prejudices of the Moslem mind."[5] His colonialist confidence highlights the important sense among missionaries that these networks were more than transmitters of messages; they were spectacular objects that could awe others into a particularly Christian reverence. Network technologies could reach where the Christian message could not: into the minds of potential converts, where they left a palpable mark of US Protestant culture as it came into being.

US Protestant missionaries, despite the complicated relationship between Protestant doctrine and materiality, saw new technology as a powerful *thing* to offer their potential converts and a crucial aspect of the Christian culture they hoped to disseminate. Moreover, missionaries understood media to bear their own power, to themselves act on what missionaries understood to be hardened hearts and stubborn minds. In missionary writing, as in Hamlin's claim, these technologies have agency for sweeping cultural change: they stand as the subjects of sentences that promise to soften minds to Protestantism, leap whole lands into a shining US American future, and unify the world under the banner of Christian civilization. An internal, belief-based process of conversion was not the only goal for these Protestant missionaries; they sought a broader cultural and material "conversion to modernity" itself.[6]

This chapter argues that religion was at the heart of where the telegraph went, how it got there, and what happened once it arrived. US Protestant missionaries in the nineteenth century used media *as* mission, equating the spread of certain technologies with the spread of Christianity. They drew on rich resources of two centuries of European-US discourse and practices of settler colonialism in North America, which identified technology as a critical partner for religion in the "civilization" of the land and its Native American inhabitants.[7] In this sense, Protestant Christianity took on a life as the material things of culture that did their own energetic mission work alongside the people, power, and doctrine attended to by scholarship on colonial religion.[8] And these material things, these spectacular media, had their own lives: they were vital participants in this troubling assemblage. That is, as much as

Protestant mission shaped and empowered the surge of network media in the nineteenth century, network media shaped and empowered the surge in Protestant mission. In both cases, particular forms of exclusion enabled promises of unity.

It may seem counterintuitive to begin a book about the relationship of US religion and network infrastructure in the Ottoman Empire, but that is perhaps the clearest place to see how US religious activity *abroad* helped form and strengthen emerging—and increasingly protestant— imaginaries of networks *at home* and how *domestic* religious imaginaries became part of a *global* technological phenomenon. The exportation of US technology and religion was a primary technique for the development of national identity and public culture in the United States. In this context, US missionaries helped build telegraph networks at home and abroad that US Americans understood to be both quintessentially American and necessarily global. Morse here serves as an apt example: hailed as a hero in the United States but with a machine many people considered inferior to its competitors (particularly the British machine invented by William Fothergill Cooke and Charles Wheatstone), Morse desperately needed international recognition; his first arrived in the form of a diamond-studded imperial decoration from the Ottoman sultan, facilitated by the demonstration that Hamlin made possible.[9] Hamlin's sponsoring agency, the American Board of Commissioners for Foreign Missions, imagined itself to represent a nation that would "find sacred purpose in commercial and imperial expansion," guided by an emphatically Protestant way of life.[10] For many of those who were involved in the ABCFM, spreading religion went hand in hand with or even needed to be preceded by spreading "civilization," in all its technological infatuation.

But human intention and activity alone did not produce these identities. Telegraphs themselves—what they made possible, how they organized communication, whom they empowered to communicate, where they worked, and where they failed—acted alongside missionary exportation of technology and the Ottoman Empire's anxious enthusiasm for infrastructural endeavors. Together, they tell an important story about the surprising activity of technology to confound powerful human intentions, not least of which was telegraphs' participation in the rise and fall of all sorts of sovereignty. In the Ottoman Empire, the regularity of failure in telegraph networks and missionary endeavors loomed starkly against the sunset of the sultanate. In this light, the story of the relationship among telegraphy, religion, and the United States begins abroad.

The Spirit Electric

The appearance of a mechanically obsessed missionary in the palace of the Ottoman sultan makes a surprising amount of sense in the double context of a struggling empire in the thick of radical reform and a wave of US Protestants convinced that industrial innovation was a sign of religious righteousness. In 1839, just eight years before dots and dashes surged through the Beylerbey Palace, Abdülmecid I marked his first year as sultan with a sweeping declaration of reform: the *Hatt-i Şerif-i Gülhane* (*Rescript of Gülhane*). This document ushered in an era of reorganization known as the Tanzimat (1839–76) that instituted new forms of inclusion of the non-Muslims in the Ottoman Empire. Alongside diverse Muslims, the vast empire was home to Jews, Greek Orthodox, Gregorian Armenians, Catholics, and Protestants. The Tanzimat reforms abolished the *millet* system—a form of limited self-governance by autonomous religious communities—and subjected all Ottomans to the same broad governmental authority. In practice, the *Rescript of Gülhane* did not inaugurate the universal equality among subjects that it declared but did establish a formal shift from a political arrangement in which different religious groups in the empire lived under different educational and legal systems, different forms of taxation, and different privileges to one in which each member of the empire was roughly beholden to the same laws.[11]

These reforms eased the efforts of Western Christians hungry to convert the religiously diverse inhabitants of the holy lands described in the Bible. As the editorial secretary for the ABCFM William Strong wrote in his 1910 history of the organization, echoing the resoundingly bigoted tone of nineteenth-century missionary reports from the area, "It seemed intolerable to its founders that Christianity's birthplace should be forever in the grip of Islam, or left to exhibit a form of Christianity, ancient and intrenched, but for the most part lifeless."[12] Beginning in 1819 with Pliny Fiske and Levi Parsons's arrival in Palestine, US Protestant missionaries made the Ottoman Empire a central site of their efforts.

Catholics were already active in the area, particularly serving the small communities of existing Catholics and protecting Christian holy sites. The arrival of the Filles de la Charité in Constantinople in 1839 marked a new era of Catholic evangelism in the Ottoman Empire.[13] Protestant missionaries were not met with a warm welcome from the Eastern and Catholic Christians or the Muslims they intended to convert; the later Tanzimat era offered increasing protections from previously permitted legal action against them in the Levant.[14]

The ABCFM began as a small sectarian organization in the early 1800s and grew to become the primary engine of US international mission in the nineteenth century. Originally made up of Massachusetts Congregationalists, the organization accepted support from the Presbyterians and elected commissioners from New Jersey, New York, and Pennsylvania by 1812, thereby establishing itself as a multistate and multidenominational venture.[15] Notably, despite its regional origins, the organization named itself the *American* Board of Commissioners for Foreign Missions.[16] As the principal organization of US Protestant mission in the nineteenth century and as a community that spanned Protestant sects, a number of states, and many foreign mission sites, the ABCFM proffered a dominant voice of US religion at the time. Historian Emily Conroy-Krutz's study of US missionary literature reveals that missionaries identified themselves parochially *and* globally; they considered themselves to be both "American Christians" and part of the "Christian world."[17] The organization also served as a vehicle for the commitment of other US Americans who participated in its ventures from home by providing financial and social support. According to Cyrus Hamlin, by 1880 a full third of the ABCFM's income was spent on missions in the Ottoman Empire.[18] *The Church at Home and Abroad*, a Presbyterian missionary journal, reported that by 1898 there were seventy thousand Protestants in the Ottoman Empire, and missionaries had established six US colleges.[19] Because US missionaries directed concerted attention to the Levant before other European Protestants, it became one of the few missionary sites in the world dominated by US efforts.[20]

US missionary enthusiasm for the area and the Ottoman push for reform shared a handful of causes that circled around the defining power and precarity of a vast empire in an era of imperial decline. As surrounding Muslim empires dissolved—only the Safavid and Mughal Empires accompanied the Ottoman Empire into the seventeenth century, and neither lasted as long—the Ottoman Empire became a central source of power in the Muslim world. At the time of the telegraphic demonstration to the sultan, the empire covered a massive and religiously important territory: it stretched around the west coast of the Mediterranean from Tunis in North Africa to Sarajevo in southern Europe (with the prickly exception of Greece), along the southeast coast of the Black Sea and most of the east and western coasts of the Arabian Peninsula, including in its span the significant cities of Cairo, Constantinople (Istanbul), Jerusalem, Mecca, and Medina. Ottoman sultans claimed the authority of the caliphate (the spiritual head of the world's Sunni Muslims) beginning in the fourteenth century, and when the Ottoman Empire conquered Egypt, the Levant, and Hejaz (home to Mecca and Medina) in 1517, the title gained legitimacy across the Muslim world. Unlike in many other places that attracted missionary attention in the nineteenth century, US missionary efforts in the Levant preceded US military and economic interests in the area. This was notably distinct from contemporary European missionary ventures since the ABCFM's efforts in the Levant did not have an accompanying system of colonial governance.[21] Missionaries were enticed by the possibility of striking at Islam from its center. Hamlin defended the extraordinary expenditure of the ABCFM in Turkey by citing the caliphate (in notably colonialist shorthand): "Turkey is the throne of the spiritual power of Islam. . . . Now success in the missionary work here would carry its influence to 'farthest Ind[ia]."[22]

The loud claims of Ottoman spiritual and imperial power reflected not just its clout but also its insecurity. In historian Selim Deringil's study of the new forms of public life that emerged in the empire in the nineteenth century, he argues that, in fact, "the continuous, almost monotonous, underlining of the spiritual aspect of the sultan's title can be traced directly to the period of decline, gaining momentum at the end of the eighteenth century."[23] By the time Abdülmecid I became sultan, the empire was in the tricky position of legitimating its power as a fading dynastic empire among emerging aggressive nation-states and as a Muslim power—in fact, the only non-Christian power—among the major European powers. It was not invited to the Congress of Vienna in 1814 that determined the great powers of Europe, and over the course of the nineteenth century the Ottoman Empire experienced incremental losses

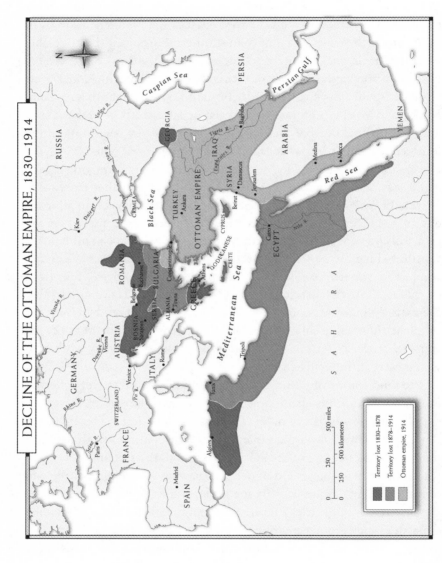

Figure 1.2. Map of the Ottoman Empire, 1830–1914. (Map created by Maps.com, LLC)

of territory largely to European colonial powers, such as the British, who were alternately allies and threats.

The Ottoman Empire inhabited this tense position by adopting what Deringil terms a "borrowed colonialism," that is, a hybrid form of its own "civilizing mission" modeled on the modern imperialists—Britain, France, and Germany—but crafted according to a hodgepodge of tried-and-true Ottoman techniques.[24] In this Ottoman modernity, the early forms of inclusive national identity came into being through Islamism, and the first appearances of a modern citizenry were framed by monarchical sanctity.[25] While drawing on long-standing precedents, the *Rescript of Gülhane* led the charge by empowering a dynastic empire through techniques of modern nationalism. Its preface is an apt example: it instituted the hallmark of modern nationalism—a guarantee of life, honor, and fortune to all subjects, regardless of religion—in order to restore the empire to a time of greatness in which "the lofty principles of the Kuran . . . were always perfectly observed."[26] In this framing perhaps it was most true to emergent modern nationalism—promising the state-sanctioned universal individual equality that would become known as secularism from a firmly religious foundation.[27]

And likewise true to other modern nations, particularly the United States, promises of equality came by way of systems of profound inequality. The ideals of inclusive nationalism were coterminous with new efforts to wrangle control over the nomadic populations at the periphery of the empire. Since the Ottoman conquest of portions of the Arabian Peninsula in the sixteenth century, the Sublime Porte had been largely only a nominal authority for the nomadic tribes whose loyalty lay with local sheikhs.[28] The Tanzimat era coupled the determination to unify the empire under the banner of Ottomanism with new land reforms that disrupted the way tribes held land in common and formal policies intended to fully integrate tribes into Ottoman taxation and military service. Thus, the Tanzimat reforms became a fully elaborated colonial project, complete with declarations of cultural superiority. Nomadism was equated with "savagery" in Ottoman discourse: the collocation "they live in a state of nomadism and savagery" was repeated in hundreds of documents.[29]

Telegraphy emerged deep in the tangle of these complicated contexts. For both the Ottoman government and US missionaries, telegraphy represented a form of salvation. For the Sublime Porte, Morse's electromagnetic telegraph was a US technology that appeared to offer a way both to modernize the empire on the model of European nation-states and to strengthen the power of the sultan by facilitating communication with local governors across a vast territory. This double move exemplified "borrowed colonialism" and was fully realized in Ottoman colonial power plays over the nomadic tribes at the periphery of the empire.[30] Establishing telegraph lines through tribal territory signaled the tighter control the Sublime Porte intended to exert over nomadic populations and activated brewing disputes about land rights, taxation, and compensation.[31] The telegraph became a strategic site for sabotage as political action for frustrated tribes, such as in Sheikh Mansur's attack on the telegraph following new aggressive measures to assert centralized control over the Muntafiq (a powerful settled tribe in what today is lower Iraq) in 1863.[32] In fact, while often described in official sources as vandalism, almost every case of sabotage of the telegraph by nomadic people in the empire can be directly linked to acts they perceived to be part of a system of oppression by the Porte.[33] Telegraph infrastructure was such a critical symbol of imperial control that a wire crossing the disputed border between the Ottoman Empire and Iran could only be built after a long-negotiated and utterly ungainly compromise of alternating wooden (Iranian) and iron (Ottoman) poles across the contested territory.[34]

US missionaries shared the conviction that new machines of industry and communication, and the infrastructure to support them, were signs of modernization and cultural dominance. The ABCFM placed so much stock in the evangelical work that machinery could accomplish that at one point it created specific missionary divisions focused on medicine, industry, and publishing; it trained people in mining; and it hired blacksmiths.[35] The emphasis on industry as part and parcel of mission reflected an early theory embraced by many missionaries of the ABCFM that "some measure of civilizing influence must *precede* any effective attempt to Christianize."[36] Debates over whether civilization paved the way for or stood in the way of Christian conversion were prominent among leaders of the ABCFM. Senior secretary Rufus Anderson in particular advocated strongly against the importance of so-called civilization to Christianization.[37] Yet, the idea that any possibility of Christian conversion required a first step of familiarity with European and US technologies resounded throughout the writings of US missionaries in the nineteenth century and ultimately became widespread policy in the organization. In part, this was the mark of a theory of mission that understood conversion to be cultural and of which religion was only one part. To take up Christianity, one also had to take up an ensemble of affiliated practices including attention to, use of, and celebration of technology.

Such missionary logic coincided with popular performances of what Fred Nadis, who writes on science and technology in US popular culture, terms "wonder shows," displays of discovery and invention in an emerging field whose ownership among artisans, mechanics, performers, and (recently named) scientists was as yet undecided.[38] The objects they displayed were, likewise, tenuously located among science, natural wonder, spiritual mystery, and hoax. Of the many machines and people exhibited at such performances, electricity was particularly important in the US imagination; this mysterious fluid (and its mythologized hero, Benjamin Franklin) featured heavily in the birth and growth of US science.[39] In 1837, two Persian princes went to Constantinople to see the electrical experiments presented by missionaries there. One had seen similar presentations in Beirut and brought the other to see, in the missionary account, "the 'fire wonders' at Mr. Goodell's. Every thing that makes such men acquainted with European superiority, and their own inferiority, political, intellectual, and scientific, helps to weaken their religious bigotry."[40] It is not simply the sense of cultural superiority that merits attention (although it merits plenty) but also the idea that political, intellectual, scientific, and religious orientations could be shifted with a demonstration of electricity.[41] These machines were crucial animating elements of broad cultural structures. In the movement of electrical current, Christianity and progress-laden ideas of advanced civilization were produced and linked, and (the missionaries hoped) Persian minds opened to that colonial ensemble.

Protestant missionaries articulated a set of technological, religious, and cultural structures that contributed to an emerging condition of Western modernity: that cultural membership depended on a kind of technological know-how. They presented mechanical and industrial skills as racially and culturally determined—natural to the British and Anglo-Americans, of course, and utterly unnatural to their colonial others—but accessible through cultural shifts including conversion to Christianity. For example, an excerpt from a journal of the *John Williams*, a vessel for the London Missionary Society, described the printing office of Stephen Mark Creagh in Maré: "He has a very nicely fitted up printing-office, and is assisted in it by some of the natives belonging to his own station, who make very good attempts in the various branches of the work; still they require his constant supervision, and like *all* other natives in *these* seas—if not elsewhere—are unable to do a tidy job of mechanical work without some one to plan out, arrange, and direct them."[42] Christianity's imbrication with mechanical arts is presented as a corrective to what one report from the London Missionary Society described as the "innate indolence of the natives," which, thanks to missionary efforts, "has given place to industrial pursuits, and in several instances to the acquisition of industrial arts. Many of the natives have become useful mechanics."[43] *Industry*, at the time, was both the practices of production that increasingly defined the emerging capitalist nation-state and the moral virtue of diligence and hard work, and these definitions held little distinction for the missionaries who took it upon themselves to inculcate industry among those whom they encountered at home and abroad: becoming like a capitalist citizen was to become morally upright.

One missionary gained particular attention from the ABCFM for his successful use of industry in mission: Cyrus Hamlin. Hamlin understood technology to sit at the center of mission, perhaps even trumping explicit evangelism. In his account of his time in the Ottoman Empire, he wrote, "Now, whatever the missionary can do to promote industry, and to guide to the right objects of industry, is in the line of his calling, and places him in the apostolic succession, although he may not be a tent-maker."[44] Hamlin spent thirty-five years in the Ottoman Empire, originally appointed by the ABCFM in February 1837 to head a high school in Constantinople. Hamlin arrived in 1838, and in the midst of political upheaval that directed attention away from the unwelcome incursion of Protestantism, he opened the Seminary of the American Board in Bebek in 1840.[45] Hamlin often involved mechanical proficiency in his evangelical endeavors, from a seminary bakery to a laundry service for British soldiers during the Crimean War.[46] Hamlin used experiments in physics, a particular interest of his since his early education, as

Figure 1.3. Cyrus Hamlin. (Middlebury College Special
Collections)

a means to attract "gentlemen of high standing" to the seminary.[47] He
understood technology to be a critical step on the path to conversion.

Hamlin's work to spread technology, even training students in mechanic arts at the seminary he founded, was recognized by the ABCFM.
According to one board member, "The best work yet done by any native
pastors or preachers has been done by men who were trained to industrial habits and pursuits at the Bebek Seminary by Dr. Hamlin."[48] In fact,
Hamlin's well-known interest in mechanical engineering earned him an
ironic nickname. As Hamlin explained it, "The Turks ascribe mechanical invention to Satan. . . . I have myself, for some supposed mechanical ability, been seriously introduced by one Ottoman to another as 'the
most Satanic man in the empire!'" Hamlin's repetition of this story word
for modest, astonished word in both of his memoirs belies any supposed
offense, although he did lament that it "is not favorable to mechanical

progress."[49] In case the meaning escaped his readers, he helpfully clarified in *My Life and Times* that the nickname "meant simply the most
skillful."[50] Hamlin, satanic technophile and Protestant missionary, epitomized the ABCFM's commitment to technology as part and parcel of
Christian mission.

As missionaries like Hamlin avidly attended to the dissemination
of "civilization," a powerful metaphor took hold: that technology acted
directly on the mind. In missionary writing of the time, technology
promised a physical effect on the minds of others: "impress[ing]," "softening," and, in one case, "enkindl[ing the] desire" for Christianity.[51]
Heathen minds, according to missionary writings, were hard and closed
to Christianity but strikingly passive to the power of technology and
awe-inspiring performances of it.[52] This physical metaphor drew on
the paternalism of eighteenth- and nineteenth-century pedagogy (and
its amplification in the paternalism of the concurrent colonialism), in
which learning was understood as a process of impressing and imprint-
ing on malleable young minds.[53] And it spoke to a primary ambivalence
in both the concept of the mind and emerging concepts of technology
in the nineteenth century. The mind was, at that time, largely considered
to be immaterial consciousness or intellect. But perennial debates over
the relationship between the (immaterial) mind and the (very material)
brain haunted the century. Emerging scientific, medical, and psychological ways of knowing posited a *location* for cerebral activity and recognized the *corporeal* effects of conscious experience, indicating just how
tenuous the mind's immateriality was.[54]

I use the anachronistic term *technology* to describe the mechanical,
industrial, and infrastructural interests of missionaries and the Sublime
Porte because it articulates these elements together as they were identified at the time. Moreover, technology, which at first seems so obviously
material, is like the mind a strange intra-action of the material and the
immaterial, pathways and habits, electricity and imaginaries.[55] Leo Marx
tells us that the term *technology* was applied retroactively to explain the
dramatic cultural shifts of the nineteenth century. The single machine
used to represent a technology always stands in for a vast array of materials, forces, practices, and assemblages.[56] As missionaries saw minds and
technology interact, both situated in a tense ambiguity between materiality and immateriality, the metaphor of technology's impression on the

minds of others took on a power that extended the metaphor into a nearly physical reality. For Hamlin, the spread of US science and technology promoted what he understood to be the prosperity of the culture as a whole, but, more important, the new machines of the nineteenth century bore their own evangelical effect. As in the quote from Hamlin at the beginning of this chapter, the work of technology to "soften" the minds of the people Hamlin encountered in the Ottoman Empire became a recurring theme in his monographs. Hamlin described scene after scene of technology producing a reverential awe for the power of the Christian God.

According to Hamlin, the presentation of the telegraph to the sultan Abdülmecid I in 1847 provided a perfect opportunity to illustrate the deep links between theology and mechanics. The sultan, Hamlin reported, took great interest in the machine and how it worked and was especially intrigued by the apparent fact that iron semicircles only magnetized when in contact with an electric current:

> [The sultan] took the iron semicircles, laid them on the coil, laid the coil on them, and placed them in every possible position, with no result; but when he passed the ends within the coil, they instantly cohered with a *click* that surprised him. At length, throwing them down, he turned to me, and said, "Why is this so?" I replied, "Your majesty, science makes known to us facts, but God only knows the reasons of those facts." He immediately bowed his head reverentially, and said no more.[57]

There is an ambiguity here—was the sultan reverential because of Hamlin's theological ingenuity or because of the magnets' resounding *click*? If it was the former, Hamlin cast technology as the gateway drug of Christianity, making Muslims in the Ottoman Empire open to a religiocultural shift. But if it was the latter, Hamlin saw technology *as* that shift, and its appearance in the Ottoman Empire signaled a matrix of cultural change already underway. In this latter sense, technology did not pave the way for a future change; it enacted a present one.

Ottoman Muslims shared the sense that the telegraph might draw people away from Islam. A didactic treatise probably written by a Turkish provincial religious scholar (outside the official ulema) in the last quarter of the nineteenth century expressed tremendous concern about the persuasive power of telegraph technology. The author identified the telegraph as a thing "which first appeared from the unbelievers" but even as such was "there by God's creation and by His decree."[58] The telegraph was a tempter: "God, Who is exalted, has created this kind of thing through the hands of the unbelievers, in order to lead astray, and deceive, the sinners, and the shameless. . . . If they see something like the aforesaid telegraph, they will flee away [from Islam]."[59] The telegraph for this author was marked by its non-Muslim origins, and this represented its power and its danger. From plural perspectives in the Ottoman context, the telegraph bore the power to catalyze religious and cultural transformation.

Media as material enactments of a culture coming into being defy common understandings of media as the pathways along which messages are sent from senders to receivers. In this "transmission view," as James Carey so helpfully names it, missionaries used media—from the Bible to the tract—as vehicles for the message of salvation they bore.[60] Missionaries certainly thought of media in terms of their power of transmission. But missionaries also considered media to be radical embodiments of God's favor for the West and an awe-inspiring expression of the glorious civilization that Christianity promised. New media, including Bibles and tracts, were understood by many to be spectacular manifestations of God's work on earth. Thus, the American Bible Society, another US Protestant missionary group active at the time, joined the ABCFM in putting concerted effort into the distribution of Bibles and tracts in the Levant.[61] The materiality of media became definitional for emerging US evangelicalism; in the words of historian of religion Candy Gunther Brown, the physicality of the Bible and other Christian publications represented the power of "the Word to transform the world."[62] In this sense, media were much more aligned with James Carey's alternative to transmission: ritual. In the ritual view, the media at stake matter not for what they transmit but for the fact of their presence, the relationships they establish, and the cultural conventions they embody.[63] Carey considers ritual communication to hark back to pretelegraphic technologies, but here the ritual model, especially with supplemental emphasis on materiality, is appropriate to the way missionaries used various media, from tracts to telegraphy.

A robust account of missionary media requires a reorientation in our understanding of what media do or, even, what they are. John Durham

Peters offers a definition of media that attends to this kind of communication. Media, as he defines them, are "ordering devices."[64] They organize our experience of the world. As Peters urges us, "Once communication is understood not only as sending messages—certainly an essential function—but also as providing conditions for existence, media cease to be only . . . messages and channels, and become infrastructures and forms of life."[65] Media in the context of US mission in the nineteenth century are best understood as the historically, culturally, and materially specific structures that organized particular ways of being in the world.

New media technologies played a critical role in US mission as marvels that embodied the progress and power that missionaries understood Christianity to offer. In Henry Harris Jessup's account of his half century in Syria, he offered a long list of technological accomplishments as evidence of missionary success:

> With regard to the material gains to Syria through the missionaries, it is worthy of note that Rev. Isaac Bird introduced the potato in 1827. . . . Mr. Hurter, our printer, introduced kerosene oil and lamps in 1865. . . . Americans also introduced the first steam printing-press in 1867, photographic camera in 1856, iron building beams in 1871, wire nails, sewing-machines, parlour organs in 1854, mimeographs, typewriters, dentistry in 1854, and agricultural machinery; Dr. Hamlin of Robert College, Constantinople introduced the Morse telegraph apparatus, and now the empire is netted over with telegraph wires.[66]

The work of mission was to spread the potato and the sewing machine, for these were the signs of an intertwined religious and cultural rectitude.

Take, for example, the Leyden jar displayed by US missionaries at a wedding party in Persia. They demonstrated the ability of this jar to store an electric charge: "The whole party seemed to be wrapped in amazement, declaring that the mysterious engine possessed *unlimited*, as well as *unseen* power. A more favorable opportunity for such an exhibition could not possibly have been presented; and we trust that some desire for knowledge and improvement may have been enkindled in the minds of these scores of the Persian nobles, and the multitudes of people who thronged the court to witness it."[67] In the scene painted by the missionaries, technology awed the party and spurred the desire for "improvement" (presumably both religious and cultural, with no way to distinguish the two). Technology bore a God-effect, marking the minds of the Persians as religion would. These stories of media technology reveal a particular relationship between machines and mission; they should be understood as the strategic use not so much of media *in* mission but of media *as* mission.

The Matter of Networks

Since James Carey first conferred fame on the telegraph as the marker of a radical split between information and its human carriers on their various forms of transportation, the telegraph has often signaled the dematerialization of communication.[68] This study is, instead, curious about the materiality of telegraphic communication (Carey, however ambiguously, provides an important consideration of the materiality of telegraphy, as will be discussed in chapter 4). New materialist theories from scholars such as Karen Barad, Jane Bennett, and Bruno Latour, drawing on the much older theories of Spinoza and Lucretius, insist that we consider the *life* of *things*: their actions, their power, and their refusal to behave according to our rules and desires.[69] A healthy regard for the vital capacity of the telegraph allows us to attend to the boats that creaked against the weight of the cables, to the uncooperative ocean that tossed them about, to electricity that surged through the line, to the insulation that melted at the heat of all those dots and dashes, to the slight flick of delicate mirrors that caught transatlantic electric messages for the first time in history. In these activities of matter, the telegraph network came to life.

And such material activity brought more life—for the ABCFM, specifically Christian life—along with it. According to the prominent administrator for the ABCFM the Reverend Judson Smith, a confluence of technology, industry, and commerce paved the way for Christianity and, on its own in his syntax, created the change that missionaries hoped for in China:

> Commerce is penetrating to the very heart of China, and is bringing new ideas into the midst of the people. The telegraph is beginning to spread its network of new life over the land. Mining has begun to develop the

prodigious wealth that lies restored up in the mountains. Railroads will soon still further hasten the collapse of old customs and conceits, the quickening of a new and better life. There is evidence that the existing religions of China are losing their hold, old faiths are falling, the sense of approaching revolution and change is widely diffused. All these things make the very opportunity we seek.[70]

For Smith, new technologies and industrial processes bore the capacity to bring a fundamental force of life into places he considered bound by dying customs and old religions. Matter—in its exhilarating newness— was an agent of life, quickened and Christian.

Privileging human actors calls attention to all those people who invested meaning, money, and power in the telegraph, whether inventors, promoters, or tactical saboteurs. Missionaries championed technology as inherently Christian progress, and Ottomans celebrated the machine, sabotaged the lines, built a network, and ultimately undid an empire with it (as discussed in the next section). The telegraph, however, is reduced in such accounts to a passive bearer of meaning supplied by missionaries, sultans, and revolutionaries as if the telegraph only ever was an emblem of imperialism or nationalism. The telegraph's disruptions of such meaning get hidden beneath discursive determination. The story of the telegraph, full of faults and failures, demonstrates that it never successfully bore such meaning, certainly not without its own interruptions and revisions.

Privileging the power of technology, on the other hand, tends to root networks in the inevitable force of progress and cannot account for the ways the telegraph was made and remade by ambitious, if often bumbling, people. Moreover, technological determinism does not resolve the reduction of technology to a seamless vehicle for imperial meaning. In fact, it seems to compound it. In one missionary account, Japan was swept up in an explosion of divine and technological agency without any mention of people at all, but the technology remained beholden to the missionary imagination: "The waters of the coasts of Japan are now plowed by steamers in every direction, nearly 2,000 miles of railroad are in operation, and thousands of miles of jinrikisha roads are found, while a network of telegraph wires is spread over the land, and the postal facilities extend to the remotest hamlet, and these railroads, steamers, telegraphs, and post offices are all the ready servants of the messengers of the Cross."[71] Both social constructivism and technological determinism fall far short of the rich interplay of connection and disconnection that fueled network technology and the multiple actors wound up in its web.

And, as Bruno Latour insists, the attempt to strike a dialectical balance between these two perspectives is also doomed to fail. Both technological determinism and social constructivism retain the same investment in mastery despite disagreeing on whether humans master machines or machines master humans. Dialectical accounts of technological and social change get stuck against the apparently indelible difference between the subject and the object. A better option, Latour contends, is the recognition that people and things are all "participants in the course of action."[72] Broadening the ontological field of agency opens an escape route from the bind of the binary choice of who (or what) is on top—humans *or* technology—and paves the way for a rigorous consideration of the multiple forms of agency at play.

Once humans and nonhumans are recognized as actors, agency can no longer be located in any single body, let alone a human one. For Jane Bennett, "an actant [a human or nonhuman actor] never really acts alone. Its efficacy or agency always depends on the collaboration, cooperation, or interactive interference of many bodies and forces." Agency becomes, in Bennett's terms, "distributed across an ontologically heterogeneous field, rather than being a capacity localized in a human body or in a collective produced (only) by human efforts."[73] A robust account of the telegraph network in the Ottoman Empire depends on the expansiveness of such ontological heterogeneity. The network was not simply a wire here and a machine there but also the codes, the alphabets, the electricity, the powerful desires of sultans and nations, the momentum of multiple forms of colonialism, the enthusiasm, the flubs, the sabotage, and the wonder. This sort of ontological promiscuity is true to the capaciousness of the term *technology* itself, which, as discussed earlier, offers a machine to stand in for a vast array of practices, materials, forces, habits, and forms of communication.[74] Technology, especially network technology, thus always represents a tangled assemblage of, in Bennett's phrasing, "vibrant matter."[75]

Attending to the material agency at work in missionary practice and discourse highlights the promises of network technology in all its active glory: global reach, instantaneous communication, and cohesive global culture. For US missionaries in the nineteenth century, wiring electric communication across the globe would suture the world into Christian congregation link by link. Yet, attention to missionary media as vital matter also reveals a current that runs against the sweeping tide of enthusiasm for global connection that marks descriptions of networks then and now. The telegraph betrayed Hamlin and his technologically infatuated missionary compatriots. Its story was one of gaps and failures. There was death and international drama. And above all, there was *dis*connection. The telegraph's tense relationship to the promise with which it was varnished offers a new understanding of the disconnection that underwrites networks and issues a call for a more robust account of disconnection in materialist theories. While US Christian missionaries held up networks of various kinds as divine mandates for global conversion and the unique promise of a new era of evangelical reach, Morse's telegraph stumbled its way across the ocean, arrived broken, drowned in a river, fought off competing European machines, and made use of war. Any connection it managed to forge was made possible by political machinations, colonialism, various forms of violence, and the failures of the technology itself. In the case of the telegraph in the Ottoman Empire, do not imagine a shining system of binding wires. Imagine a tangle of cables tarnished by sea salt and domination; knotted up in seaweed, politics, and money; and rife with both literal and figurative fracture. Imagine the gaps where those cables were not.

A Network of Rapture/A Network of Rupture

The story of the telegraph in the Ottoman Empire often begins with US innovation and, in a tale charged with excitement and exoticism, quickly lands at the port of Constantinople. But then the telegraph stumbles and falters, the heady thrall of expansionism stopped in its tracks by faulty wires, shaky boats, and political schemes.[76] After Morse's telegraph machine arrived in Constantinople, it took a circuitous eight-year journey from Constantinople to Hamlin's seminary in Bebek, up to Vienna for repairs, back to Bebek, and only then on to the sultan's Beylerbey Palace across the Bosporus. From there it took another eight years and an unruly confluence of colonialism, capitalism, and war to wire the first Ottoman telegraph line. Within decades the Ottoman Empire boasted a large telegraphic network, served as an important route for global communication, and became the recipient of half of Britain's wire production—but only through a winding path of loss, missteps, and sabotage.[77] Understanding this history demands that we see the failure and fractures of the telegraph's development not as obstacles overcome by the steady march of technological progress but as integral parts of what religions, the telegraph, and the Ottoman Empire became as they entangled themselves in these new cables.

From the telegraph's arrival in the Ottoman Empire to its meeting with the sultan eight years later, it needed the missionary. The lack of an electrical power source and missing parts thrust the telegraph machine into Cyrus Hamlin's hands not once but twice. Businessman Mellen Chamberlain brought Samuel Morse's electromagnetic telegraph to the Ottoman Empire in 1839 as part of his work with Morse to win international patents for his machine in competition with European versions.[78] Hearing that Hamlin had a galvanic battery in his seminary, Chamberlain took the machine there. Morse's machine worked but was unreliable, and its transmissions were error-ridden. Hamlin and Chamberlain decided to have a new and improved machine constructed in Vienna before attempting to sell Morse's telegraph to the Ottoman Empire. According to Hamlin, Chamberlain and five others set out on the Danube "with high hopes and enthusiasm" only to lose their lives (and the machine) when the rapids claimed the boat: "Thus perished this early attempt to introduce the telegraph into the East."[79]

Eight years later, John Lawrence Smith, a US chemist and mineralogist working in the Ottoman Empire, ordered a new telegraph machine from America. It arrived with parts missing, and Smith turned to Hamlin to supply the missing parts, fix the machine, and set it up in the seminary to practice before presenting it to the sultan. At the long-awaited presentation, the sultan considered the missionary and the mineralogist before him and sent Smith to the other room, desiring to put the "great magician" at a distance and keep the "less[er]" one close by. Thus, it was the missionary who transmitted the sultan's first telegram.[80]

The life of the Ottoman telegraph always included this strange mix of connection and fracture, both the products of the relationship of religion and media. The sultan was impressed with the demonstration of

Morse's telegraph machine and invited Hamlin, Smith, and Brown back to repeat it before a gathering of high-ranking government officials. Many of the officials shared the sultan's excitement, and it was decided that a telegraph line would be established to Adrianople (present-day Edirne), approximately 150 miles to the west. But a portentous disconnection haunted even this moment of telegraphic connection: Hamlin and Smith later discovered that one of the wires in the palace had been separated after the first successful telegram was sent. Hamlin suspected sabotage by someone opposed to the establishment of an Ottoman telegraph. Indeed, the preemptively celebrated line to Adrianople was not built for nearly a decade due to opposition by influential members of the Ottoman political system.[81]

It was an international war over religion that finally motivated the construction of the Ottoman telegraph line. Among the myriad causes of the Crimean War (1853–56) were conflicts over the rights of and protections for Christian subjects of the empire in the Holy Land, exacerbated by missionary activity in the Ottoman Empire that spurred religious tensions.[82] (Catholic) France and (Orthodox) Russia aggravated the struggle as the war ballooned into an international battle for land and power. The allied British and French wrestled with a five-day transmission time between troops in Crimea and authorities in London. Messages would travel two days by steamer from Crimea to Varna, then three days by horseback to Bucharest, and then by telegraph to London.[83] In 1855, France and Britain laid the first telegraph lines in the Ottoman Empire: France laid an overland line from Bucharest to Varna, and Britain laid a submarine line under the Black Sea to connect Varna with Balaklava, the British army headquarters in Crimea.[84] While the Black Sea line was at the time the longest submarine cable in the world, additional length would have helped: the British laid the line with so little slack that it failed in under a year. With the war nearing an end, the British abandoned the effort.[85] With French support, however, a series of telegraph lines connected Balaklava with London via Bucharest, Jassy, and Varna within the year.[86]

Hamlin marveled at the suddenly speedy development of telegraphy in the Ottoman Empire: "The Crimean War made it a necessity; and the lines have become numerous, uniting Constantinople with all the world. From the distant parts of the empire, from India, from

America, from all parts of Europe, the telegrams pour into the capital, and are published morning and evening."[87] The spreading vision of a rapidly cohering world cast the telegraph as the great unifier; disconnections, faulty cables, and the fracture of war were emphatically omitted from Hamlin's narrative as the rapidly shrinking Ottoman Empire found itself woven into a complicated and fragile web of empires and nations, which Hamlin described as a single and complete "all the world."

After the war, the Ottoman Empire bought the lines and equipment to help cohere its territory and reinforce the centralized power of the sultan. The first project of the Ottoman Ministry of Public Works was the construction of the originally proposed line between Constantinople and Adrianople.[88] Historians, missionaries, and the sultan himself have seen the early years of Ottoman telegraphy as an epoch of centralization of power under the Sublime Porte.[89] By 1874, Jessup sent a letter to a friend about the Ottoman Empire in which he stated, "They have a postal telegraph service, defective enough, and yet enabling the central power in Constantinople to move the whole empire like a machine."[90] The Ottoman Empire owned the network and supported its development, and the British and French remained deeply involved, particularly given the British interest in submarine and overland telegraph routes to India after the Indian Rebellion of 1857.

But local resistance to the network by religious leaders complicated the narrative of consolidation. As civilians increasingly used the telegraph system, Muslim clergy began to voice concerns for the power of the technology to erode Ottoman culture and religious life and extend Satan's influence.[91] Rooted in the long history of prioritizing oral media in Islam, suspicion of this imported tool increased in tandem with the rising threat to the empire from Europe.[92] New media had long performed as flash points for concerns about global politics and religious authority and became contentious touchstones for debates about authority and cultural change among Muslims. In 1727, the Ottoman pasha Sa'id Effendi was the catalyst for the Muslim adoption of print technology, and in 1729 the Ottoman diplomat and historian Ibrahim Muteferriqa was the first Muslim to open a printing press with movable type in Arabic. Muteferriqa argued that the adoption of print would restore Muslims' intellectual superiority.[93] Thus the Ottoman sultan Abdülhamid II

(1876–1909), who inherited the burgeoning Ottoman telegraph system, met the concerns of the telegraph's detractors with a strategy familiar to the empire. He claimed the telegraph as a particularly Islamic invention and, with the railroad, as a symbol of "Pan-Islamism"; the viability of his interpretation was helped in no small part by the construction of a line from Damascus to Mecca.[94]

In addition to religious resistance, local landowners and tribal authorities at times actively sabotaged the telegraph for its role in facilitating the Tanzimat restructuring of local administration and land rights.[95] It was a particularly effective way to get the attention of the distant Porte intent on cohering the empire over alternative deep-seated structures of power. In response to such sabotage, there was a flurry of production of regulations, laws, and inspection positions all designed to protect the telegraph system.[96] Thus, these disconnective processes and events were creative, resulting in new identities, technologies, relationships, and administrative procedures. A striking example of this dynamic is the report in the *Examiner* of the signing of an 1864 British-Ottoman convention to construct the Indian telegraph line, immediately followed by the report of a supply of British weapons given to the Porte for the Imperial Guard.[97]

Fracture not only participated in the establishment of the Ottoman telegraph network but also became a central effect of its construction. While the Sublime Porte supported the expanding network as a way to consolidate the sizable empire and impose a series of broad administrative reforms, it also became a way for distant subjects to send speedy complaints to the government at a time of tremendous social and political transition. Ultimately, the Ottoman telegraph played a key role in the disintegration of the empire.[98] In 1908, Abdülhamid II, who had made great use of the telegraph in his reign, found himself deluged by telegrams of complaint demanding dramatic governmental change, which historian Roderic Davison calls "revolution by telegraph."[99] The telegraph was a key organizing tool of the 1908 Young Turk Revolution and allowed leaders like Talat Pasha (originally a telegraph clerk) to grow the movement outside the view of the sultan.[100] Britain, France, and Russia cut Ottoman telegraph lines in 1915 (sixty years after building the first line in the Ottoman Empire) in the Gallipoli Campaign of World War I. Despite the Allies' optimism that doing so would be a defining coup

(Louis Edgar Browne's punny headline in the *Chicago Tribune* reads, "bold stroke cuts off line") Gallipoli was the only major Ottoman victory in the war.[101] The drastic defeat of the Ottoman Empire in World War I (a war in which all sides made great use of the telegraph and other network technology) paved the way for the dissolution of the empire by internal revolt just a few years later.

Ottoman nationalism, with roots in the Tanzimat reforms, grew exponentially when faced with Allied occupation. Kemal Atatürk, a "master in the use of the telegraph," used the Anatolia line to organize nationalist resistance through telegraphic communication with sympathizers in Istanbul.[102] In 1919, representatives from all of the Anatolian provinces met at the Congress of Sivas and issued a series of demands to the sultan. The telegraph played a central role in this critical turn of events. Atatürk (then General Mustapha Kemal Pasha) and Reouf Bey took the resolution of the congress and, according to Browne, "gave the Sultan one hour to get out of bed, proceed across Constantinople to the end of the telegraph wire in Stamboul to hear and accept the ultimatum of the Sivas congress." The refusal of various ministers to appear at the telegraph office initiated the terms of the ultimatum and cut Anatolia off from Istanbul. According to Browne's report, Atatürk and Reouf Bey were able to secure the agreement of all of the important unoccupied cities in Anatolia from the telegraph office: "I have never heard of more efficient communication than I witnessed that night."[103] In Atatürk's famous six-day speech, *Nutuk* (*The Speech*), he described how he unleashed a "telegram tempest" on Istanbul as part of his campaign.[104] When later asked how he won the war of independence, Atatürk responded, "With telegraph wires."[105] Which is to say, the very telegraph that was brought by Hamlin to convert Ottomans to Christianity, built by the French and British to secure military prominence, and developed by the sultan to strengthen the empire was embedded in establishment of the secular Republic of Turkey.[106]

In the frame of human and nonhuman agency, causal links and gaps come to the fore. For Latour, action reveals itself always to offer a "slight surprise": "There are events. I never *act*; I am always slightly surprised by what I do. That which acts through me is also surprised by what I do, by the chance to mutate, to change, and to bifurcate, the chance that I and the circumstances surrounding me offer to that which has been invited, recovered, welcomed."[107] A full understanding of activity and agency cannot focus only on the connections between cause and effect; it must include the unexpected disconnections that creatively upset intention. The linearity of cause and effect crumbles in the face of the deviations, disruptions, and defiance of expectations that a materialist approach reveals.[108]

US and British missionaries wrestled with materiality's disobedience to their intentions in the middle of the nineteenth century. Despite early widespread celebration of civilization as a necessary precursor to conversion, a lively debate over the ultimate effectiveness of civilizing measures marked the middle of the nineteenth century. Particularly in the context of opium use, British missionaries raised concerns that the negative effects of civilization were worse than its benefits, in one case calling attention to "that nervous pain which is called 'tic,' a short word for long, throbbing agonies . . . [which] is the product of civilization."[109]

The spectacular technologies meant to mark cultural assimilation fell short of producing the religious effects that missionaries so ardently desired. Missionary accounts in both the ABCFM's *Missionary Herald* and the various journals of the London Missionary Society began to include a repetitive trope of the failures of material changes to secure permanent Christian conversion. An example is the Reverend Josiah Tyler's dismay when a promising Zulu convert, who had left his home and traveled abroad for sixteen years, returned to South Africa:

> Now comes the sad part of this story. He had not been in his heathen
> *kraal* more than a fortnight, before he dropped all his civilized clothing,
> and put on the skins of wild animals, like the rest of his heathen friends.
> He chose a wife from among the heathen, and is now living with no apparent desire for civilizing influences. His heart was not changed, alas!
> and he is a heathen still.[110]

In 1884, Smith, an early technological enthusiast and vocal supporter of the power of industry in mission, offered this reversal in the *Missionary Herald*:

> In countless instances through all the centuries Christianity has heralded civilization and prepared its way and thrown around it a favoring

atmosphere and cherishing guards. The life and institutions of all the Western nations are thus permeated and colored and shaped throughout by the Christian faith. But the reverse is not true; civilization does not always and necessarily lead to Christianity and open the way for its spread; it has often been found in high degree for great lengths of time, without any perceptible relation to the kingdom of Christ. Now our aim is to Christianize and not to civilize.[111]

Despite a robust rhetoric of the power of civilization, the missionaries found that the techniques of civilization confounded their determinations for it. The technologies missionaries promoted left tics, losses, and disconnections in their wake.

The trick with a materialist consideration of disconnection is that disconnections, by definition, are not there. They are an absence that makes a difference. Just as technology (in codes, protocols, etc.) exceeds tangibility, matter cannot be reduced to that which is accessible to sensory perception. Lots of things are material and imperceptible, from electrical charges to the frantic dance of atoms in the most solid of steel. The materiality I embrace here takes up the new media theorist Jussi Parikka's expansive sense that "materiality is not just machines—nor is it just solids, and things, or even objects."[112] Networks, especially, are ontological multiplicities built of actions, forces, and matter that often elude observation and include plenty of what Parikka calls "real . . . non-solid things," including "modulations of electrical, magnetic, and light energies, in which also power is nowadays embedded."[113] In other words, recognizing matter as assemblage entails refusing an equation of matter with solids or things immediately available for perception. As Bennett reminds us, "Materiality . . . is as much force as entity, as much energy as matter, as much intensity as extension."[114] Even solid objects are made up of moving atoms, and thus no matter is ever passive; it is always already a complicated series of interactions among atoms, space, movement, structure, and force.

The commonsensical affiliation of networks with connection is an old habit. Even the missionaries understood the gaps, fractures, failures, and discontinuities that arose as minor obstacles to be overcome by connection's pure force. The network derived its particular power from its omnivorous appetite to incorporate. One missionary writing on recent innovations in network technologies marveled at their ability to create systems out of lines: "Railways, the telegraph, and the public mails had grown from isolated lines into systems and networks, knitting the whole country together."[115] In such an imaginary, technologies wove themselves into networks and, in so doing, knit a country into connection. Yet discontinuities were useful to the network, and not only when they were overcome; they were themselves productive. Lacks, gaps, needs, and breaks shaped networks in unique ways, and networks required and produced discontinuities. In fact, US Protestant mission, while oriented toward visions of global religious unity, required gaps in religious homogeny as license to missionize. In other words, missionary discourse and practice focused on global connection but were fueled by a profound need for and commitment to disconnection.

Religious involvement in the establishment of telegraph networks highlights the persuasive power of matter on spirit and the constitutive ruptures of a network meant to cohere community (whether religious or imperial). Connection and disconnection worked through each other in tense tandems, dyadic tropes that played on paradox and impossibility: a whole world created by important forms of exclusion and the promise of proximity to people adamantly characterized as strangers. The final sections of this chapter examine these two pairings in turn. These tropes were utterly unsuccessful—each fell apart in some way—and it is their failure that made them particularly productive participants in this network. Attending to the matter of global telegraphy contributes to a call for more attention to the deep relationship between religious and material agency in networks and to the power of disconnection, gaps, and failure in matter, particularly as a force that built and sustained networks.

Incomplete Whole

During the demonstration of Morse's machine to the sultan, something quite strange happened. Brown, Hamlin, and Smith set up the telegraph with one station in the throne room and another in a corner room of the palace, winding a wire between them. They asked the sultan to come up with a message they would send from one room to the other. Facing a telegraph system firmly confined by the palace walls, the sultan asked, "Has the French steamer arrived? And what is the news from Europe?"[116] Before the telegraph connected even one building to another, the sultan imagined the machine in global terms. His message was like many of the test messages that were used in early demonstrations of telegraphy, which in Lisa Gitelman's illustrative catalog of them read like a litany for the mundane artifice of modern capitalist globalization: "The enemy is near!" "Steam boat Caroline burnt!" "Attention the Universe!" and "Send 56 copies."[117] That was the particular magic of the telegraph: even disconnected from a *local* network, it seemed to bring a *global* network and the whole world it encapsulated into being.

Such an imaginary was not entirely a fantasy; the machine had crossed continents and oceans and appeared at that very moment in a surprising confluence of transnational politics, technology, and religion. Within a decade the first telegraph line was built in the Ottoman Empire; within two the empire was connected to India, Crimea, and Europe; and within three it boasted the eighth-largest telegraph network in the world, spanning more than seventeen thousand miles.[118] The telegraph participated in a host of other coordinating activities that were shoring up a sense of the global, from contemporary efforts to synchronize time across space to protocols that standardized the conventions of media (e.g., Morse code).[119]

For US missionaries, however, ambitious promises exaggerated the possibilities that appeared when this tangible circuit began to encircle the earth, fueling the potent image of a whole world turned to Christ. In the words of one Protestant publicist when California came under US control, "Home and foreign missions have struck hands on the Pacific. Bible and tract operations have girdled the globe."[120] Emerging networks of communication and travel animated missionary imaginaries of the world as a whole and bounded Christian entity. The ambitious universalism charged by new technologies became a clarion call to missionaries in the nineteenth century. In this sense, US missionaries embodied the spirit of Western modernity, affirming Arjun Appadurai's maxim, "Modernity belongs to that small family of theories that both declares and desires universal applicability for itself."[121] The paradoxically simultaneous declaration of and desire for global Christianity point to the energetic tension between presence and possibility, between tangibility and intangibility, and between connection and disconnection at play in emerging missionary imaginaries of a networked world.

US missionaries heralded the developing network of communication and transportation technologies as the dawn of a new age that would make their evangelical endeavor uniquely possible. Along with enabling wide and speedy dissemination of missionary messages, networks seemed to reshape the world into a thing with fixed borders inside of which missionaries might now, tantalizingly, have absolute access. Hopkins remarked on the novelty of this experience of the world in his "Semi-Centennial Address" at the fiftieth anniversary of the founding of the ABCFM: "For the first time since the dispersion of men, is the world waking up to the consciousness of itself as one whole."[122] The Reverend Leonard Baker remarked at the 1836 annual meeting, "God seems to be opening the whole world to missionary effort and enterprise. The walls which formerly separated us from the heathen empires have fallen down."[123] Christian missionaries considered this new openness to constitute permission if not demand for missionary incursion. In the words of the "Annual Survey of the Missions of the Board" in 1851, "Not in vain has [God] opened so large a portion of the whole world for the labors of Christian missionaries."[124]

US missionaries framed new global imaginaries in terms of the connection they understood networks to offer, particularly the bounded totality they made out of unfathomable space, the unprecedented access they promised within those borders, and the intimacy they would apparently forge within its scope. Hopkins stated, "Now [the ABCFM's] mission stations belt the globe, so that the sun does not set upon them, and the whole world is open."[125] He continued, "The circuit of that globe, with every continent, and island, and ocean that it rolls up to the sunlight or buries in its shadow is now known; and this it is that we are to conquer for Christ."[126] The world now wrapped—both figuratively and literally—in mission networks fueled the imagery of the earth's boundedness and the concomitant possibility of global Christian community. These imaginaries of a networked globe emphasized universality: in the face of the suddenly possible *all*, *some* barely counted. The world in this ideal form would be both complete and completely converted.

Naming the whole world as the site of mission produced an imaginary of the world as a comprehensive and complete totality without remainder. As missionaries of the ABCFM repeated throughout the

1800s, the mission field was the world itself, and the whole of it would be conquered for Christ. Only two decades after the ABCFM's founding in 1810, it adopted the ambitious goal of evangelizing the entire world.[127] In 1836, the annual meeting of the ABCFM unanimously passed the following resolution: "In view of the signs of the times, and of the promises of God, that the day has arrived in which the work of converting *the world* to God should be undertaken with a definite scheme of operations based upon the expectation of its speedy accomplishment."[128] Despite the optimism of this initial call, the ABCFM was calling for the same, with the same urgency, fifty years later. The Reverend Arthur T. Pierson of Detroit, Michigan, wrote in the *Missionary Herald* in 1881, "The time has fully come for concluding the colossal scheme of the world's evangelization as an enterprise of the united Christian Church . . . by a division of the field which is the world." ABCFM historian Clifton Phillips notes that "the directors of foreign missions had no grand strategy for the Christian conquest of the heathen world," but that did not seem to stop the board from trying.[129] The ABCFM stated regularly that its primary goal was to evangelize the whole world throughout the nineteenth century, including in the annual reports of 1836, 1859, 1878, and 1895.[130]

The apparent futility of these enthusiastic declarations did not diminish their popularity. In fact, the futility seems to have preserved a productive discourse for the ABCFM across nearly a century of its existence. By the late nineteenth century, the call to evangelize the whole world became an assumed mark of commitment to Christian mission in general.[131] In the words of the Reverend A. N. Hitchcock of Chicago, "Now beyond a doubt, this spirit of our body is vitally related to the evangelization of the world." Hitchcock was not satisfied that it be merely the central commitment of missionaries and demanded that it be the central commitment of the church as a whole from the individual pastor to every corporate entity:

> When pastors are installed let us ask this question, "Brethren, do you believe that the evangelization of the whole world is the final end of your ministry?" And when churches are recognized let us ask the same questions. Let us put it into our articles of faith, into our covenants, and into all the constitutions of our associations. Here is described the

normal sphere and the appointed function of the entire church in all its membership, and all its machinery, and all its associate life.[132]

Hitchcock's words illuminate the zeal with which the whole world became a new and demanding missionary object. Christian ideas of the whole world date back to biblical literature and were a cornerstone of the ways the Pauline epistles imagined a coherence for a scattered community.[133] Biblical uses of the idea of the whole world are regularly quoted by the ABCFM; new technology reactivated this old idea.[134] At this moment in the nineteenth century, when advances in travel and communication were part of a new dominance of the global over the local, the novelty of the whole world commanded a pressing power.

The wholeness of this new world was equal parts external boundedness and internal unity. Missionary unity discourse, however, reveals the importance of difference for their networked world. For Hopkins, the association of numerous Protestant sects in missionary ventures sparked a "blessed upheaval of great truths, where, as upon a high table land, Christians could walk and work together, and look down upon their differences, and claim the same promises, and with the eye of faith sweep the horizon of the whole world as their common field, and feel how much more there is that united than there is that divides them."[135] A single Christianity emerged at the vantage point of great global diversity.

The declaration of Christian unity flew in the face of the robust sectarianism of Christian—and particularly US Protestant—history, requiring rhetorical twists and turns in which unity was named only through the differences that underwrote it. Hopkins, echoing the founding documents of the London Missionary Society, repeated their apophatic enumeration of the many different sects that make up this supposedly natural and universal unity: "It is declared to be a fundamental principle of the Missionary Society that our design is not to send Presbyterianism, Independency, Episcopy, or any other form of church order and government, (about which there may be a difference of opinion among serious people,) but 'the glorious Gospel of the blessed God' to the heathen."[136] Missionaries enchanted by their own pan-Protestantism celebrated new alliances through the sectarian differences that made such unity discourse meaningful, just as they celebrated mission through the religious difference that served as its mandate.

Hopkins's list of the denominations that composed Protestant unity and, indeed, his citation of the founding documents of the London Missionary Society—an only occasional ally to the ABCFM—epitomized the rhetorical convention among missionaries of celebrating unity by detailing difference. Cyrus Hamlin's autobiographical description of the Praying Circle he encountered at Bowdoin likewise elaborated distinctions to depict unity: "The Praying Circle brought together the religious element of the college without any distinctions. In that there were neither Congregationalists, Baptists, Methodists, nor Presbyterians. Its influence in college was unobtrusive, but was very great."[137]

Investment in pan-Protestant international unity as a representation of what Protestantism could offer a divided world reflected a religious context that both spurred and collapsed sectarian distinction. The period of the ABCFM's rise was marked by the transatlantic revivalism that contributed to the creation of and alliance among new forms of Protestantism on both sides of the ocean. Emerging tract, home missionary, temperance, and Bible societies marked and erased the differences among these new expressions of religion. These social movements and religious practices, which multiplied difference and relied on unity across denominational divides, motivated many of the missionaries in the field and the investors who funded them.

Likewise, the global spread of colonial Christianity coincided with the rise of the nation-state, a new and critical form of both structural similarity and political difference.[138] The forms of globalism that rose in the nineteenth century were sustained by transnational projects, like the telegraph, and an emerging parallelism made possible by the establishment of nation-states around the world.[139] As much as missionaries understood moral reform to supersede national difference, they also understood the formation of nation-states as a mark of successful mission.[140] Strong's 1910 history of the ABCFM chronicled missionary activity in present-day Hawaii in this way: "The transformation of the Sandwich Islands from a land of savages to an ordered nation was now accomplished."[141] (Of course, this transformation was soon superseded by the machinations of the United States to facilitate a coup and annex the islands to its own territory as Hawaii.) While nation-states presented the possibility of equality among like civil forms, national difference was reinforced by the ABCFM's practice of distinguishing between foreign (i.e., US) and native mission workers. Missionaries kept records that made and maintained this distinction. While the role, power, and value of native mission workers were a source of conflict among US missionaries, it was understood that the native workers' responsibilities were determined formally by the foreign missionaries.[142] The goal of Christian unity was wrought by critical differences in Christian power.

In addition to the tension between unity and difference played out through sectarian, cultural, and geographic encounter, the missionary imaginary of complete global totality relied on a key form of *incompletion*. Missionary writing reveals a sense of two worlds at work in the whole world: the Christian world and the world to be made Christian. In 1812, an address to the "Christian Public" at the third annual meeting of the ABCFM declared, "All the power and influence of the *whole Christian world* must be put in requisition, during the course of those beneficent labors which will precede the millennium. . . . The utmost exertion of every Christian now living, so far as his other duties will permit, is required in this glorious service."[143] The Appaduraian gap between the declaration and desire for global Christianity was the mandate mission required. In the words of the Reverend A. N. Andrus, "When Dr. Newman, of Washington, journeyed from India through the Persian Gulf, up the Euphrates and Tigris on his way across the Turkish Empire to the Mediterranean, he was surprised to find no traces of missionary labor until he reached the gates of Mosul! Indeed, the chain of missions which connects the whole world with the Christian Church has a break here; a link is missing."[144] The missing link was the missionary's raison d'être.

The missionary imaginary of unified global totality came into being through a simultaneous imaginary of a world split down the middle between Christians and their others, and both were understood in various ways to be bound by new networks. Often, missionaries declared certain religious populations to be out of reach of conversion, as in Smith's account of Turkey:

> Cities, towns, villages, hamlets, and homes are reached in a steady widening of the field, until all Asiatic Turkey is covered with a network of

stations and out-stations, of churches and schools, that bring the new impulse to well-nigh every home and heart in the non-Moslem population of the empire. The Moslem population soon became inaccessible, and has remained so to this day. Hence the aim of missionary effort has been to bring a pure gospel to the nominally Christian peoples, the Armenians, the Greeks, the Syrians, and through the internal reformation of these old churches to make ready for the time when the gospel could be freely preached to all nationalities.[145]

The network of missions able to spread across the vast expanse of the Ottoman Empire and into hearts and homes was halted in its voracious tracks by the refusals of the local Muslims.

Missionary affiliation of ambitious universalism with absolute exclusions points to the failure at the heart of network imaginaries: the wholeness of any network is always incomplete and necessarily so. A report in the *Missionary Herald* on Christian missions in India in the late 1870s provides an illustrative metaphor from the Protestant missionary M. A. Sherring: "The land is spread over with a network of Christian congregations, which, like the stars in the sky, are so many small luminaries shedding light upon the surrounding darkness."[146] Sherring described the network in expansive terms: spreading over the land and composed of nodes as numerous as the stars. And yet his racist metaphor also reveals that networks produce and require a background that is not, and cannot be, part of the network itself. Thus, Sherring could understand the linked Christian congregations as bright lights that have nothing at all to do with the dark sky in which they are housed. The inclusive impulse of a totalizing network is predicated on a primary exclusion that networks disavow.

Intimate Strangers

Networks reanimated an old Christian trope: the sense of the whole world subject to a singular God. In biblical texts, the wholeness of the wide world demonstrates the expansive majesty of its creator, but by the nineteenth century the whole world offered the particular power of a smaller size: the promise of intimate access. Close relationships seemed possible with distant strangers and played on the motif of tensions between presence and possibility, matter and spirit, and connection and disconnection. These intimate stranger relations were animated by the electric friction of making proximity out of distance.

It was a sort of global bait and switch: missionaries claimed that the grand material stretch of wires and rail collapsed the vast extension of geographic space. Proximity and reach despite, or rather in defiance of, distance became a reigning trope in descriptions of new communication technologies and the world they appeared to produce. At the annual meeting of 1890, Smith presented a paper titled "The Missionary Outlook," in which he stated,

> With the introduction of steamships and railways, and the constant improvements in machinery, with the network of telegraph lines covering the great continents, and sunk beneath the seas, and binding all parts of the world into the circuits of swift intelligence, space and time are almost annihilated, the continents are near neighbors, and even the islands of the sea have lost their isolation and form a part of the closely linked system of the world.[147]

These rapidly connecting lines of emerging networks bore the curious ability to thread their way through land and sea to overcome both. Proximity and reach framed communication as connection and set such connection against the foil of the distance it supposedly overcame. In that way, any intimacy that US Americans attributed to emerging networks was underwritten by the distance and gaps that were used to define previous modes of communication. The network was not important if it only replicated what a walk across the lane could accomplish—the marvels of the telegraph shimmered in the light of conquered expanses.

Expansive intimacy as a result of emerging networks of communication became a refrain for Smith. A paper he delivered in 1890 celebrated the "growing ease of communication between all parts of the world" as the catalyst for a rapidly shrinking globe:

> The ends of the earth are thus brought together; the effect of near neighborhood is thus increasingly realized, in better acquaintance, truer appreciation, kindlier sentiments, and a deepening sense of mutual duty

among the nations. The world is one, its inhabitants one race, its nations kindred, its hopes and fortunes one. Travel and commerce feel the impulse of this widening circle of human life; the civilization of the foremost nations tends to spread itself far and near; common interests grow up to bind nations and people into a living unity.[148]

Smith's enthusiasm for the technological capacities of the nineteenth century promised a vast world made up of strangers who were both geographically bound and emotionally close. His "near neighborhood" echoed the prominent theologian (and father of Harriet Beecher Stowe) Lyman Beecher's similar claim about communication networks sixty-three years earlier: "The intercourse between different parts of the globe is becoming daily more frequent and easy, contracting the dimensions of the world, and bringing the most distant parts into near neighborhoods. . . . By the rapidity and ubiquity of commercial intercourse, the whole world is more accessible to missionary enterprise now, than the Roman empire was in the days of Paul."[149] Space morphed under the bind of cabled networks and produced affects of intimacy among the global inhabitants of a suddenly "near neighborhood."

The idea of a global neighborhood engaged two fused Christian definitions of neighbor: one who lives near whom one should love deeply, and the stranger to whom one has an ethical and emotional obligation. The books of Matthew, Mark, and Luke not only repeat the divine commandment from Leviticus to "love your neighbor as yourself" but also depict Jesus naming this commandment the second greatest, bested only by the commandment to love God.[150] In the account in Luke, when asked, "Who is my neighbor?" Jesus tells the parable of the Good Samaritan, identifying the neighbor as a stranger who shows mercy to another.[151] The metaphor of the neighbor is governed by an equation of stranger, friend, and self and thus equipped missionaries with a rhetoric of geographic, ethical, and emotional proximity that could span the world and overcome nation-state and sectarian difference.

This theological appreciation of the neighbor as a way to forge intimacy among strangers was given new contextual life in the pan-Protestant revivalism of the nineteenth century. For example, the itinerant preacher Lorenzo Dow's autobiography contains a long discourse on the requirement to prove one's love for God through love of neighbor. According to Dow, a neighbor is "thy friend, enemy, acquaintance and stranger, and whosoever is in distress, no matter who."[152] Charles Grandison Finney, one of the most innovative preachers of the nineteenth century, expanded the definition of the neighbor in his 1836 lecture on the Christian duty of reproof. While offering his thoughts on the mandate to rebuke one's neighbor for sin, Finney extended the idea of the neighbor to accommodate new technological capacities: "Neighbor, here, means any body that sins within the *reach* of your influence; not only in your presence, but in your neighborhood, if your influence can reach him, or in your nation, or in the world."[153] New modes of contact expanded who the neighbor could be. They also enabled new definitions of neighbor in terms of reach, a strikingly physical metaphor for new communication technologies' abilities to exceed the physical limitations of embodied presence.

A primary focus for US missionaries as they emerged out of the fires of the Second Great Awakening was to recognize that the whole world was made up of neighbors. In their descriptions, the neighbor served as a prime example of imagining the whole world through ideas of proximity and unity. As James Taylor preached to the Hampshire Missionary Society, "I am bound to call every human being, my neighbor, my friend, my brother; my Saviour has taught me to do so. Whether he be the person, that is within the reach of my arm; or the man that treads the antipodes of the earth—he is my neighbor."[154] The nearness of the neighbor stood in for a particular collapse of distance and difference made possible by new networked technologies. Missionary discourse took up this logic fervently. In a plea for aid for efforts to address famine in western Turkey, a local missionary, Mr. Farnsworth, wrote, "Tens of thousands of old men and old women, of young men and maidens, and little children, are today suffering this very torture. By means of steam communication and the telegraph they are *your neighbors*."[155] For many US missionaries, networks bound new world citizens into close, ethically demanding relationships.

In a celebration of the advances of missionary work since the early years of US mission, the Reverend J. D. Davis wrote from Japan, "China and Japan were almost unknown. It took six months to reach them, and when reached they were not accessible. But to-day the whole world is open. Steam and electricity have annihilated distance, and the

700,000,000 of the heathen world are now our near neighbors. We can hear their cries, we can feel their heart-throbs, the scattered family of Adam are reunited, we are brothers."[156] The emotional intimacy that so enchanted these missionaries found context in the emergence of sympathy as an ethical mode of relationship popularized in eighteenth-century England.[157] Feeling the pain of another as a particularly moral act rendered these newfound communicative modes into an affective and familial intimacy.

The trope of the neighbor in this newly networked moment functioned through a commanding concentric expansion of intimacy: love your neighbor as yourself, the stranger as your neighbor, and the distant stranger as your near neighbor. Yet this idea relied on a particular logic of disconnection that belied the equality that the neighbor seemed to offer. The stranger became the neighbor only when first made not strange at all. Carolyn Marvin's study of new technologies in the nineteenth century addresses the affiliation forged between new technologies and dreams of cross-cultural community. Marvin cautions, however, that "the vastly extended eyes- and ears-to-be of new machines of communication anticipated few cultural puzzles to unravel, and showed their inventors only the most reassuringly echoic and potent images of themselves."[158] To feel neighborly about the stranger, US missionaries first made the stranger into a (failed) copy of themselves.

Copy as identity abounds in Christian history. From *imitatio Christi* to Paul's encouragement of early Christians to model themselves on him, mimesis has been a primary mode of Christian relationship and was, as biblical studies scholar Elizabeth Castelli asserts, a strategy of power.[159] This was an old mode of relationship. Castelli's rich examination of mimesis traces the long-standing "erasure of difference through the call to imitation" from Greek antiquity to its reassertion in Paul as a way to secure his claim of authority as an apostle of Christ. This early way of relating to others has thrived through Christianity and remains, as Castelli amply demonstrates, a power-ridden demand that reaches toward a dangerous universalism.[160]

In the thirty-seventh annual report, the ABCFM announced, "It would almost seem as if a single missionary in a city, or a dozen in a kingdom, might speedily transform an ignorant, sensual, idolatrous, and selfish community into a nation of intelligent, moral, Christian freemen;

or as if a hundred or two such laborers might, in a few years, put a British or American face on the whole Chinese empire."[161] Missionary imaginaries of the world in the nineteenth century presented a particular inversion of the imitative practices that have long been foundational to Christian life. They were less an encouragement to model oneself on a saintly other than a vision of a lesser other in terms of an empowered self, less mimesis than synecdoche. The ABCFM imagined the whole world through an idealized part, and that Christian "British or American" part was understood to represent what the whole world could—in fact, would—be. Synecdochical logic enabled ideas of the network and the neighbor by obscuring the insistent underlying determination to make vast, fractured, and foreign cultures and places become a single, suddenly familiar, whole. In the racist parochialism of mission logic, the cultural and religious difference that licensed mission and defined the strangeness of a would-be neighbor became the invisible background to the shining light of the promised echoic part made whole.

In this inversion, the trope of reach fit better than that of copy as the primary model for mission. Mr. Trowbridge described "the extension of Christ's kingdom through the whole world."[162] In 1897, J. Rendel Harris and Helen B. Harris, British Quaker missionaries often published in the *Missionary Herald*, wrote of their time in Armenia: "The civilization of Asia Minor is American; it is covered by a network of American agencies."[163] In this imaginary, the whole world could be understood, made proximate, and imagined as a site of unity because it would be built as a networked extension of the known, although idealized, core of portable Anglo Protestantism.

British and US missionaries used the idea of a shared race, language, culture, and religion—whether or not that actually existed—as the idealized part that stood in for the united global whole. Rufus Anderson wrote in 1850, "We can suppose the Anglo-Saxon race to fill the myriads of sunny islands on the bosom of the broad Pacific; and the genius of American and English enterprise to preside in great commercial cities, (other New Yorks, or even Londons,) reared on the Sandwich Islands, New Zealand, and Australia."[164] The alliance of British and US mission here became particularly salient, and the spread of an imagined Anglo culture stood in for the spread of Christianity. For example, in a report from the ABCFM Prudential Committee in 1854, the committee on the

Home Department resolved to accept a recent offer of aid from British missionaries, with the hope that "England, Scotland, Ireland, America and all of every tongue who love our Lord Jesus Christ, shall constitute one 'allied army' for the subjugation of the whole world to God."[165] These English-speaking missionaries understood themselves as the center of the effort to convert the world and the heart of the culture that they would spread across the planet. All their linguistic others followed, syntactically and metaphorically. Missionaries' efforts to make neighbors of strangers led them to efface strangers under the world of their imagining.

Synecdoche, like mimesis, is a troubling way to relate to a stranger. First and foremost, the stranger falls almost completely out of view beyond these violently superimposed Anglo faces. The other was overwritten by the familiar in missionary accounts and bore few ways to figure in colonialist discourse beyond the faint durability that haunts any palimpsest. Even theorists who disagree about whether one can ever truly know an other agree that baldly overwriting otherness with sameness is no way to have a relationship. Fundamentally, and with serious political consequences, synecdoche never makes good on its representational promises: a part can only stand in for a whole by failing to represent the all it lays claim to.

Second, the part that struggled to stand in for this disastrously effaced whole was itself a mess of fracture and fissure. While many British and US missionaries traded in the fantasy of shared culture, which included the English language, expansive Protestantism, and technological innovations, none were unaware of the simmering tensions between these two newly separated nations. As Tracy Fessenden has thoroughly demonstrated, US English not only was determinately unlike British English but also was taught to children with a hefty dose of antimonarchical instruction until nearly the end of the eighteenth century.[166] The War of 1812 and the founding of the ABCFM as a national venture occurred in the same year. British and US missions, fueled by nationalist commitments, were emphatically considered separate ventures in their early years. The first possibility for a formal British-US missionary alliance withered under national sentiment. Within two years of the ABCFM's inception, it sent missionaries to British India but was sorely lacking in funds and knowledge and starkly aware of both needs. The ABCFM sent Adoniram Judson to London in

1811 to request British financial support and advice. The British society refused the ABCFM and offered instead to employ the US missionaries themselves. The ABCFM rejected the British offer.[167] Religious ties were forged through shared history and the spread of transatlantic revivalism in the eighteenth and nineteenth centuries, as well as movements such as temperance and antislavery, and US-British missionary ventures improved in time.[168] But those religious alliances were complicated by conflict in that same history; England and the United States existed in tense political relationship through the first half of the nineteenth century.[169]

To forge a unified whole world, US missionaries engaged in rhetoric that aggressively overlaid difference with a representative sameness. Empowered by the Christian trope of the neighbor and fueled by a technologically charged expansion of who could be a neighbor, US missionaries imagined an intimate and expansive worldwide network. Impassioned feelings of global closeness were animated by emphatic disconnection; this neighborly intimacy was forged by erasing the strangers' very strangeness. Failure underwrote this logic: "Anglo culture" could not represent global difference, nor could its own multiple fractures pretend to represent a global unity. That is, not only could the part not stand in for the whole, but it never really existed as a part to begin with. Anglo missionaries were not loving strangers as themselves but loving themselves as strangers. This tense dance between intimacy and unfamiliarity never resolved; it persisted as a durable refusal undergirding the imaginary of unity.

* * *

While missionaries celebrated unprecedented possibilities of connection, they saw, struggled with, and made use of particular kinds of disconnection, from the religious others whom they hoped to convert to the gaps in mission fields that motivated investment in their expansionist project. Networks in the nineteenth century emerged as extensive connections set against a scene of geographic, social, and temporal disconnections. The other way to say this is its inverse: networks relied on exclusion to enable the specificity of inclusion. Or, networks relied on disconnection to enable specific connections. This interplay between connection and disconnection served as a crucial frame for how missionaries imagined and inhabited the world and still empowers our love affair with communication media and their salvific promises. Materialist commitments direct our attention to the ontological multiplicity through which networks came into being. What we call networks were the entanglement of missionaries acting as agents for Morse, colluding chemists and Christians, the rise and fall of an empire, the intimacy of strangers, and the strangeness of global intimacy; it was the world made vast and close and whole and broken at once.

And it was the making of a vast, close, whole, broken nation. Cultural expansion constituted the US nation; the imaginary of the global produced the imaginary of the local.[170] Just as US missionaries were spreading formal Protestantism around the world, diffuse protestantism was helping create a very particular sort of United States. Just as aspirations of global unity fueled techno-missionary activity abroad, aspirations of national unity fueled religious and technological discourse at home. Chapter 2 takes up the forms of fracture and fragmentation that attended the entangled rise of nineteenth-century religion, nationalism, and infrastructure in the burgeoning United States, producing a nation that was anything but united.

2

The Great Fizzle

Protestant Affect, Obsolete Telegraphs, and US Nationalism

That there have in all ages, in almost every nation, existed a
nation within a nation—a people who although forming a
part and parcel of the population, yet were from force of circumstances, known by the peculiar position they occupied,
forming in fact, by the deprivation of political equality with
others, no part, and if any, but a restricted part of the body
politic of such nations, is also true.
—Martin Robison Delany, *The Condition, Elevation,
Emigration and Destiny of the Colored People of the
United States, Politically Considered* (1852)

The Honorable William D. Kelley, a founder of the recently formed
Republican Party and an avid advocate of national rail and telegraphy,
declared that the first laying of the Atlantic Telegraph Cable in 1858 had
"made the whole earth vocal . . . and brought the nations of the earth face
to face, that they may enter into social converse."[1] Of course, it hadn't.
The Atlantic telegraph made a select few people, companies, and nations
vocal for the very short span of its life. And it did so amid the multiple
silences and fractures rending the young nation on the brink of civil war.
Moreover, Kelley attributed the power of the telegraph to the Christian
God, which significantly restricted the universalism he claimed for this
unprecedented public. Yet the idea that certain technologies provide
specific conditions for expansive public life appeared regularly in public
discourse in the nineteenth century and has been a hallmark of foundational scholarship about mediated publics since.

   In the mid-nineteenth century, as the very things that would come to
be called networks (railroads, telegraph systems, nerves, societies) were
being built, discovered, and described, the term *network* had not yet

entered colloquial discourse.[2] As railroads and telegraph lines began to snake across the United States, they were a phenomenon in the making. Their expansion preceded the literalization of the metaphor that made networked media indistinguishable from the sociality wrought through it. Close examination of this period of unfolding allows us to see how networks came to bear material and social agency at once. How did the first cabled network—the telegraph—come to stand for both electric communication and social cohesion? How were imaginaries of connection produced through conditions of fracture? And precisely what kinds of sociality emerged from technologically inspired declarations of grand national and global publics?

Networks did not (and do not) have natural meanings; the intimate slippage between technological infrastructure and social form (network as a set of cables and network as a mode of human relationships, respectively) was not inherent to any of the component parts of networks or their sum. Rather, networks came to bear meaning and to matter for modern US Americans through affective investment secured and made durable by emerging relationships among other aspects of US life, including what we now call technology, nationalism, early globalization, slavery, utopianism, and antebellum racialization. As Lisa Gitelman persuasively argues, technologies themselves do not bear intrinsic affordances but are retroactively attributed with extrinsic capacities and limits that emerge through protocols developed in use.[3] Networks are not naturally or inherently connective but are now read as such because of the particular conditions through which networks became legible as technological and social at once. This obliges a closer examination of the particular emergent context through which networks came to mean techno-social connection (and connection alone) and to matter so much to US life that we now have trouble thinking about relationships outside of these terms.

The answer to how particular imaginaries adhered to network media lies, in part, in the early manifestation of networks by the telegraph. Unlike network, *telegraph was* named in all sorts of discourse in the nineteenth century, but in these diverse discourses it bore multiple mobile meanings without any real consensus on them. There was the *optical telegraph*, the practice of using visual codes (like lights or flags) along lines of sight to send long-distance messages. There was the *spiritual telegraph*, that mode of communication with the dead through coded rappings or knockings that catapulted a few attuned communicators to fame on a wave of passionate religious experimentation in the mid-nineteenth century and then quickly ushered them into disrepute as the practice became the object of scrutiny in an age obsessed with evidence. (Harry Houdini was an avid debunker of Spiritualism.) There was the *grapevine telegraph*, the word-of-mouth communication among free and enslaved African Americans to facilitate survival, escape, and revolt. There was even a *teaching telegraph*, invented by the popular nineteenth-century pedagogue Joseph Lancaster, to communicate orders for bodily comportment to large groups of children, particularly African American and Native American children.[4] And, of course, there was the *electromagnetic telegraph*. Or not so "of course." The fact that we now refer to this technology simply as *the* telegraph and that the others have been rendered archaic tells us something important about the techniques that established a dominant meaning for telegraphy and affiliated it with a particular sort of publicity.

It is my contention that religion—particularly religion's capacity to marshal social energy—forged a meaning for the telegraph as an electromagnetic technology that unified expansive social groups, and that it forged these meanings by displacing other meanings for telegraphs that mattered. Religion's power to generate and direct affect produced an imaginary for telegraphy that we now consider to be inherent to the technology. Religion's affective force in the context of public protestantism in the United States stabilized these meanings so that they have lasted, extended to networks in general, and—despite all this affective effort—appear natural and inherent, unrelated to the complicated contexts in which the telegraph came to life.

Had a different telegraph become "the" telegraph, networks might mean something quite different today. These other telegraphs, while still networks, had alternative protocols and meanings. The grapevine telegraph was not broadly public and moreover relied on secrecy and personal trust. Not tied to a fixed mechanical infrastructure, it was a highly mobile and dynamic network. Likewise, the spiritual telegraph depended most heavily on the receptivity of its human operators, rather than the reliability of wires or machines. The optical telegraph was entirely contingent on the weather. Had a different telegraph gained affective investment the way the electromagnetic telegraph did, and a few of these came close, we might think of networks as private, even secret, mobile, contingent, perhaps even fickle, spiritual, and independent of large-scale structures.

Religion has been a privileged site of affective investment in the United States. This was particularly true in the nineteenth century, a time of innovative religious techniques that emphasized emotive performance and intensity. The highly charged revival Protestantism that swept through the nineteenth-century Atlantic world—marked by attention to and performance of energetic emotion—extended and amplified religion's regular trade in emotional investment, social meaning, and the habits of everyday life. Religion is, of course, not the only social practice that forges affiliations, institutes habits, and so on, but it is particularly effective at doing so. Paired with the lingua franca of conventional public protestantism, this diffuse and affectively saturated religion was a dexterous vehicle for the affiliation of network technology, connective sociality, and implicit Christianity, expressed as a burgeoning (Christian) nationalism in a globalizing (Christian) world.[5]

Religious language conventionally appeared in public texts, such as newspapers, political speeches, and displays, and its effects exceeded institutional forms. When the success of the 1858 cable was confirmed, William Hudson, captain of the USS *Niagara*, which laid the western half of the cable, sent this paean to his family in Brooklyn: "God has been with us. The Telegraph Cable is laid without accident, and to Him be all the glory."[6] The Mechanics Bank in Brooklyn, New York, posted a transparency of the dispatch, and it was reprinted in the unfortunately titled article "Atlantic Telegraph: Absolute Success of the Enterprise," in the *New York Times*. Religion's coherence across diverse discourses— science, technology, capitalism, print publicity—also served to suture these areas together into a meaningful assemblage that came to be known as "America." The diffusion of protestantism with its affective gravity was the stuff of nation making.[7] Yet the presence of religion also marked a significant restriction on the nation. While public speeches declared the "whole world made vocal," they clarified that the whole world and the vocality they were celebrating were Christian.[8] Reigning imaginaries of the world and the nation were forged through a particular form of Protestant Christianity, and, as such, the comprehensive universality these imaginaries pretended to were impossible from the get-go.

Contingency, discursivity, and even impossibility do not preclude a public from having real effects. Something was called into being for a moment in 1858—these speakers, writers, telegraph operators, and others organized themselves according to their imagined membership in a national and global public. But if this public existed, even for just twenty-three days, it did so in the live, crackling tension between universal aim and bounded specificity, between new imaginaries of national and global unity and erupting fragmentation. It existed not despite but through the condition of its own impossibility. And while the cable itself held strong in 1866, the promises made then of a whole and united world must also be read in this tension between expansion and exclusion, between momentary arising and collapse. The technological successes that followed also participated in failure and fracture. To trace further along this thread of history: these copper cables were replaced by the fiber-optic cables of the internet, running along the same submarine routes, which today are said to promise a global democratic forum that will allow access to social converse and commercial exchange for all members of the world. This too is a public imagined into being only in the condition of its own impossibility.

This chapter charts a number of telegraphs at play in 1858—the ship *Telegraph*, the grapevine telegraph, the spiritual telegraph, and the optical telegraph—to excavate the work religion did to help establish electromagnetic telegraphs as *the* telegraph and produce its durable pairing with an impossible expansive sociality. By examining how other telegraphs worked, this chapter complicates the naturalization of a number of characteristics that we now think of as inherent affordances of networks: that they are national, global, politically neutral, technological, connective, and even fully functional. The flattening of telegraphy into a single technology with fixed attributes depended, first and foremost, on exuberant affective investment in the electromagnetic telegraph as all of these things. The heart of this chapter focuses on the public US protestantism that percolated into a full-blown national celebration of electromagnetic telegraph networks, fireworks and all.

Religious Publicity: The *Telegraph*

There were, in fact, two telegraphs that crossed the Atlantic Ocean in 1858. The Atlantic Telegraph Cable bore universalist promises of a newly united world and the grand entrance of a young and vocal nation to a global communicative scene. The other was a ship, the *Telegraph*, which flew a US flag and took 654 enslaved Africans from West Central Africa to Sagua, Cuba.[9] Vice Consul of the United States Thomas Savage submitted his report to Secretary of State Lewis Cass on the slave trade with this commentary: "This expedition is reported to have proved a disastrous one from the great mortality sustained on the passage."[10] Only five hundred survived. The United States had formally abolished the Atlantic slave trade fifty years earlier; the presence of the slave ship *Telegraph* on top of the sea that year while the Atlantic Telegraph Cable came into being below points to the wide, churning gap between the formal discourse of US public life and the multiple marginal and meaningful alternative forms of US existence and infrastructure. This is not the story of one telegraph trumping another or of universalism ultimately winning out over the violence and fracture of slavery. Nor am I pitting an expansive fiction against a violent reality. Rather, both of these networks came into being and meaning through each other; the grand nationalist and globalist imaginaries of unity entailed other modes of life.

The slave ship *Telegraph* called little attention to itself, and little by way of historical record survives today. The Atlantic Telegraph Cable, however, was greeted with booming, bustling public celebration: parades, fireworks, cannon, illuminated buildings, lithographs, hymns, speeches, memorabilia galore. In 1865, at the advent of the subsequent attempt at an Atlantic telegraph cable, the *New York Times* reflected on public reaction to the transatlantic telegraph seven years earlier, which the sardonic author named "the great fizzle." The fizzle and its greatness were occasioned by the 1858 Atlantic Telegraph Cable, the communication revolution of which it was part, and the cable's failure, but the great fizzle was none of these things exactly. It was, the author asserted, "popular enthusiasm," which at this first possibility for relatively rapid communication with Europe rose to a "fever heat" and marked a defining aspect of US culture: "Then succeeded the great fizzle of the nineteenth century, a fizzle which developed the Americans as the most enthusiastic believers in fables, the most implicit dupes of 'statements,' the most credulous in all that pertains to glorious achievement . . . in the world."[11] It is an unfortunately fair description: many US Americans ranging from small communities of utopian communists to President Buchanan had, in utter contradiction of the realities around them, celebrated the improbable promise that the telegraph would unify the world into a grand global society of Christianity, prosperity, and peace. Their effervescent celebration of global telegraph infrastructure was unmatched among their new international partners. The British regarded what they understood as a local colonial communication line with a significantly stiffer upper lip.

While we might agree with the reporter for the *New York Times* that the wild enthusiasm for global telegraphy was more froth than substance, let us not see those who participated as "dupes." Gullibility is a poor frame in which to understand the great fizzle because it is an accusation of failing to carefully weigh evidence. These US Americans did not fall for a con. The evidence that communication networks would not spontaneously unite the world was clear—the cable itself was riddled with failures, encounter at distant shores was fraught with conflict, and the burgeoning form of a US nation was rocked by violence over slavery and attempted conquests of Native American people and the land they inhabited. US Americans knew that their dream of a young nation connected to a unifying world was set against a profoundly conflicting reality; the investment of social energy into this dream was never simply a matter of rational choice. Enthusiasm, which might compensate for rational inadequacy, also falls short as a frame for the great fizzle not because of its absence but because enthusiasm alone cannot account for the work the great fizzle accomplished. The great fizzle was not merely a surge in national feeling; it produced a strong sense of what telegraphy was and what it would do for the United States, powerful new meanings for networks as unifiers of national and global community, and a durable fantasy of the United States as a coherent participant in a global public.

The fizzle was widespread, and accounts attended to the emotion with which US Americans greeted the transatlantic cable. A report from Buffalo on August 7, 1858, read as follows: "Upon receipt of the news of the Cable's being successfully landed, a strong desire took possession of the people of Buffalo to celebrate the event in a manner becoming its importance." The celebration included illuminated buildings, bonfires, ringing bells, and firing guns. The report described celebratory crowds: "Bands of music are also parading the streets, which are literally packed with an excited and joyous throng."[12] Similarly in Nashville, reports proclaimed a "general joyful feeling throughout the city," and accounts from Rutland, Vermont, stated, "There is great rejoicing here to-night, in appreciation of the greatest event in the history of the world. . . . The people are full of enthusiasm." In cities from Cincinnati to Columbus, flags, bells, fireworks, lights, guns, and celebrants thronged the streets. Even these reports, according to the New York Times, did not come close to representing the energy of the populace: "The columns of the Times would be insufficient for the accommodation of a tenth part of the expressions of enthusiastic rejoicing over the success of the Cable, which reach us from all parts of the country."[13] In an 1858 account of the Atlantic cable (published before the cable failed), Charles Briggs and Augustus Maverick claimed that "the whole Union rejoiced together. Every city, town, village, and hamlet in all parts of the country sought to testify its sense of the importance of the work."[14] The "spontaneity and wild enthusiasm" of these public demonstrations spurred Briggs and Maverick to include a summary of them in an appendix to the volume.[15] Even when rendered in a more somber tone, the mood of universal attention prevailed; the Weekly Wisconsin Patriot dryly reported, "Every man is more or less absorbed in the subject."[16]

The emotional intensity that marked this moment was more than sound and fury; this affectively charged celebration of the Atlantic cable in 1858 forged new forms of public life in the United States and new meanings for networks. The telegraph was understood early in its life as a public technology, that is, one that would cohere the world, give voice to all people, and, in so doing, make a United States to reckon with.[17] Reports on the celebrations of the telegraph attributed the emotional outpouring to "the people," "every man," or "the public." The San Antonio Ledger described the unflappability of "public confidence" as the Atlantic telegraph was laid.[18]

Cheering the telegraph in the voice of the public called the public into being. Samuel Morse, in his quest for federal funding, tripled down on this move by attributing recognition of public gain to the universally held judgment of a coherent community: "I believe *there can scarcely be two opinions*, in such a *community as ours*, in regard to the advantage which would result both to the Government and the *public generally*, from the establishment of a system of communication by which the most speedy intercourse may be had between the most distant parts of the country."[19] Clearly *the* public imagined by those writers and speakers who believed all human beings had been united into one human family for the first time and forever was *a* public, a rather small public, and a very fragile one at that. But the contingency of this public does not mean it did not exist. Rather, the failure of this public was the very means by which it was constituted.

In some ways, publics flirt with impossibility by definition. Publics are modes of relationship organized around an imagined and indefinite group of strangers.[20] They name a sort of relationship that exists among people who, for the most part, do not know each other in any real way. There is no one thing that holds a public together; it is not determined by identity, formal protocols of membership (like citizenship), geographic location, or a shared characteristic. Think of the US public, composed of strangers, with all sorts of relationships to the idea of the United States itself, bearing various types of citizenship and immigration status, people at home and people abroad, in astounding diversity. Publics are not determined by space or by a fixed oppositional relationship to private life. The most public acts can take place in spaces deemed private, and the so-called private is given form by the modes of publicity in which it participates. Examples abound: female missionaries to Korea traveled around the world to model US Christian domesticity in the nineteenth century, suburban bay windows framed disciplined performances of home life for the neighbors in the mid-twentieth-century United States, and communities on opposite sides of social issues agree that the personal is political.[21] For the landmark theorist of the public sphere Jürgen Habermas, the public sphere depended on the private realm since it was only with a sense of private citizens that a public could exist.[22] For Benedict Anderson, nations came into being as people read shared news in shared time, but each reader read "in silent privacy."[23] Publics are multiple and overlapping, highly determined by context and power, and dependent on sustaining labor.

Most important, publics are deeply entangled with media. Dominant theories of publics relate these social forms to specific media: Hannah

Arendt argues that we become political beings through speech; Habermas traces the emergence of the public sphere to the existence of new modes of publicity and particular forms of address (e.g., the salon) through which public discourse could emerge; Anderson links the emergence of the nation-state to print capitalism; and Michael Warner understands publics and counterpublics to emerge through mere attention to a circulating text.[24] In 1858 in the United States, the Atlantic Telegraph Cable became wrapped up in loud claims that a certain public was *the* public. This public was not mediated by the telegraph itself, unlike the modes of publicity proposed by the canonical studies of modern Western publics mentioned earlier, which were mediated *by* speech, salon, print, or broader ideas of text. Rather, this public was called into being by a kind of affective and imaginary work organized *around* the Atlantic Telegraph Cable. Celebrations of the cable claimed a coherent public as its cause and its effect, understood that public not just to be US American or to have global reach but to *be the United States* and to *be the whole world*, and proclaimed wild success in the face of likely and then actual failure.

The accounts of this public among those who were speaking the language of public protestantism did not differ greatly from each other: they promised a certain unity, and that unity guaranteed peace, involved every human being, and was ordained, if not accomplished, by God as part of God's plan for human destiny. This public was said to arise directly out of the event of the Atlantic Telegraph Cable. In this way, there were two central conditions of this public: the telegraph as the material means of connection, and Christianity as the mode of coherence both as a framework for the imagination of the public and as the presumed identification of its members. Both conditions have interesting implications for thinking about public media and public imaginaries. If we consider the actual telegraph wire, we could understand the failure of the newly united global family as the result of the failure of the cable on which it was said to depend. That seems fairly commonsensical. But that move cannot account for the persistence of global network imaginaries after the 1858 cable failed and before a new one was constructed eight years later. Understanding the failure of a social imaginary through a material failure does, however, force a recognition that the discursive practices that constitute a public must include material practices, in this case communication technology. This is an extension of the provocative line with which Karen Barad begins *Meeting the Universe Halfway*: "Matter and meaning are not separate elements."[25] Alternatively, if we consider the restrictive religion called to constitute this expansive public, we could dismiss this imaginary as nothing more than a fleeting fiction. But we know that the omnivorous expansion of networks as social and technological publics persists even as those networks reinscribe the landmark values of protestantism: the priority of belief, texts, and individuals and the assumption that membership is voluntary.[26]

The discursive and material practices that forge publics are inextricably entangled, and this was utterly so in the case of the Atlantic telegraph and its equation with national and global sociality. While the transcripts of the first transatlantic telegraphs were mostly communications to check connectivity and develop a protocol for transmission on a new medium (chapter 4 will address this in depth), these were interrupted by public telegrams from the British queen, the US president, business leaders, and military personnel. This public was called into being not only by the literal address of it by Buchanan (he refers to this public as "the kindred nations" and "the nations of Christendom," which he hoped would be bound by the cable into "perpetual peace and friendship") but also by the means of his address, the very fact that he could address the public in this way. Content, form, and medium cannot be disentangled.

The turn to a specific sort of Christianity as the mode of coherence for this expansive subject inscribes failure into this imaginary long before the cable went silent. In some ways this is the old trope of Western colonial universalism—the determination to view all of humanity through a Christian lens as a way to both resolve the encounter with difference and fold it into a hierarchy that constructs the "West" and constructs it as superior, as addressed in chapter 1. This proposed global universality based on the specificity of religion shares form with many publics—to forge cohesion among strangers, one must, according to Ernesto Laclau, manufacture concepts or demands that are so empty of meaning that they can stand in for all sorts of meanings for all sorts of people.[27] The "whole world" meant very little in these accounts. Its necessary specificity—that is, its orientation to European and US contexts and Protestantism in particular—constantly interrupted its global reach.

But this particular public could only be imagined to cohere *through* this Christian specificity. *Both* its vague, expansive inclusion *and* its specific orientation were productive even while mutually undermining. Both contributed to the fizzling attention to the world precisely because the form and meaning of that world were not fixed.

Reflecting on the ill-founded zeal that met the 1858 Atlantic cable, the reporter who coined the "great fizzle" continued: "The *Times* teemed with dispatches from all parts of the country, descriptive of the universal joy which the tidings inspired. . . . Such a week of excitement, such days of wondering, such hours of prayerful thanksgiving, such never-ending transports as our people indulged in, we hope to never see again."[28] We have, of course, seen such fizzles again. Networks in material and metaphorical form seem to attract fever-hot enthusiasm in the United States. Whether the ardent belief that the internet is an inherently inclusive global forum for free speech, the conviction that social media platforms will fuel democratic revolutions in local and global settings, or the increasing difficulty we have imagining that social life can take anything but a networked form, fizzles seem to wax at the advent of new network technologies and coalesce into a tumultuous fusion of pure, inspiring, unrealistic *promise*.[29] The imaginary of a technologically empowered united world thrived then and thrives now in vital contradiction with lived experience. The great fizzle, it seems, never fizzled out.

Fizzle, of course, connotes both effervescence and failure. The ambiguity of the great fizzle—that is, energetic investment and failure together—was a critical element in the establishment of networks as agents of national and global unity. The great fizzle provides a valuable lens into the particular—and particularly US—activity that sustained the impossible imaginary of a world united by network technology. Aspirational ideas of what connection could offer affiliated networks with promises of unity, peace, progress, and perfection, and these network imaginaries thrived in the context of overwhelming evidence to the contrary. The cables failed, the codes were garbled, the materials disintegrated, the ships tossed about. Indeed, fizzling enthusiasm and the fizzling out of fiasco went hand in hand in this modern global imaginary.

When read in the context of technological change, failure is often considered a misstep on the path of progress, and success is framed as an end *despite* failures along the way. But, given the multiplicity of failures at stake in these telegraph networks and US imaginaries of a united nation and world, and their simultaneous growth at this time, the Atlantic cable of 1858 demonstrates that this fizzle continued to percolate *by means of* its multiple failures. What made an empty, effervescent fizzle that wouldn't fizzle out? A tongue twister at the heart of the techniques that constituted US public culture: failure was the fuel of fizzles.

The US public that we so regularly take for granted has never actually come into being. There has never been a single coherent public or even a core public around which the rest of us muster some sense of belonging. At the heart of US publicity is a great gaping hole. This is a problem attended to by a number of scholars who think about public life. Janet Jakobsen and Ann Pellegrini illustrate how references to the "general public" in discourses of tolerance in the United States have served to constitute not a broad mainstream but various exclusionary publics.[30] Benedict Anderson asserts that every nation-state is imaginary insofar as it exists without any real relationships among its members. Ernesto Laclau argues that every "people" is "not a *given* group, but an act of institution that creates a new agency out of a plurality of heterogeneous elements."[31] Michael Warner insists that publics are "a kind of fiction."[32] Christian Lundberg takes up Laclau and Jacques Lacan to characterize publics according to a "failed unicity" coupled with a "feigned unicity," such that subjects and their social worlds come into being by pretending to a coherence they can never have.[33] Contemporary attention to public life situates failure at the core of its becoming. The constitutive failure of publicity is a defining element of the affective investment in network sociality and locates disconnection at the heart of whatever we might imagine network society to be. As described by Lundberg, "Failures of unicity in speech, subject, and the sign are put to work as forces that call forth our investment in the supplements, fantasies, and imagined totalities that work to cover over failed inequities: instead of becoming fatal in the life of speech and the speaking subject, failures in unicity become the driving forces that animate human existence."[34]

The nationalist and transnationalist socialities that emerged around networks are best understood as forms of affect. Affect is "the social energy through which subjects, meaning, and cultures are produced, organized, and undone."[35] While this social energy can flow and shift in nimble ways, it can also create habituated formations that adhere to and sustain certain forms of social life, whether a nation or a world. The inclusion of affect in the processes that constitute sociality interrupts the narrative of smooth causal movement between the affordances of a particular technology (e.g., print) and the formation of particular forms of social life (e.g., a national public). Despite the fizzling declarations of direct effect, the telegraph did not produce a united nation in a united world, nor has any network since. Affective investment—the weighting of certain components, such as the idea of a national telegraph, the unity of the states, or the wholeness of the world, with a power that thwarts even obvious evidentiary contradiction—was a critical participant in the establishment of networks as both material and social connective media. The next section will address the particular role religion played in establishing networks and their publics as global through an extraordinarily local imaginary.

The Very Local Global

There is a deep irony to the opening line with which Kelley began his oration at the Philadelphia jubilee celebration of the Atlantic cable: "The occasion is not a local one."[36] He was referring, at first, to the many US cities celebrating that night. However, he quickly elaborated the reach of the cable's impact to include "every member of the human family." In the history of human scientific discovery, he claimed, "no event has occurred which is to work so large an influence upon nations and people, upon the social, political, commercial and economical relations of mankind—no event, the influence of which is to be so far-reaching, or so all-pervading."[37]

The universality of the cable did not lie merely in its impact. Kelley spent the next ten pages of his oration thanking every person he considered to have had some hand in the making of the Atlantic telegraph, from the naval lieutenant who commanded the ship that made the soundings of the ocean floor to a lawyer who ten years earlier had put a memo before Congress urging it to note that there was a table of land beneath the ocean that stretched from Newfoundland to Ireland. The memo was sent to committee and floundered there, but Kelley honored the lawyer alongside the sailors, the inventors, the machinists, the congressmen, and the funders, not to mention all of the famous "experimenters" in electricity he could think of from Benjamin Franklin to Alessandro Volta. Kelley did so to insist that the Atlantic cable was the work "not of members of a single community or state, not of a particular nation, not of any one of earth's named localities" but of "various nations and races." The work all these people ultimately accomplished "was for the world and man; and it was fitting that the *human family* should have its hand in it."[38] According to Kelley, a vast and diverse group of people worked somehow in concert over great stretches of time and space to create the Atlantic cable.

Kelley included in his expansive list of participants a particularly unique actor as the primary agent. The "great Omnipotent One" created the earth, gave humanity dominion over it, and then bestowed the telegraph as a last great blessing.[39] Kelley averred, "When the Almighty permitted that cable to be laid, He made public announcement to man, that He had registered a decree for the early completion of the Pacific Railroad. . . . God in His providence has ordered the work to be done."[40] Kelley's mention of God was more than just the addition of another global participant. At the heart of the venture was God, and it was God who made this imagined global public cohere. Rather than a scattering of inventors, sailors, lawyers, and congressmen working independently, these agents were the "highest ministers [of God] on earth."[41] This project, according to Kelley, was not merely the twisting of copper to survive submarine currents but rather a collective project to realize a divinely ordained human destiny in the unification of the whole world.

Kelley's insistent Christianity serves as an important example of the role of religion in the articulation of network technology to national and global imaginaries: through diffuse public protestantism, an infrastructural project became the foundation for an impossibly cohesive global community. Kelley posited this community as both a cause and an effect of the Atlantic telegraph, and in both roles this global community was cloaked in divine purpose (they were, after all, God's ministers, despite the likelihood that the machinists, sailors, and lawyers were unaware of their place in the divine employ).

Yet, similar to other renditions of this global imaginary, when we look more closely at the names Kelley cited, every single one is from Europe or the United States (except God, although that is perhaps debatable in this case), and Kelley paid particular homage to those from

Philadelphia. This not-so-local event turned out to be rather local after all. Indeed, the God that drew these multitudes of laborers into a singular human family was familiarly Christian, even parochially Protestant. Kelley's whole world functioned as one unit by virtue of its God-given vocation, and yet this particular God-givenness ensured that Kelley's whole world was rather limited. As with the American Board of Commissioners for Foreign Missions (see chapter 1) and the Oneida Community (see chapter 3), this global community cohered through a specifically US version of public protestantism.

Kelley's speech conferred two related meanings on the telegraph, both of which enriched the submarine cable with affective power. First, Kelley's insistence on God's role as the director of this invention and the unifier of this inventing community imbued the cable with religious significance and authority. The power of Kelley's discussion of God did not rely on proof of divine involvement. Rather, Kelley assumed the public protestantism of his audience, which he then used to lend his account importance, grandeur, and emotional clout. Kelley harnessed the spirit of US protestant imperialism, particularly the racist and religious self-assurance of manifest destiny (coined by Jane Cazneau in 1845), without inciting the controversy that attended manifest destiny as a political project.[42] At the time, religion served as a rich and reliable source of affective attention and an effective vehicle by which such attention could be invested in the dream of a unified world.

Second, Kelley premised unity on the physical fact of this electric communication technology rather than on a process of communication. The presence of the cable (itself already riddled with material fractures) between two continents held no more guarantee of connection than the ocean it spanned. His assertion that a physical link would forge a family out of the world's population and bring recently warring nations "face to face" diverged from the probable into energetic, not rational, investment. This was also a trope of manifest destiny, robustly illustrated by John Gast's painting *American Progress* (1872), in which an angelic Columbia, trailing a telegraph wire in her hand, leads railroads, agriculture, and white settlers across the plains as Native Americans retreat in front of them. Through these meanings, particularly as they were animated by the social energy that religion wielded, a copper line sufficed to foster a sense of whole-world unity and national

Figure 2.1. George A. Crofutt's chromolithograph of John Gast's *American Progress*, ca. 1873. (Library of Congress)

promise that was able to overcome the material gaps, failures, and ruptures that violently excluded much of the nation, let alone the whole world.

In the United States, descriptions of the Atlantic Telegraph Cable lauded it as an utterly global event, an expression of greatness, an inhabitation of a transcontinental ocean, and the cause of new capacities for speech that appeared to create a new sense of what the world could be.[43] Indeed, the 1858 cable brought new forms of transnationalism into being, sutured the United States into a cabled network with Europe, and signaled the real possibility of electric global communication. The world in its wholeness came into sharp focus as a newly accessible site of communication and cohesion. But all the imaginaries of unity and universality that emerged around the telegraph cable were premised on exclusions, limits, and fracture that these same imaginaries glossed over, obscured, or adamantly denied even while calling them into service.

On August 16, 1858, the first public transatlantic message was sent from Queen Victoria of England to US president Buchanan. He responded three days later, heralding a Christian universality made possible by the telegraph:

> It is a triumph more glorious, because far more useful to mankind, than was ever won by conqueror on the field of battle. May the Atlantic telegraph, under the blessing of heaven, prove to be a bond of perpetual peace and friendship between the kindred nations, and an instrument destined by Divine Providence to diffuse religion, civilization, liberty, and law throughout the world. In this view will not all the nations of Christendom spontaneously unite in the declaration, that it shall be forever neutral, and that its communications shall be held sacred in passing to the place of their destination, even in the midst of hostilities.[44]

Buchanan made a striking series of moves in this short missive. First, he established vast forms of sociality—the "world" and "mankind"—as preexisting and real. At the same time, he asserted the priority of the "nations of Christendom" as the agents of any unity to be had by the world. The difference posed between Christendom and the world was not ontological but temporal—empowered by the telegraph, the world would soon be drawn together by a swift infusion of religion, civilization, liberty, and law as a result of the divine instrument of telegraphy. Even as Buchanan declared it, he also called the spontaneous unity of Christendom into question; he flagged the fragile politics between England and the United States of America in his insistence that the cable should remain neutral and his haunting reference to the hostilities, potential or actual, that would surround it. Buchanan's world was whole and real and holy and insecure. He celebrated a universalism that he hinged on tenuous US-British relations and an as-yet-inaccessible Christian coherence.

Promoting Protestantism in both its formal and diffuse forms was not specific to the Atlantic cable; it was, in fact, never far from the life of the telegraph in the United States. In the midst of Morse's first five years of work on the telegraph, he led a public life as a nativist: he ran for mayor of New York as the Nativist Party's candidate in 1836 and published a long, paranoid text about the essential opposition of Catholicism and democracy in 1835, *Foreign Conspiracy against the Liberties of the United States*.[45] "Popery," he claimed with bluster, "is a Political system, despotic in its organization, anti-democratic and anti-republican, and cannot therefore co-exist with American republicanism."[46] His anxieties were sparked by a recent wave of immigration, particularly from Ireland, and he articulated his anti-Catholicism to an equally vitriolic anti-immigrant stance. He developed this perspective in the subtly titled text *Imminent Dangers to the Free Institutions of the United States through Foreign Immigration*, published later that same year.[47] The religious exclusivity of the global telegraph was woven into its invention.

This imaginary of telegraphically empowered global unity was particular to US Protestantism. Religious groups that did not identify with the emerging Protestant mainstream, such as Reform Jews and Mormons, provided different imaginaries of telegraphy, including concerns over the telegraph as a fracturing, not unifying, medium and enthusiasm for its local impact rather than its global reach. For example, the *Israelite*, the primary publication of US Reform Judaism in the nineteenth century, edited by Rabbi Isaac Mayer Wise, expressed concern that the telegraph might hasten the spread of anti-Semitism.[48] Mormons lauded the telegraph for its ability to connect their community across a growing *local* territory. Brigham Young and his counselors advocated for the construction of a telegraph network among Mormons: "We now require to be united by bonds which will bring us into more speedy and close communication with one another; the center should be in position to communicate at any moment with the extremities, however remote; and the extremities be able, with ease and speed to make their wants and circumstances known to the center."[49] It was this commitment to local connection that sparked the Mormon construction of the Deseret Telegraph line, the only major line built and operated by a religious organization.[50] In the Mormons' alternative imaginary, the telegraph not only was local but also facilitated separation from more expansive publics: various reports claimed that Mormons used the Deseret Telegraph line to warn community members during antipolygamy raids at the end of the nineteenth century.[51] Alternative imaginaries, as the next section will address in depth, offer a glimpse at the different publics that emerged through telegraphy and the labor that went into empowering a particular protestant alignment of telegraphy with expansive public life.

The United States That Weren't: The Grapevine Telegraph

The adamant affiliation of the Atlantic telegraph cable with an emerging US nationalism obscured other telegraphs, the deep fissures constituting the nation, and the Ireland-to-Newfoundland path of the cable itself. As the electromagnetic telegraph was becoming a household term, the *grapevine telegraph* was circulating as a name for the secret transmission of messages relating to survival, existence, resistance, and rebellion among free and enslaved African Americans.[52] Much like the Underground Railroad, this was an imaginary of an emerging network without machinic technology. As one newspaper report on Harriet Tubman put it, "Special signals, passwords and figurative messages became so comprehensive that they were known as 'the grapevine telegraph.'"[53] A striking example included in Sergio Lussana's study of resistance among enslaved African Americans came from George Washington Albright, a former slave, who said this about communication: "We slaves knew very little about what was going on outside our plantations, for our owners aimed to keep us in darkness. But sometimes, by grapevine telegraph, we learned of great events."[54] In Booker T. Washington's autobiography, he recalled whispered conversations about the approaching Civil War: "These discussions showed that they understood the situation and kept themselves informed of events by what was termed the 'grape-vine' telegraph. . . . Often the slaves got knowledge of the results of great battles before the white people received it."[55]

This name for the secret medium of communication among African Americans during slavery gained traction and pulled along with it connotations that violate some of what networks have become today. The grapevine telegraph functioned through specific protocols of *private* access, select participation, and techniques of secrecy; it was highly contingent, received no public or private funding, used no dedicated mechanical infrastructure, and became the cause of no public celebrations. A report on the process of emancipation edited by W. E. B. Du Bois included this lament of the exclusive nature of the grapevine telegraph: "[President Lincoln] referred to the really astonishing extent to which the colored people were informed in regard to the progress of the war, and remarked that he wished the 'grapevine telegraph' could be utilized to call upon the Negroes of the interior peacefully to leave the plantations and seek protection of our armies."[56] Far from acting as the herald of national unity, the grapevine telegraph relied on the deep divisions among publics.

In stark contrast, the electromagnetic telegraph was regularly couched in claims of national coherence. Any declaration of US unity three years before the Civil War can make no bones about its falsehood. Trish Loughran notes that the project of nation building was unfinished in the mid-nineteenth century, as her inclusion of the photograph of Lincoln's inauguration in front of the half-built Capitol building makes visually plain.[57] But the great fizzle produced a fiction of a unified nation that was generative and durable. Electromagnetic telegraphy was understood to be a mode of national sociality, a capacity that later colloquial and scholarly discourse extended to networks more broadly. Yet, the assertion of telegraphy as a mode of national sociality was produced through forms of cultural labor that obscured the many ways the telegraph was never a national project and the nation never cohered as such.

The power of the imaginary of national unity relied on profound national exclusions—corporeal, material, and discursive—and all were bolstered by multiple modes of violence. There is no mention of slavery in the overjoyed descriptions of global unity apparently presaged by transoceanic telegraphy. To gloss Paul Gilroy, techno-nationalism thrived on the fiction that "the reflexive cultures and consciousness of the European settlers and those of the Africans they enslaved, the 'Indians' they slaughtered, and the Asians they indentured" were "sealed off hermetically from each other."[58] The discourses of slavery and the discourses of transatlantic telegraphy were apparently discrete then and have remained so in scholarship since. Despite their disarticulation in US public discourse, the establishment of network infrastructure and practices of slavery occurred in the same time, space, and publics. An extraordinary example is William Kelley's remarks as the representative of Pennsylvania to the House of Representatives on both slavery and another emerging network infrastructure, the railroad, in two emphatically separate discussions, later published as one document with two discrete parts.[59]

Telegraphy and slavery were not so clearly distinguished in practice. The USS *Niagara* provides a striking illustration of this.[60] The *Niagara* was a uniquely large steam frigate, which allowed it to carry the heavy load of its half of the 1857 and the 1858 transatlantic cables. It was celebrated in public discourse and featured in memorabilia along with its captain for the journey, William Hudson. After laying the 1858 cable, the *Niagara* made three other important voyages. Also in 1858, shortly after bearing the US half of the Atlantic telegraph, federal law prompted the *Niagara* to transport 271 enslaved people from the captured slave ship *Echo* to Liberia. Only two hundred survived.[61] The second was the United States' first diplomatic mission to Japan. And the third returned it to the issue of slavery as it fought for the Union in the Civil War.

The trope of networks as connective, expansive, technological, and public was (and is) not politically neutral; it was written through a racist history fueled by public protestantism and over another telegraph that facilitated resistance to and overthrow of slavery. The electromagnetic telegraph became *the* telegraph while the grapevine telegraph has now nearly passed from colloquial speech. Its only current popular reference is in the plaintive lyrics of "I Heard It through the Grapevine," written in 1966 and recorded within two years by Gladys Knight and the Pips, the Miracles, and then, most famously, Marvin Gaye. (It is, in striking coincidence, a song about rupture.) Why one telegraph shaped the affordances of networks and one fell into near obscurity has little to do with the natural capacities of a technology and everything to do with race, power, violence, and the energetic attention a specific form of white US protestantism brought to bear on an imaginary of a technologically united world blessed by a very specific sort of God.

Paul Gilroy urges us to see that the forms of nationalism in circulation around the Atlantic were forged through particular incarnations of transnationalism and racialization.[62] Public attention to the tight tether connecting telegraphy to national and global social life as an isolatable causal relationship missed a matrix of other factors that supported the emergence of global sociality, nationalism, and telegraphy. While the role of racist nationalism in the creation of the United States should surprise no one, its close cousin—the implicit raciality of technology—is not as widely recognized. The telegraph's emergence as a common good and its apparent innocence of the concurrent industry of slavery were written over a history of its involvement in both slavery and its abolition. Ultimately, this discourse established national habits of displacing fissure to foreground aspirational unity as a key element in US imaginaries of new technology and the publics sutured to them.

In an unfortunately similar vein, the telegraph was already snaking into the western frontier as an explicit tool for dominance over Native Americans and their land. Agreements between Native Americans and the US government, from treaties to reservations, were required to include rights-of-way for telegraph lines and additional rights to the natural resources needed for their construction, such as timber.[63] As the telegraph network became an important object of strategy and sabotage in the escalating violence between the settler colonists of the US government and Native Americans of the West, its role as a tool of racist domination was clear. In a striking example in the historian of communication James Schwoch's thorough study of westward telegraph expansion, the transcontinental telegraph line was used to start a prairie fire of such magnitude that he rightfully considers the telegraph to have been a "weapon of mass destruction" against Native Americans and an entire prairie ecosystem.[64]

To be clear, even had this single cable unified the United States, claims that the Atlantic Telegraph Cable of 1858 was the landmark US innovation were already empty; the Atlantic telegraph was not "American" in its origins, its use, or the communities it constructed. It was, as Jeremy Stolow urges us to see, an *Atlantic* phenomenon.[65] It emerged from a particularly Atlantic set of relationships and shaped the Atlantic world in turn. Casting the Atlantic telegraph as a US project renders its politics as simple nationalism, but the Atlantic politics of the Atlantic telegraph were far more complicated and less amenable to the fantasies of unity that fizzled in nationalist discourse.

The cable was uniformly described in the United States as a bridge between it and England, but it was actually strung between Ireland and Newfoundland. The British envisioned the Atlantic telegraph as an entirely British venture that linked the United Kingdom with its colony, Newfoundland. For example, in October 1858, the *New York Times* reprinted a report from the *London Daily News* that illustrated how President Buchanan's strong suggestion of the cable's neutrality in times of war was met on the other side of the pond: "Perhaps Mr. Buchanan would like to secure the neutrality of the British *fleet* also, in case of war."[66] The *New York Times* continued,

The Telegraph is regarded as thoroughly and exclusively a British institution,—just as completely British property as the Cunard steamers; *and so it will remain.* It is owned mainly by British capital: it is mainly in the hands of British directors:—its ends are upon British soil,—and its operators are British subjects. In the event of war it will be used, solely and exclusively for the promotion of British interests:—and that, too, in spite of all the promises, negotiations and pledges that may be entered into.[67]

Only from a US perspective was the Atlantic cable a US event.

Adam Weingärtner's commemorative lithograph for the 1858 cable illustrates the particular nationalism that greeted the telegraph. He titled the lithograph *Torchlight Procession around the World—Dedicated to Young America.* His heavy-handed racialization of people from "around the world" laying the cable under the electric lights of liberty posited a globalizing cause and effect for the Atlantic telegraph. The world made the cable, and the cable unified the world. This globalism was framed by a strong nationalism. The dedication to "young America" signaled that the cable (and its unified world) was *for* the United States, in all its youthful exuberance. It also referenced the Young America movement, a mid-nineteenth-century nationalist movement that championed free-market capitalism, modern infrastructure projects like the telegraph, and a uniquely US art and literature (and which became an important shaping force in the Democratic Party). The United States' primacy was echoed in the Very American Men (Benjamin Franklin, Samuel Morse, William Hudson, Cyrus Field) at the corners. Undermining the signs of British-US partnership and the celebration of global unity and underlining, instead, the rather charged relationships at stake, a New York fire laddie shoots electricity at Britain.

Moreover, while US nationalism and Atlantic telegraphy were enmeshed in each other, US investment in the Atlantic telegraph was not a national project per se. Unlike the postal system and early terrestrial telegraphs, which were funded by the US government with the specific mandate to unite the nation through communication, the Atlantic telegraph did not receive federal funding. Rather, an ad hoc public-private mix allowed for moneyed men to represent national interests while the US government provided logistical support, boats, and expertise.[68] The

Figure 2.2. Adam Weingärtner, *Torchlight Procession around the World—Dedicated to Young America*, 1858. (Library of Congress)

Atlantic telegraph thus held a tenuous place at the center of emerging US nationalism and, likewise, a tenuous place at the center of a new set of discursive-material practices of globalization. The cable was neither national nor global but was imagined as utterly both.

The preceding terrestrial telegraph might have become a national enterprise. Morse was ready with nationalistic ambitions in his efforts to encourage Congress to fund his terrestrial telegraph. In 1838, Morse wrote to the chairman of the Committee on Commerce of the House of the Representatives, Maine representative Francis Ormand Jonathan Smith, to say,

> From the enterprising character of our countrymen, shown in the manner in which they carry forward any new project which promises private or public advantage, it is not visionary to suppose that it would not be

long ere the whole surface of this country would be channeled for those nerves which are to diffuse, with the speed of thought, a knowledge of all that is occurring throughout the land; making, in fact, one neighborhood of the whole country.[69]

Knowingly or not, Morse was borrowing the rhetoric used for an earlier network technology: the US Postal Service. In an 1829 essay on the importance of union cohesion published in the *Christian Examiner*, Unitarian theologian William Ellery Channing wrote of the postal system, "It binds the whole country in a chain of sympathies, and makes it in truth one great neighborhood."[70] But while the postal system was indeed a national and nationalist project, the telegraph was in the end a far more private venture. Morse received early federal funding to establish the first telegraph line from Baltimore to Washington, DC, but private companies funded the later development of a national telegraph system and, ultimately, Western Union owned the network, making it the first national industrial monopoly.[71]

Even in the early years of the telegraph, when it was still potentially a federal project, it was inaccessible to anything resembling public communication. It was largely a medium for political, journalistic, and commercial use. As media historian Menahem Blondheim makes plain, even after the Baltimore–Washington line became publicly accessible, it was "rarely employed for social exchanges."[72] In its first years, while the telegraph system became more widespread and familiar, transmission rates were prohibitive for the vast majority of US Americans. Historian of technology Gregory Downey details the astronomical cost in his history of the messenger boys who were integral to the telegraph system in the United States: "A ten-word message from New York to Philadelphia cost 30¢ in 1873, 15¢ in 1883, and 25¢ in 1908."[73] The average daily wage in the United States in 1873 was $2.35½.[74] The decidedly nonpublic nature of communicating by telegraph was only more true for the less accessible transatlantic cable. On the 1866 cable, the first opened for commercial use, the original minimum cost for transmission was $100 ($10 per word with a minimum message length of ten words), or roughly $1,700 today.[75] The limited use of the telegraph was not an accident of commerce. The telegraph was not designed as a mass medium and was not intended for use by the national population. Only in 1910, after sixty-five years of commercial telegraphy in the United States, would the telegraph be reconfigured for popular use.[76] The telegraph was not public, and the idea of networks as *inherently* public is itself a powerful fiction that persists today.[77] Similarly, the idea that telegraphs are technological or scientific achievements also rests on a strange story of fantasy, hybridity, and erasure. The electromagnetic telegraph came into being through yet another telegraph, the spiritual telegraph, which reveals even more (and even more haunting) involvement of religion in networks.

Science and Spirit: The Spiritual Telegraph

Looking back at early networks—before they were even named as such—from a time invested in its own secularism, it may feel commonsensical to consider these technologies as scientific. The language of experimentation, rubrics of invention formalized in patent applications, even the prickliness of people with training in the sciences toward those who came to invention from other directions (like the artist Samuel Morse) all appear at first glance to secure the telegraph its proper place in the realm of science. But the very designation of *scientific* is highly contextual and brings to the fore the particular porousness of the boundary between religion and science at the time.

Randall Styers's lucid genealogy of the tripartite distinction among religion, science, and magic illuminates the instability of these mutually dependent categories in Western modernity and their animation by various forms of circulating power. In Europeans' effort to distance themselves from the so-called primitive encountered through colonialism, they used magic as a foil for the emerging concepts of religion and science. Magic— "far too elusive and indeterminate to remain a stable and contained rhetorical tool"—was a particularly compelling foil because it was a faulty one.[78] All of the effort that went into putting magic (and the "others" who practiced it) in its place—and its repetitive, Houdini-like escape from those bonds—made magic a potent and persistent subversion of modern subjectivity and regulatory norms. As Styers warns, "The scholarly effort to reify and contain magic has regularly had the inadvertent effect of making more magic."[79] According to Styers, the unstable function of magic becomes in modernity a source of pleasure, an enticing cultural labor around which modern subjectivity is always inadequately organized.[80]

In this sense the telegraph was truly modern. Today, it may appear at first glance scientific but was an essentially ambivalent technology that flitted among religion, science, and magic and participated in constituting these categories through its dynamic engagement of them. Contextually, this makes a great deal of sense; none of these categories had fixed boundaries when the telegraph emerged. For example, as late as the 1810s, sound morality was considered a standard for patentability in the United States.[81] The value of an invention was measured in ethical terms alongside any industrial and scientific contributions. Thus, when Frances Ormand Jonathan Smith promoted Morse's telegraph to the House, he did so with claims not for its scientific or technological contribution but for its *moral* contribution:

> It is obvious, however, that the influence of this invention over the political, commercial, and social relations of the people of this widely-extended country, looking to nothing beyond, will, in the event of success, of itself amount to a revolution *unsurpassed in moral grandeur* by any discovery that has been made in the arts and sciences, from the most distant period to which authentic history extends, to the present day. With the means of almost instantaneous communication of intelligence between the most distant points of the country, and simultaneously between any given number of intermediate points which this invention contemplates, space will be, to all practical purposes of information, completely annihilated between the States of the Union, as also between the individual citizens thereof. The citizen will be invested with, and reduce to daily and familiar use, an approach to the HIGH ATTRIBUTE OF UBIQUITY, in a degree that the human mind, until recently, *has hardly dared to contemplate seriously as belonging to human agency, from an instinctive feeling of religious reverence and reserve on a power of such awful grandeur.*[82]

Smith linked the moral promise of telegraphy to an explicitly "religious reverence" for a newfound spatial and temporal unity through a new capacity in human agency. Alexander Pope originally coined the desire to "annihilate . . . space and time," which became a primary expression of telegraphic potential. In Pope, the power to produce such miraculous proximity is reserved for the gods. In telegraphy, it is a newly human power.[83] This is not the old story of secularism in which science and technology elbow religion out of the realm of ultimate concern. This is science and technology getting their footing on religious ground.

Given the electromagnetic telegraph's emergence into the reigning entanglement of science, religion, and magic, its co-constitutive relationship with a far more mystical telegraph appears quite reasonable. In 1848, just four years after Morse's public demonstration of telegraphy, two young girls ignited a religious movement when they began to talk to the dead with coded knocks. The twelve- and thirteen-year-old Fox sisters spent the evening of March 31 trying to communicate with whatever had been producing the strange noises in their supposedly haunted house in upstate New York. There are various accounts of this origin story. The noted Spiritualist practitioner, lecturer, and author (and active campaigner for Abraham Lincoln) Emma Hardinge gave this version in her history of Spiritualism:

> At length the youngest child, Kate—who, in her guileless innocence, had become familiar with the invisible knocker, until she was more amused than alarmed at its presence—merrily snapped her fingers and called out, "Here, Mr. Split-foot, do as I do!" The effect was instantaneous; the invisible rapper responded by imitating the number of her movements. She then made a given number of motions with her finger and thumb in the air, *but without noise*, and her astonishment and childish delight was redoubled to find that it *could see as well as hear*, for a corresponding number of knocks were immediately given to her noiseless missions. "Only look, mother!" she cried, "look, it can see as well as hear!" What an announcement were these few simple words! *It can see as well as hear* should have been a text which all the doctors, professors, sceptics, and scoffers who have subsequently tried to crush out the sublime truth of spiritual intercourse with earth should have studied and learned by heart ere they entered on their rash and irreverend crusade.[84]

Hardinge referred to these earthly and supernatural communicators as "spiritual telegraphers," and the words *Spiritual Telegraph* served as the name of a weekly Spiritualist newspaper.[85] Not only was the mode of communication reminiscent of Morse's code, but the unseen power that motivated the knocks seemed to work according to the same principles as the unseen power of more terrestrial telegraphs. In Hardinge's words, "They referred to the house at Hydesville as one peculiarly suited to their purpose from the fact of its being *charged with the aura requisite to make it a battery for the working of the telegraph*; also to the Fox family as being similarly endowed."[86]

The causal relationship between spiritual and electromagnetic telegraphy was utterly mutual; they were inextricable. Each was used to garner interest in and prove the validity of the other, and much of the engineering and investment in telegraphy occurred through Spiritualism, including the efforts of the electrician of the Atlantic Telegraph Company who spearheaded the 1866 cable, Cromwell Fleetwood Varley, an avid Spiritualist practitioner.[87] Telegraphy and Spiritualism, in lockstep, offered new and expansive imaginaries of community that extended the sense of the world to its farthest limits and beyond, whether in ways that exceeded prevailing senses of space and time or in ways that slipped past the border of the living into the realm of the dead. In this way, the resonance between Spiritualism and telegraphy (and other new media) is hardly surprising.[88] As US historian R. Laurence Moore notes, "The professional medium appeared in America at about the moment Thoreau heard a locomotive whistle penetrate the woods around Walden Pond."[89]

Both the spiritual telegraph and the electromagnetic telegraph emerged through negotiation with significant disconnections in their infrastructures. Spiritualism was organized around overcoming the evocative absence of the voices of the dead. And, as media theorist Bernard Dionysius Geoghegan illustrates, the Fox sisters and the movement they spurred also contended with gaps in the emerging infrastructures of western New York, spreading in creative negotiation with the absence of a railroad station, a telegraph station, or even a mention of their hometown of Hydesville on maps of local infrastructure.[90] Just like the electromagnetic telegraph, as discussed later in this chapter, the spiritual telegraph functioned through its ability to integrate itself with other, multimodal systems: "kinship, the community, technologies of trust and witnessing, the printing press, and ultimately the canal and city of Rochester itself, which spirited the [Fox] girls and their family away."[91]

As the telegraph spread, so did Spiritualism.[92] Anecdotal estimates of US practitioners of Spiritualism ranged from forty thousand to eleven million.[93] As a movement that never cohered, never bore a formal leadership structure, and never framed itself through institutions, Spiritualism is notoriously hard to trace. It was an ad hoc confluence of a number of globally circulating practices that all held a significant interest in communication with the dead. Jeremy Stolow includes Theosophy and French, Brazilian, and Cuban Spiritism alongside US, British, and Canadian Spiritualism in this assemblage.[94] His study makes clear that recognizing the Atlantic orientation of Spiritualism and telegraphy illuminates the participation of both in a new set of Atlantic exchanges. The intimate relationships between Spiritualism and telegraphy bore tremendous effects on emergent forms of "sociability and subjectivity . . . inviting us to revisit some of the reigning assumptions about how these terms relate to one another and also how they relate to larger social transformations gathered under the sign of globalization."[95] Spiritualism helped to usher emerging forms of global—and public—life into being. Many demonstrations of Spiritualist practice were hosted in public settings, and the spirits themselves occasionally demanded entrance into public discourse. Hardinge cited an instance of a spirit demanding that an exchange not be kept private but published in the *Democrat* or *Magnet*.[96]

In part, Spiritualism's publicity, like the telegraph's, was spurred by equal measures of fascination, appreciation, and the tantalizing possibility of scandal. Telegraphy and Spiritualism emerged at a time in which concerns over national identity and destiny mingled freely with anxieties about and excitement for new technologies. As a new movement that paid a great deal of attention to technology and concerned itself with a practice that was met with a heady combination of desire and skepticism, Spiritualism stood at the anxious intersection of science, religion, and magic and became another site for their mutual constitution.

Spiritualists actively aligned their practice with science in a variety of forms. Spirits were, by Spiritualists' accounts, familiar and prodigious with new technology. They asked mediums to turn down the gaslights or use graphite pencils, and spirits invented numerous machines, including a mill, a machine for riving shingles, and, of course, the celestial telegraph itself.[97] Notably, many Spiritualists, including the movement's eminent Fox sisters, saw apparitions of Benjamin Franklin, who apparently extended his earthly fame for his experiments with electricity to become something of a "technological saint."[98] In one early Spiritualist text, *The Philosophy of Spiritual Intercourse*, Andrew Jackson Davis, the "Poughkeepsie Seer," claimed it was Franklin who discovered "this electrical method of telegraphing from the second sphere to the earth's inhabitants."[99]

Most important, Spiritualists considered their practice to be a process of knowing, not faith. Spiritualism hinged on its empirical validity; everything depended on whether the spirits were *really* communicating. Thus, while Spiritualists described their practice as a religion, they also, and often more strenuously, described it as a science and as the realization of the legacy of scientific thought. Hardinge was explicit about this in her text:

> Chemistry, Physiology, Phrenology, Magnetism, and Clairvoyance have all been steps leading up through the once-forbidden mysteries of nature into the realm of imponderable forces, bearing the student onward to the very gates of the temple of mind, within which are now heard the low, telegraphic knocks of the spirit, inviting the earnest inquirers to enter, and prophesying the great day of revelation, when man may ascend as on a Jacob's ladder, that mighty column where Physics is the base, Science the shaft, Metaphysics the superstructure, and Spiritualism the coronal glory of the capital, whose starry crown pierces the overarching firmament of Heaven.[100]

Hardinge was true to the explicit commitment to empiricism in Spiritualism, which focused much of its practice on protocols of verification taken from scientific discourse. Public demonstrations were structured as controlled, reproducible experiments, and the Fox sisters ultimately included in their demonstrations an independent committee of spectators who were tasked with investigating the process and reporting to the audience.[101] In some ways Spiritualists promoted a more muscular empiricism than scientific discourses of the day. While scientists for the most part understood the mysteries of the universe to outstrip human capacities for knowledge, Spiritualists were vocal advocates of the idea that scientific investigation could reveal all, even those who spoke from beyond the realm of the living and their manifold technologies.[102]

Verifiability became another site at which the telegraph and Spiritualism crossed wires. Andrew Jackson Davis wrote, "That the conditions and principles upon which spirits answer, in this manner, to the inquiries of man, are simple and physical, philosophical and rational, can be demonstrated to the candid and enlarged understanding; because those conditions are no more complicated or wonderful than the principles upon which the magnetic telegraph is daily operating along our great commercial avenues."[103] But, just as the telegraph seemed to flicker between regimes of science, religion, and magic, Spiritualism's place within scientific discourse called forth an equal measure of magic. For the scholar of US religions David Walker, Spiritualists actively embodied the space of P. T. Barnum's "humbug," a tantalizing mix of just enough substance to be possible and persistent, active doubt that never resolved.[104] The science and magic went hand in hand, and the undecidability between them was precisely what spurred Spiritualism and made it such a modern phenomenon.

Walker locates the "most fertile religious grounds" for the Spiritualists "between Bacon and Barnum."[105] For Barnum and the Spiritualists, objects of critique invited investment.[106] Controversy incited excitement, and debate over veracity made Spiritualism a lively object of scrutiny. It thus demanded affective attention, seated somewhere between science and scandal. As described by Walker, "Mediums' own modernity lay neither in singularity of affiliation or diction, nor in the ability to collapse or harmonize cultural dichotomies, but rather in their navigations and encampments between them."[107] Spiritualists promoted their practice with demonstrations that they framed in a double rhetoric of empirical investigation and cosmic promise; the ambivalence of the practice between the two was essential to Spiritualism and the widespread attention to it in the United States. This process worked both ways: Charles Lee, a skeptic who set out to expose Spiritualist rappings as nothing more than the sound of mediums' joints, found that his demonstrations of its falsehood resulted in converting audience members *to* Spiritualism.[108] For Walker, Spiritualism did not vacillate between the investigatory modes of science and the faithful belief of religion; rather, Spiritualism inhabited that undecidability as its proper place.[109]

Such undecidability was as essential for Spiritualism as for its helpmate telegraphy. Spiritualism dealt in mysterious communication from a transcendent realm that worked through barely understood means. The same for telegraphy: it existed only by virtue of recently formed abilities to harness the electrical power of the heavens. Both telegraphy and Spiritualism traded in this charged ether.[110] Benjamin Franklin, cast as progenitor in both telegraphy and Spiritualism, understood electricity as a particular form of the ethers that filled the universe and served as media for the activities therein. Because ethers in general and electricity in particular acted in ways that often defied experimental expectations, they were ripe sites for proposals of divine agency and the more elusive activity of magic.[111]

Much of the instability among religion, science, and magic in telegraphy stems from the uncomfortable place of electricity itself. In the words of Samuel Morse,

> In the minds of many, the electro magnetic telegraph is associated with the various chimerical projects constantly presented to the public, and particularly with the schemes, so popular a year or two ago, for the application of electricity as a moving power in the arts. I have asserted, from the first, that all attempts of this kind are premature, and made without a proper knowledge of scientific principles. The case is, however, entirely different in regard to the electro magnetic telegraph. Science is now fully ripe for this application.[112]

William Kelley, who formally located electricity and telegraphy as inventions of science in his oration celebrating the 1858 cable, also attributed the origins of telegraphy to God in the same speech.[113] Electricity—or "fire wonders," "lightning subservient . . . to the will of man," was barely understood, and concerns about humbug abounded.[114] Magic tantalized in spectacles of these new wonders, while science and religion legitimated.

The congressional debate over a bill to fund Morse's first telegraph line with $30,000 in 1843 included mocking amendments by Representative Cave Johnson (D-TN) that half the money be used to fund mesmerism and by George Houston (D-AL) that some of the funds go to Millerism, a religion founded on the belief that the world would end within the year.[115] That the science of electricity could be mocked by the science (yes, at the time) of animal magnetism and a religion of doomsday prophecy signals the blurred lines among these experimental fields. Neither amendment passed; the bill did.

In the mid-nineteenth century the United States was deeply invested in its own development of scientific knowledge as a rival to Europe and, in its more ambitious forms, in locating itself at the vanguard of intellectual achievement. US celebration of the telegraph and its oceanic cable became a celebration of US vision, ingenuity, and gumption. A cult of US heroism rewrote a complicated history of international scientific exchange into a singular myth of great US inventors, with Morse and Franklin at the helm. Despite widespread US memorialization of Samuel Morse as the inventor of the electrical telegraph, the first US patent for a telegraph went to the British team Charles Wheatstone and William Cooke.[116] And long before Franklin got around to conducting his iconic lightning experiment, two French scientists captured electricity from lightning, based on a letter from Franklin describing his experimental plan. Franklin published his later, and modified, experimental results in the *Gazette*. When German physicist Georg Wilhelm Reichmann replicated Franklin's kite-and-key experiment, his actual success led to his immediate death, thus revealing that Franklin had quite fortunately failed to capture electricity from lightning and had, rather, captured less potent and therefore less lethal ambient electricity from the storm.[117]

In fact, the article that decried the great fizzle articulated the contestation among science, magic, and religion as a concern over the nation's religious fervor for Cyrus Field: "For the time being it seemed as if there was but one God, his name being FIELD, and we were all his meek and modest satraps." The author dismissed this religion of science by naming it as nothing more than magic:

Things changed. The cable no longer afforded connection for Queen or President; drygoods men could no longer send their little puffs; De Sauty–like, the current was played out, our demigods became demireps; the whole thing was voted a humbug, and every man was loud-mouthed in asserting that for his part he never believed a bit of it, and knew that those messages were not bona fide. We need not discuss these points, the great success was a great fizzle.[118]

Telegraphy skipped higgledy-piggledy among science, religion, and magic and thus highlighted the charged intimacy of all three. Religion, blurred as its boundary was, oriented affective investment to this new electrical power, which seemed to make science relevant and urgent while also regularly jumping science's grasp. Part magic, part religion, part science, "the telegraph" took center stage, getting all the credit for messages that were, behind the scenes, carried by an ad hoc assortment of other, also fragmented, systems: boats, flags, and runners.

System Failure: The Optical Telegraph

"The telegraph" was an illusion. At best, this assemblage of technologies and processes was an uneven amalgamation of the people, expertise, infrastructure, technologies, and ways of using those technologies available at any given time and place. Sending an electromagnetic telegram often required a whole host of other infrastructural technologies to come into play: optical telegraphs to cover gaps in the cabled networks, boats to cross rivers in the absence of cables under the water, and boys to run the messages from the stations to their recipients. None of the emerging network technologies (rail, post, telegraph) could be extricated from the others and still function. They were inherently multimodal, as Downey notes: telegraph networks "began and ended with young [telegraph messenger] boys but encompassed a variety of technologies, institutions, and geographies in between."[119] To say "the Atlantic telegraph" and to consider its role in forming "the nation" is already to engage in a sort of sleight of hand. The telegraph was as much bodies of water, young boys running, and cutthroat competition for patents as it ever was wires and nodes.

Despite widespread claims of singularity, speed, and ubiquity, the electromagnetic telegraph was a much more complicated beast. Comparison with the optical telegraph (a system of using coded combinations of panels to deliver messages by line of sight between towers) makes this plain. The optical telegraph did not employ the mystical power of electricity and was much more continuous with previous signaling techniques like smoke and flags in its reliance on a visual code. It may have lacked the flash and novelty of the electromagnetic telegraph, but it was far more reliable in general (depending on the weather, of course). On a clear day in 1850s France, the optical telegraph often worked faster than the electrical systems of the time. In fact, despite its limited use in the United States, the forty-plus US newspapers that sported "telegraph" in their mastheads in 1820 were referencing the *op-tical* telegraph (the electromagnetic telegraph had not been invented yet).[120] The multiplicity of media infrastructures as a sort of overlapping, intertwining, and mutually informing chaosmos is not new to an age of media saturation; rather, it is old and common to networks since their inception.

The communication and transportation infrastructures of the nineteenth century were necessarily interdependent. The early telegraph system stands as a quintessential example of McLuhan's adage that "the 'content' of any medium is always another medium."[121] Any telegram passed through multiple human operators at stations along a cabled route. Once a message arrived at the telegraph station closest to the addressee, a telegraph messenger boy then ran the message to the recipient, often using other multiple forms of transportation along the way. For example, the Magnetic Telegraph, the first private US telegraph company, had a line that ran from New York City to Philadelphia, but because it could not yet cross the Hudson River with telegraph lines, handwritten messages were physically delivered back and forth by young boys between New York City and Newark by train and boat.[122] Downey demonstrates that "the technological network of the telegraph was more than just a combination of electromechanical systems; it was also a combination of systems of labor, in which messenger boys served different functions at different moments, sometimes working as technological components in and of themselves, sometimes being sold as commodities along with the telegrams they carried, and sometimes acting as agents of change within the technological network itself."[123]

The Atlantic cable was a particularly enticing illusion of discrete invention as it appeared in its singularity to be so contained and so novel. But it too functioned only through such a multimodal network. Communication from Europe was relayed by submarine and terrestrial telegraph to England and then to Ireland, crossed the ocean on the Atlantic Telegraph Cable, and then traveled by submarine and terrestrial telegraph to Canada after arriving in Newfoundland (which was a self-governing British colony 1855–1907 and only joined Canada in 1949). In fact, the original plan for a telegraph line between Newfoundland and Nova Scotia, Canada, involved telegraph cables, steamer ships, and carrier pigeons.[124] Multiple actants, human and nonhuman, and multiple forms of transportation moved the messages attributed to the cable itself.

Thus, the complicated matrix that produced the illusion of the telegraph also produced a series of systems that worked differently in different spaces. In Downey's pithy phrasing, telegraph systems bore their own "spatial and temporal rhythms," which produced an "uneven geography" for their operation.[125] The availability of the telegraph as a medium of communication and its speed depended entirely on the distance the message was to travel, the schedules of railroads and boats, an industry of message runners, and the density of the local population.[126] In other words, despite a robust discourse of universality, the telegraph was a medium highly restricted to very specific local centers and determined by local conditions.

Likewise, the promises of instantaneity remained an unrealized fiction. US public speech hailed a new immediacy and portrayed global unity as the result of the material connection of the cable and the new technological possibility of global simultaneity. For example, the *New York Times* reprinted a notice from the *Boston Atlas* on a "most interesting fact" demonstrated in the celebrations: "By preconceived arrangement, Mr. J. B. Stearns, Superintendent of the Boston Fire Alarm Telegraph, rung all the bells of Boston connected with the fire-alarm from the office of the American Telegraph Company in *Portland*! This extraordinary feat indicates the practicability of a simultaneous ringing of bells throughout the world."[127] Here it is clear that the "world" imagined at the advent of the Atlantic cable was not understood to emerge from agreement or new relationships but from concurrence. Simultaneity stood in for unity. Later developments in democratic and communication theory that promoted discussion as a means to agreement and unity did not yet reign.[128]

The distinction between unity forged through agreement and unity forged through the cable's capacity for rapid transmission was crucial because it placed the priority on the medium of communication rather than on the forms of speech that might take place through it. This sentiment was echoed in President Buchanan's declaration of "spontaneous unity," Weingärtner's depiction of the cable that bound the world without any representation of the messages that passed over it, and Kelley's announcement of a "whole world made vocal" without any real concern for the cacophony such global vocality entailed.[129] Unity was not premised on these technologies as media of mutually transforming discourse. Rather, technological capacity was understood as the sole condition for unity regardless of what speech might transpire across these lines.[130]

Promises of spontaneity and instantaneity were widespread and widely celebrated; they completely failed in practice. Delay was integral to the system. While the speed of time is always relatively perceived, as any digital native listening to the slow tone of "instantaneous" dial-up can tell, Morse was clear in his promises of speed that the telegraph would transmit messages in literally no time at all:

> The fullest and most precise information can be almost instantaneously transmitted between any two or more points between which a wire conductor is laid: that is to say, no other time is consumed than is necessary to write the intelligence to be conveyed, and to convert the words into the telegraphic numbers. The numbers are then transmitted nearly instantaneously, (or, if I have been rightly informed in regard to some recent experiments in the velocity of electricity, *two hundred thousand times more rapidly than light!*) to any distance.[131]

In practice, the rapidity afforded by telegraphy was more varied and depended on many factors, including location and the length of the message.

Because other new modes of transmission and transportation were affecting the speed of information transmission in the United States, the time-saving capacities of the telegraph were quite small in some contexts. For example, the time lag between an event occurring in Washington, DC, and its publication in Boston was reduced by 3.4 days by telegraphy, but the decades before telegraphy (1790–1817) had reduced the time lag by nearly 12 days.[132] Menahem Blondheim calculates that transmitting the Old Testament from Boston to New York by telegraph would have taken more than 5 days; sending it by pony express would have taken less than 10 hours.[133] Likewise, the telegraph contributed to a 32.9 percent reduction in time lag from New York to Charleston or Savannah but a 63.2 percent reduction to Cincinnati.[134] Promises of speed and ubiquity were regularly thwarted by context and local conditions.

The telegraph also had to negotiate regular failures in transmission, which compounded delays. Downey notes, "For example, in 1852, a telegram traveling the two thousand miles from New York to New Orleans had to be rekeyed four or five times along the way at intermediate stations. A garbled message would have to be resent, slowing overall transmission speed."[135] Notably, another system that would become known as a network—the nerves of the animal body—was also revealing the integral nature of delay. In the mid-nineteenth century, Hermann von Helmholtz found a delay of a thousandth of a second between nerve stimulation and the resulting muscle contraction. This inevitable lag ultimately became known as "real time," ironically now the label for mediated immediacy.[136] This semantic link highlights the deep roots of our habit of attributing speed and instantaneity to media regardless of how time works in practice.

Affective Publicity

Effusive celebrations of Atlantic telegraphy as a pinnacle achievement of US scientific innovation and a fecund cause of new national and global social life reigned while no element of this fantasy held together. US Americans imagining a new networked world wrestled with this central impossibility of the very public they declared to come into being. In a stirring passage in the *San Antonio Ledger* in April 1858, social disintegration is part and parcel of predicted global sociality:

> It will be an annihilation of time and space that will bring the eastern and western hemispheres within hailing distance of each other; it will infuse a new, and perhaps, in some respects, an embarrassing intelligence into the transactions of commerce; and news of all the current events of times—the wars and rumors of wars—the calamities that men inflict upon themselves and each other, or suffer in the natural course of things, with the thousand minor items of detail that swell the catalogue of human destiny—will flash with the speed of thought from one extremity of the globe to the other.[137]

The proximity and totality of the globe would be produced through the very conflicts and "embarrassing intelligence" that would make global unity impossible. Failure was a critical generative element for the production of global public life. In fact, according to historian of communications Richard John, the inflated promises that Congressman Smith attributed to Morse's telegraph in order to secure federal funding were necessitated by Morse's *failures* to secure financial backing; in Britain, Wheatstone and Cooke had little use for such bloated publicity for their telegraph because of readily available funds.[138] What the telegraph presents is a case of publicity emerging *through* its impossibility, which points us to the generative participation of affect in the production of this impossible, vital public.

The fizzling responses to the telegraph structured and shaped the cultural field claimed as their context. The United States that emerged was constituted in part by the enthusiastic declarations that the telegraph was American (and even that such enthusiasm itself was American). Cultural studies scholar Lawrence Grossberg calls the organization of affect a "mattering map." Such organization makes possible certain objects of investment (what we can care about) and certain modes of investment (how we can care about such things), and it determines the coherence between these elements and the subjects we become in the investments we make.[139] According to Grossberg, mattering maps not only determine our investments but also structure the very practices of investment: "Mattering maps also involve the lines that connect the different sites of investment; they define the possibilities for moving from one investment to another, of linking the various fragments of identity together. They define not only what sites (practices, effects, structures) matter but how they matter. And they construct a lived coherence for those enclosed within their spaces."[140] The telegraph, the science it embodied, the whole world it brought into being, and the nation it connected all achieved their impossible coherence from the investment of affect at a key moment in the antebellum United States. This particular "mattering map" produced the impossible social forms that have become naturalized to networks. These elements—the telegraph's whiteness, protestantism, publicity, technicity, nationalism, and globalism—were nodal points of investment that became saturated with affect, particularly through the adept vehicle of religion. As these points attracted more affect and shaped more of the field around them, the fizzle gained momentum.

Affect produced meaning for these elements and also rendered certain meanings more culturally important than others. Affect can help us understand why the Atlantic cable as a unifier of the world surpassed other meanings of the cable and how the electromagnetic came to be "the telegraph" at a time when multiple telegraphs abounded. Affective investment explains why US enthusiasm for the cable as the connector of the United States with Europe only grew as the cable was strung between Ireland and Newfoundland. The meaning of the telegraph as an exclusively British institution carried no weight for people in the United States. It may have been true, but it did not *matter*. The cable was understood by US Americans, facts be damned, as their link with the world. Likewise, the assertion of a dominant white Protestant mode of public life as *the* US public charged the electromagnetic telegraph with meaning and mattering while obscuring the grapevine, spiritual, and optical telegraphs and their inventors and users, who were not at all incidentally predominantly black, female, and French, respectively. That the slave ship *Telegraph* was not part of public discourse about telegraphs then and has since largely fallen from the historical record naturalizes the whiteness of US public culture and its networked media.

This US affective formation commanded little influence in Europe. In editorial comments submitted to the *New York Times* from Heidelberg on September 3, 1858, shortly after the initial success of the telegraph cable, the effect of location on the experience of the cable was clear:

> We, in this region, have been greatly amused at the reports of the celebration in America of the successful completion of the Atlantic Telegraph, of which recent numbers of the American journals have been full. By the time this reaches you, the excitement will have died away, and very likely the whole affair will be well nigh forgotten. You may, therefore, be able, in some degree, to sympathize with the astonishment felt by Europeans at demonstrations so greatly transcending the achievement.[141]

Undeniably, by the time this report was published in the *New York Times*, the line had failed and excitement had indeed died away. But the very lack of investment in celebration on the European side underscored the striking investment on the part of some US Americans. Celebration of the Atlantic cable was a US affective practice for a US imaginary.[142]

There was a surprising amount of explicit reflection on the emotional investment in the cable in public texts. Much of affect theory relies on the idea that social energy functions through circulation that often does not reach a conscious register.[143] In the case of the cable, however, US affective formations around the telegraph cable became news. At times regretful and at times celebratory, newspapers from New York to Georgia included reports on the growing affective investments of US Americans in the possibilities of the cable. This news was particularly notable because these same articles also included discussion of the persistence of this collective energy—what the *San Antonio Ledger* called the "public confidence," as cited earlier—in the face of repeated failures and frustrations. The role of failure in generating the depth of this enthusiasm was evident in a report from New Hampshire:

> This announcement [of the Atlantic cable's success], at a moment when hope had almost ceased to be felt for the successful termination of this magnificent enterprise, created the greatest surprise and excited joy all over the land, and has been followed, from one end of the land to the other, by demonstrations of the interest and enthusiasm it has occasioned, in the ringing of bells, illuminations, firing of cannon, and other tokens of joy.[144]

The possibility of failure made the joy of success exuberant.

In those rare cases in which the news was met with different responses, reports mocked, chided, and justified them. For example, the *New York Times* reported on the less effusive reactions of some northeastern cities as a curiosity, explained them away, and then described the people's ultimate participation in the enthusiasm:

> It is very curious to observe the skepticism with which the first news was received in such quiet, conservative places as Boston and Hartford, and even the little town of Rutland, in Vermont, at the West, and in the backwoods settlements. The event came upon the good people in those parts too suddenly. It unsettled them, and discomposed their nervous systems. But when, *like doubting Thomases*, as they were, they couldn't help believing, then they all went mad together, and the consequence was a general outbreak of enthusiasm.[145]

The report from Columbus similarly indicated an initial absence of celebration but assured readers that celebration would surely come: "The citizens here are very much excited. They have been deceived once, and are awaiting certain confirmation before having a great celebration."[146] This pattern was especially true in a report from the *Boston Atlas* on the reactions of the people of Boston:

> Boston was cautious. It was prudent. It looked up and down, it went forward and backward, it scratched its head and stroked its nose, it ran its hands into its capacious pockets, it guessed yes, and it guessed no; and finally concluded to sleep on it before it went into very large and outward demonstrations. And so no guns were fired, and no bells rung, no shouts thundered, nor bunting flung to the fluttering breezes on Thursday. Boston held itself, martingale-like, back. But it was only to give vent to its pent-up Utica of enthusiasm upon another occasion and time. This was yesterday, when the city authorities set the ball of rejoicing in motion. Hardly had the hour of high noon arrived, when bell and cannon proclaimed the "glad tidings" that Boston, too, felt to its center the great event. For a full hour the bells of the city pealed forth their blessed and blessing tones, never before so cheerful, and the guns of the Boston Light Artillery, directed by Capt. Nims sent forth from their capacious throats such a grand international salute as Boston ears are unaccustomed to hear. One hundred voices of earthquakean quality rolled out and out, over city, country, over sea and land and into the ocean of blue above. Then it was that Boston threw off its reserve and threw up its hat; then it was that it pulled its hands free from its pantaloons and clapped and applauded for the Cable.[147]

In these cases and others, the demand for a certain affective formation was expressed in the insistence that any lack of enthusiasm was temporary and would indeed be overcome by the national joy.[148] Explanations were offered to justify any response that was less than fully celebratory, and each narrative of resistance to the celebration cast that resistance as wariness that would succumb to inevitable delight. These news reports show that the fizzle was not as spontaneous as it appeared—it was, as Sarah Ahmed notes of other affects at other times, pedagogical and disciplined.[149] It did not arise out of nothing but created empowered subjectivities that could enthuse about a copper wire as the communicative salvation of the young nation and the whole world.

The regular failures of the cable fueled enthusiasm for it and cast the cable in a teleological narrative that ended in success no matter the fractures that unfolded in the present. Even reports that highlighted the difficulty and shortcomings of this venture couched their concerns in an optimistic sense of the world's speedy progress toward global connection. By 1858 the tension between failure and success had become a standard motif in news reports on the cable's progress. These descriptions of the telegraph were decidedly celebratory, particularly given the daunting nature of this endeavor, the absence of a historical precedent, and the history of failed past attempts. This affirmative tone did not deny past and potential failures but, rather paradoxically, foregrounded them as reasons that guaranteed vindication. In the following report from the *San Antonio Ledger*, the pattern of subsuming any disappointment into a progressive narrative of ultimate success prevailed even after the earlier failed attempt at an Atlantic cable (1857–1858) was irreparably damaged with no chance of resuscitation:

> The failure of the attempt last summer to lay a telegraphic cable between the continents of Europe and America, caused a universal feeling of disappointment throughout the United States and England. Immense interests were bound up in the experiment, and thousands looked anxiously to the expected achievement. There was comparatively but little doubt entertained that the formidable obstacles which interposed would be eventually overcome, for so certain in their results are the means selected by modern science to effect its object, that people have come to consider it as almost omnipotent. The public confidence, therefore, was great that the experiment would have a satisfactory termination, and that a triumph would be achieved unparalleled in the history of the world. The unfortunate accident which caused the failure shook that confidence to some extent; but the general opinion still is, not only that the project is practicable, but that a second trial will have a fortunate result.[150]

After the 1858 cable failed, attention to affect in the news continued. Public confidence was again directed toward optimism and continued investment in the cable's sure success. The promise of success despite failure became a standard element of reports on Atlantic telegraphy, thus making sense of the regularity of failure through teleologies of progress despite the fact that disconnections remained part of the system even when the cables functioned at their best.

These reports on the affective formation around the cable taught US Americans to hold fast to the imaginary of a united global community and the promise that technology is progressive. They often dismissed and ridiculed doubt and concern and encouraged celebration and optimism. They directed social energy into a particular formation that invoked failure as a site of investment while interpreting failure as a sign of progress and eventual fulfillment. The gaps between the desired world and the experienced world served as the locus for affective investment. Thus, a formation of affect that orbited failure—the great fizzle—gave shape to this imaginary, powered it through repeated failure, and used that failure to sustain commitment in the impossible dream this global imaginary offered.

One report on the success of the 1858 cable put it succinctly: "A result so practical, and yet so inconceivable; so pregnant with consequences which prophecy alone can fathom and estimate; so full of hopeful prognostics for the future of mankind, must in all time designate this period in the annals of the race as one of the loftiest moments; as one of the grand wavemarks in the onward and upward march of the human intellect."[151] The unknowable future and the teleology of progress joined uneasy hands in a contradictory declaration of contingency and inevitable success and made the moment a site to which passion could adhere.

* * *

Public discourse produced "the telegraph" as a singular US invention that would be the pinnacle of scientific achievement, unrivaled in its capacity to unite the nation. This discourse contributed to later meanings for networks more broadly as singular, scientific, connective, unifying, public, social, politically neutral, and functional. To this day, networks appear to promise the annihilation of space and time and a new unity for humanity.[152] Alongside these emerging attributes for networks are other, conflicting attributes that were also produced by this discourse. Networks have a wide mesh, producing gaps as they connect nodes. They rely on equality of information and monopoly of industry at the same time.[153] They are scientific by virtue of being religious and magical. And they are global and national by means of highly local practices that produce and reify a certain localness *as* national and *as* global. They appear politically neutral while reverberating with a history of slavery, racism, protestant dominance, capitalism, and colonialism.

The US public wrought through the rise of some network infrastructure (e.g., electromagnetic telegraphy) and the eclipse of others (e.g., the grapevine telegraph) was a creative inhabitation of a social reality that extended beyond and even defied the world of experience. While dreams of national and global unity emphatically contradicted the fractures constitutive of nation and world, these imaginaries were not simply fictions about the future. They were lived in the present. Chapter 3 takes up the failures of imagination at the heart of such utopian orientations to network unity.

3

The End of Distance and the End of War

The Oneida Community and US Techno-Utopianism

By thy divine Messiah—
That true celestial wire—
　　To Heaven we're bound!
Whisper thy message low,
Swift let the tidings go,
Till grace run to and fro,
　　The whole earth round.
With thy word-woven cord,
Bind all men to the Lord,
　　And Man to Man!
—hymn sung at celebration of the Atlantic telegraph in
Walpole, New Hampshire, on August 19, 1858, reprinted in
the Oneida Community's *Circular*, September 2, 1858

Only a cough stands between us and utopia. At least, that is how Thomas More portrayed the titular island in the first edition of his landmark book *Utopia*, published in 1516. Just as the traveler Raphael Hythloday is about to reveal the location of the magically ideal land to the narrator, one man whispers, another coughs, and access to Utopia is rendered unintelligible.[1] More pokes fun at his readers by repeatedly ushering access to Utopia out of reach: he loses track of characters who know where Utopia is, he structures the text to confuse fact and fiction, and he presents his account as the transcript of another's report and admits that it is probably full of errors.

The immutable distance of the island Utopia reflects a problem that haunts the concept: utopia provides an enticing alternative to the status quo, but we can never reach it from where we are. This double meaning of idealism and inaccessibility can be blamed on Thomas More himself, since he coined the term *utopia* with this essential ambiguity. In the text, utopia is no-place, prefixing the Greek *topos* (place) with *ou-*, a prefix of negation. However, More included an introductory poem with a pun that draws on the Greek prefix *eu-* (good).[2] We inherit the concept of utopia as a good place *and* as no-place, such that its promises of the good life are premised on its spatial or temporal inaccessibility. Much of the scholarly literature on utopia, as well as the colloquial use of the term, posits utopia with both meanings intact: as an unreachable happy future or an impossible ideal.

The distinctive modern global imaginary developed in the United States in the mid-nineteenth century around network infrastructure—an imaginary that promised global unity, universal peace, and the end of distance itself—should be understood as utopian. It offered important ruptures with the status quo and enacted the desires of a population wrestling with a host of new technologies, awash in religious reinvention, and on the brink of civil war. This imaginary described a world that would solve the problems plaguing the age. Yet to say that this network imaginary is utopian appears also to say that it was an ideal that was inaccessible in space and time, the no-place of More's original (if sublimated) formulation of utopia as *ou-topia*. Indeed, this imaginary self-consciously reached for the impossible, for a world that was extraordinary because it was perfect. That said, the participants in this network imaginary understood it as neither distant nor future but near in both space and time. In public discourse inflected by diffuse protestantism and in the new religious movements that appeared in the middle of the century, telegraphy appeared to offer a radically new and radically proximate shift in the world.

How did the telegraph land at the heart of such utopian imaginaries? It was a remarkable conjuncture of technology and religion. Network infrastructure (particularly the Erie Canal) and the emotive revivals of the Second Great Awakening threaded their way through upstate New York.[3] The "extravagant excitement" of these religious gatherings led to western New York becoming known as the *burned-over district*, scorched as it had been by the fires of revivals.[4] There and in the surrounding states, a number of religious experiments were born or revived, feeding a wave of utopianism spreading west in step with the canal, railroad, and telegraph: the Shakers, the early Church of Jesus Christ of Latter-day

Saints, New Harmony, the Kingdom of Matthias, Brook Farm, and others. This religious experimentalism—particularly attempts at utopian intentional communities—and new ventures in network infrastructure all organized themselves around the ambitious assurance that they could make a perfect world in the present.[5]

A quintessential example of such a utopian endeavor was the Oneida Community, an intentional community founded on the belief that moral perfection was possible and on the determination to, thus, live perfectly. Although relatively small (about three hundred members at its peak), the Oneida Community was one of the longest-lasting utopian communities that cropped up in the mid-nineteenth century. And while some of the community's most notable aspects—particularly the marriage of all of the men to all of the women and vice versa—ended with its dissolution, the name lives on, imprinted on the back of silverware and dishes produced by the flatware company it founded. The Oneida Community understood itself as radically different, and it is generally included in histories of nineteenth-century US religion as an emblematic fringe religious movement. But in one aspect, the Oneidans were utterly like their US contemporaries: they were obsessed with the telegraph.

The Oneida Community newspaper, the *Circular*, began to report diligently and regularly on the Atlantic Telegraph Cable six years before its first success. From the initial report, an article reprinted from the *New York Observer* in November 1852, through the 570 articles that followed on telegraph technology and the possibilities it opened, the Atlantic telegraph became a focal point of Oneida attention and a critical means through which to frame the community's religious endeavors.[6] The headline in its newspaper, upon the success of the 1858 cable, announced in absolute present tense, "NO MORE DISTANCE! NO MORE WAR! THE CONTINENTS UNITED. Instant Communication with EUROPE, ASIA, & AFRICA BY MEANS OF THE OCEAN TELEGRAPH."[7] This imaginary never equated impossibility with inaccessibility. Rather, the Oneidans took a Christian logic in which the impossible (e.g., the incarnation, death, and resurrection of God) functioned as the particularly achievable and added the urgency of perfectionism, in which the impossible could be achieved here and now. They greeted the success of the Atlantic cable with an assured sense that moral and technological perfection went hand in hand, despite the problems that plagued both their ethical lives and the telegraph. The community's attention to the telegraph upended the regular workings of utopia. In the context of new entanglements of religion and technology, the radical otherness of this unified, peaceful world was precisely what made the announcement of its present arrival so important.

The declaration of global peace and the eradication of distance through telegraphy by the Oneida Community—admittedly a unique experiment in Christian communal life—should not be read as the dotty pronouncements of a misguided and short-lived religious fringe. Just as Oneida silverware became a mainstay of US kitchen tables, the community's enthusiasm for and ways of making sense of the Atlantic cable participated in a broader US excitement over what the telegraph could make possible. The way that the Oneidans described the Atlantic cable and the celebratory practices they developed around it echoed, assimilated, and mimicked descriptions and practices from around the country. As we saw earlier, missionaries of the American Board of Commissioners for Foreign Missions also announced the end of distance. In the words of Judson Smith, "With the network of telegraph lines covering the great continents, and sunk beneath the seas, and binding all parts of the world into the circuits of swift intelligence, space and time are almost annihilated."[8] The epigraph to this chapter, a hymn that exalted the "celestial wire" that bound all people to each other and God, rang with Christian tropes of global unity similar to the kinds of public protestant discourse discussed in chapter 2.[9] The hymn was sung at the Atlantic telegraph celebration in New Hampshire and reprinted in the Oneida Community newspaper two weeks later; the convoluted circulations of discourse through print and other media meant that the Oneida Community was already entangled with other publics. Despite the idiosyncrasies of the Oneida Community, it shared in a popular imagination of a world united and pacified by electric communication technology.

Utopia proves to be a useful construct to explain the emergence of this network imaginary, but only with the caveat that modern US techno-utopias significantly qualified More's attendant pun of temporal or spatial inaccessibility. The emergent imaginary of networks requires an alternative definition of utopia as *proximate*; by articulating this redefinition and mapping its particular form in the Oneida Community, we can see how religion contributed to the potent techno-utopianism that has been integral to network imaginaries since. The modes of utopia that emerged in the mid-nineteenth-century United States—the surge in utopian communities, the burgeoning idea of America itself, and the novel (and now ingrained) habit of making sense of network technology through the promise of connection—made use of new forms of protestantism to refigure the classical conception of utopia in favor of the now-here over the no-where.[10] Understanding the proximity of these US utopias—neither future nor distant but close at hand—allows us to delve into the ways in which imaginaries of networks helped to produce a new world that was both radically disconnected from reality and inhabited as real.

The Religious Logic of Proximate Utopia

The article in the Oneida newspaper that announced the end of distance and war continued with equally grand claims for what this single cable could accomplish: "Thus humanity, under God, marches grandly on to its destiny; step by step the barriers of nature fall, and we enter upon the kingly inheritance that God intended for us when He made the world."[11] The Atlantic Telegraph Cable fueled the Oneida Community's dreams of what a morally perfect world could be. Oneida celebrated the milestone of the 1858 Atlantic cable with a daylong event that included a parade, a lecture on telegraphy, music by the Oneida Community Brass Band, toasts, and supper outside under the butternut tree.[12] On that same day, as fireworks across the nation boomed for oceanic telegraphy, the cable conveyed its last garbled messages.

The Oneida Community was founded on John Humphrey Noyes's assertion that Christ had already returned, making moral perfection achievable in the present.[13] As a young theology student at Yale, Noyes resolved to calculate the date of Christ's return. After statements he found in the Gospels that Christ promised his own return within the apostolic age, Noyes was convinced that, as promised, Christ returned in 70 CE while the first generation of his disciples was still alive.[14] According to Noyes, the first and second comings of Christ reconciled humanity to God. Christ not only forgave all sin but also purified humankind, making it possible for the earliest Christians and their successors to live without sin in the first place.[15]

The religious community Noyes founded and led endeavored to live out this possibility. The Oneida Community and smaller associated communities at Wallingford, Connecticut; Newark, New Jersey; Brooklyn, New York; Cambridge, Vermont; and Putney, Vermont, were known as Bible Communists.[16] Oneidans lived together under a commitment to perfectionism, which they primarily oriented around eradicating the sin of selfishness. They shared all property and work in common and, as noted, famously developed "complex marriage," a radical refusal of what they understood as the selfishness of having a single marital partner. Children conceived in the community were raised by the community as a whole; after a few years given for nursing, particular attachments between parents and child were discouraged. Later in the life of the community, the Oneidans attempted to breed more perfect human beings through "stirpiculture," the arrangement of morally advanced mating pairs by a special committee.[17] These practices were grounded in their conviction of the very present possibility of achieving moral perfection in the here and now.

The religious movements that emerged from the revivalist fervor that surged through the new republic alongside new technology and attendant forms of national and transatlantic mobility birthed new forms of US utopianism. Shaped by John Wesley's perfectionist theology, the urgency of salvation stressed by Jonathan Edwards and others, and shifts in Calvinism that promoted a person's ability to act for his or her own salvation, a new Protestant emphasis on moral action joined the burgeoning sense that this moment in the United States offered unprecedented possibilities.[18] Religious passion rose alongside dreams of manifest destiny, and both empowered a widespread sense that new forms of life were achievable in a new land. A number of the groups born from the Second Great Awakening declared novel forms of divine contact: the Shakers understood their leader, Mother Ann Lee, to be an incarnation of God; Joseph Smith's revelation of new scripture led to the founding of the Mormons; the Millerites predicted that the Second Coming of Christ would occur in 1843–44; and the Oneida Community believed that the Second Coming of Christ had already occurred. These forms of divine communication were the foundation for diverse settlements across the United States that ambitiously attempted to realize a perfect way of life through communal living, new agricultural techniques, specialized diet, and refigurations of sexual relationships.[19]

Which is to say, nineteenth-century US utopias were never merely mental experiments—they were lived. These were no inaccessible islands or distant futures; they were new ways of inhabiting the here and now. Many of these utopian communities used Christianity's declaration of the radical rupture of the status quo with the incarnation, death, and rebirth of God to enable their radical reconstruction of life in the present. In this context, the Oneida Community represents a broader and emphatically mainstream US movement that saw an ideal reality become accessible in unprecedented ways.

US religious utopias in the mid-nineteenth century represent a significant shift from the imagined utopias of their forebears in fiction and philosophy. The Oneida Community, like many of the utopian movements in the United States and Europe at the time, was deeply influenced by Charles Fourier, who wrote his *Design for Utopia* in the 1830s.[20] Fourier intended his utopian vision as a thought experiment concerning the destiny of humankind. In the text, he laid out elaborate plans for a society organized around certain modes of agrarian labor in which communication and pleasure would meet the needs of society.[21] Fourier presented his work as a realizable (nearly inevitable) future, and many phalansteries (the community buildings at the heart of Fourier's plan for utopia) were built across Europe and the United States according to his descriptions. However, in Fourier's understanding of utopia, the agrarian civilization he described was only a near goal that remained far from the ultimate utopian destiny of humankind.[22] The alterity of that future was so extreme that he could only offer an intermediate step in the form of his text. As in More's *Utopia*, the radical rupture promised by utopia distanced it from the present. But in the Oneidan elaboration on Fourierism, the distant and unrecognizable future became daily life.

The central branch of the Oneida Community—all 306 members at its peak—lived together in a grand mansion house in Oneida, New York.[23] One account of the Oneida Community published in the *New-York Tribune* described the bounty of the gardens, the plentiful sheep, and the success of the industries that supported the community. This account, so idyllic that it was used by the Oneida Community in its own *Handbook*, is worth quoting at length for its detailed illustrations of the pleasures of life at the Community Mansion House, the Oneidans'

Figure 3.1. Members of the Oneida Community on the east lawn, 1870s. (Courtesy of the Oneida Community Mansion House)

commitment to new technology and print circulation, and the way these aspects of the community were understood to be part and parcel of their religious experiment:

> All eat in one large hall, at many tables. They provide neither tea nor coffee, and seldom meat. Vegetables, fruits, milk, butter, cheese, cakes, puddings, and pies are abundant. Rarely have I eaten meals so well cooked, so neat and so good. They equal, to my taste they excel, those at the best hotels.
>
> They have a fine library, and they take the leading daily and weekly newspapers. They publish a minute daily paper, which none but

themselves see. A handsome hall, furnished with chairs and small tables, is occupied by the members in the evening, in the same manner that a family gather around the hearth. All rooms are heated through registers and pipes. At each table are lamps; the women knit and sew, and I saw men knitting. Meanwhile, one will read a daily paper, or letters from friends, or short addresses. Then they talk over their affairs. In this way their evenings are spent till bedtime.

They employ no physician, for they need none; no lawyer, for they are peaceable; and no preacher, for they are perfect. They never pray. Musical instruments sound through the halls. They do not work on Sunday, but they do not call the day sacred. They neither baptize nor partake of the sacrament. Their lives are continued worship.[24]

The Oneida Community was strategic about its image in the world, particularly since many of its practices invited criticism and scandal. The Oneidans established their first newspaper, the *Free Church Circular*, within two years of the community's founding, joining a wave of evangelical print media that historian of journalism David Paul Nord identifies as the first mass medium in the United States.[25] The *Circular* replaced the *Free Church Circular* and became the weekly voice of the community from 1851 to 1876. It was then replaced by the *American Socialist* upon John Humphrey Noyes's resignation from formal leadership of the community. The *Circular* held a vital function of representing the community to itself and to outsiders, as well as sharing news and ideas from the rest of the world.

Those private and retrospective accounts that were later published or archived often strike a discordant note to the glowing descriptions of community life that the Oneida Community promoted and circulated. Even as late as 1947, descendants of the Oneida Community burned a treasure trove of community documents, including letters and diaries, that had been stored in an archival vault.[26] There was, unsurprisingly, significant difficulty with various community practices. Archival papers indicate that male continence, the sanctioned practice of preventing male orgasm as a means of birth control, was psychologically and physically trying for many of the male participants.[27] More disturbing, a striking account by an outside gynecologist who was granted an opportunity to speak with and examine a number of community members highlighted the implicit power dynamics that made it difficult for women to refuse sexual partners despite the community's overt commitment to consent.[28] When the surviving Oneida Community archives were made public in 1993, three edited editions of community members' diaries and letters described deeply troubled lives negotiating the complications of Bible Communism.[29] The majority of published accounts from the time, however, described a life of communitarian enjoyment, filled with leisure, friendship, passionate religious reflection, and shared work made lighter by entertainment, good food, and pride in the community's financial, social, and religious successes.

Perhaps it was this brimming sense of present possibility that animated the Oneidan obsession with telegraphy. The widespread US enthusiasm for the cable as the realization of an ideal future became part of the Oneida Community's admittedly unique religious undertaking to realize perfection in the present. The Oneidans' self-description shifted with the advent of the Atlantic cable; a vocabulary of electricity and telegraphy began to infuse their speech. For example, one author recalled the "Bible-Game," a practice in which community members read from the Bible every day: "If the letter of the Bible is a telegraph wire or a conductor for God's spirit, then a good work was done of laying down cable in that old Bible-Game." The entrance of telegraphic vocabulary into the Oneidans' discourse reflected the mundane ways the telegraph became a compelling metaphor for understanding their religious experiment and the world in which they located themselves.

The Atlantic cable struck a particularly pertinent note for the Oneidans. The religious logic of realizing a perfect future in the present tethered the highly *local* Oneidan religious project to the prevalent *global* imaginary of a world united by communication technology. Almost half of the articles printed in the *Circular* that referenced telegraphy focused on the crossing of the Atlantic by telegraphic communication (237 out of 570). Many of the articles on the telegraph provided highly technical information on elements of telegraph technology that one might doubt had anything at all to do with the avid religious experimentation of the Oneida Community, including minutiae such as the extension of the Morse patent, the laying of cable lines between Agra and Calcutta, and the total miles of Western Union telegraph lines (112,191 as of July 1, 1870). Such technical articles illustrate the Oneidans' interest in telegraphy, but they do not explain it. However, these articles were accompanied by a number of other articles that explicitly linked telegraphic communication to Noyes's dreams of salvation in the form of global unity, the primary importance placed on communication with heaven, and the framing of the Oneidans' religious endeavor as overcoming what was thought impossible.[30] On the night of September 1, 1858, at the Oneida Community's celebration of the Atlantic telegraph's apparent success, H. M. Waters closed his after-dinner toast with an illustrative junction of the Oneidan and telegraphic projects: "J. H. Noyes and Cyrus W. Field—one the layer of the spiritual telegraph; and the other of the Atlantic telegraph. May God send us more such men."[31] This toast reflects three important ways in which the Oneidans understood the significance of the Atlantic telegraph: as a compelling metaphor for their own utopian endeavor, as a sign of the bridging of this world with God's, and as a primary means for the unification of humanity through communication technology. This toast linked Noyes and Field for accomplishing unprecedented acts that shattered the status quo.

The Oneidans' claims at the advent of the Atlantic cable were hyperbolic and, even couched in the enthusiasm of the time, recognizably exceeded the limits of reality. The Oneidans were not unaware of the ways in which their discourse reached beyond the possibilities of the known world. Many of the descriptions of the Atlantic telegraph made use of the very idea of impossibility to secure the cable's relationship to the Oneida Community and as further evidence of God's action in the world: "Every such onward movement as that of the Atlantic telegraph, that raises the faith and courage of mankind toward things that seemed impossible, makes it more and more easy to reach forward towards victory over death; and we may expect that progressive people will henceforth be found looking in that direction, and will become familiar with the hope we have."[32] The Oneidans believed that Christ returned to earth within the apostolic age and "finished salvation."[33] In light of their perfectionist stance, "victory over death" was, in part, already grasped by humanity. The "impossible," toward which courage and faith were raised, had already been achieved. Their "hope" here must be read in the double sense of already and not-yet; it was a hope secured by history. While it was clear to the Oneidans that not all of humanity yet shared their view, the

Atlantic telegraph in its similar overcoming of impossibility predicted the moment for them when "progressive people" would also believe that the impossible was accessible.

The affinity for impossibility also figured in W. A. Hinds's toast at the jubilee. He asked, why should the Atlantic Telegraph Cable "excite our enthusiasms as Bible communists?" The primary reason was that "*it was accomplished in the face of unbelief*": "There is something in the successful resistance of unbelief, which cannot fail to insure our sympathy."[34] That something was the accessible impossibility that served as the premise of the Oneida Community; the Oneidans' fascination with the telegraph as a connective technology stemmed from their commitment to build a new reality radically disconnected from the one they knew.[35]

Like many other US Americans, as seen in the preceding chapters, the Oneida Community embraced a conviction that the telegraph made a new world possible. The Oneidans were, for all of their many idiosyncrasies, deeply imbricated in a discourse of telegraphic utopia that emerged in a variety of forms in diverse discursive publics. They subscribed to multiple newspapers, including religious, women's, and socialist papers, and frequently reprinted news from other newspapers in the *Circular* (a practice that was only reciprocated for accounts of the Oneida Community specifically).[36] They were aware of broader discussions of the Atlantic Telegraph Cable and integrated outside reports into their own discourse of telegraph utopianism (the epigraph to this chapter is a prime example). Likewise, others were alternately fascinated and scandalized by the Oneida Community's experiment in utopian life, and reports on the community were included in many major newspapers of the time.[37] These entwined communities produced overlapping and mutually informing imaginaries (telegraphic, religious, utopian), and all contributed to the same moment of passionate announcement of new possibility.

Those US Americans who declared the arrival of a new world made possible by the telegraph accomplished two things simultaneously. First, they invented. The unified, peaceful world whose reality they announced resembled little of what they saw around them just ten years after the Mexican-American War and three years before the American Civil War. Second, they instated that fiction as their lived reality. Both of these moves—invention and inhabitation—were central elements of the utopias of the time. These were utopias not simply as a mode of thought; they were kinetic, material, lived. The imagination of this new world and the announcement of its arrival served as a calling-into-being of a present utopia. This is not to say that the world was actually peaceful or unified. Rather, the US Americans who participated in this modern global imaginary imagined *and inhabited* a world that had only a little to do with what they encountered. Utopia enacted a vital fiction as a way of life. The Oneida Community set this way of life a standard no less than perfection. Perfection for the Oneidans was theological in nature—a new possibility to live free from sin after the Second Coming of Christ— but their attention to innovations in science and technology drew on and amplified a widespread US discourse that regularly declared new technologies to be perfect.

Perfection

Commitment to the presence of perfection was the bedrock of the Oneida Community. It held, following Noyes's idiosyncratic biblical interpretation, that Christ's return signaled not merely the forgiveness of sin but, rather, complete freedom from sin in the first place. According to Noyes,

> When therefore Christ is called the "Lamb of God, *that taketh away the sin of the world,*" we understand the language as meaning more than that by the atonement he has provided for the *forgiveness* of mankind, and so has taken away the legal *consequences* of sin. The "*taking away of sins*" is spoken of in Heb. 10:4, as equivalent to a cleansing, by which the conscience is *purged from sin*, and by which "the comer thereto is *made perfect.*"[38]

For the Oneida Community, a commitment to salvation thus entailed not merely atonement for sins committed but a more radical refusal of sin in the first place. In a more plainspoken "Home Talk" reprinted in the *Circular*, Noyes called perfection "great freedom from habit."[39]

The real possibility of perfection required a drastic change in how one lived. The Oneidans' primary critique of Fourierism was that it was merely an idea, not a description of experience. From the Oneida perspective, Fourier offered a "splendid theory, constructed with infinite pains, written down on paper, but not proved by experiment. . . . But theories are always suspicious; and in every art which we study, the living teacher, qualified by practical acquaintance is essential to perfection."[40] Their embodied commitment to the accessibility of perfection distinguished their experiment.

As lived and present, perfection was not an abstract concept. It took shape in the most mundane and material of forms, and the Oneida Community regularly used scientific and technological discovery as prime examples of realized perfection. One *Circular* article posited moral perfection as the root of scientific development—"The science of *moral perfection* . . . is the central science, and the other sciences as they are gradually developed, show correspondences, and furnish interesting illustrations to this science"—and gave horticulture as a primary example.[41] The possibility of perfection was given to humanity at the Second Coming of Christ, but it had to be lived out by each successive generation. Evidence of perfection's possibility lay all around and was exemplified by new technological and scientific discovery: "In every experimental science there is a tendency to *perfection*."[42]

The Oneida Community, for all the peculiarity of its *theological* perfectionism, was quite mainstream in its zeal for equally unlikely *technological* perfectionism. The perfection of science was a popular trope in US public discourse, which the Oneidans regularly borrowed from other sources and inflected with their particular context. They saw science and technology as fields of knowledge that proved their theological convictions. The preceding quotation, for example, was reprinted from Lord Thomas Babington Macauley's *History of England from the Accession of James the Second*, published in 1848. Likewise, the *Circular* included regular reports of the "perfection" of new technologies, including daguerreotypes, microscopes, photographic printing and engraving, and watchmaking, often reprinted from sources like *Scientific American, Popular Science Review*, and the *New-York Tribune*.[43] The Atlantic telegraph was no exception: the *Circular* reprinted a speech by Cyrus Field in which he declared the cables "almost perfect," and it titled the article "Perfection of the Atlantic Cables."[44]

The particular utopian fervor of the Oneida Community echoed widespread declarations of perfection that resounded in news reports on the

telegraph leading up to the 1858 attempt. The perfection discourse surrounding the Atlantic telegraph identified the cable as absolutely perfect
in the context of a near guarantee of failure. These cables were new technologies that were endangered every time they were moved, adjusted,
fixed, coiled, unwound, and fused. In one instance, it was reported that the
entire cable ceased functioning because of a small hole in the insulation
caused by a nail protruding from a worker's shoe.[45] The salvaged cable
from the failed 1857 attempt was put into tanks to await the next attempt.
There, it was revealed that "the cable was injured either by the coiling and
uncoiling, or by the original exposure to heat; and several bad places were
cut out where the copper wire had forced itself through the gutta-percha."
While some tests revealed significant loss of conduction, the cable could
not be tested in water without risking additional corrosion.[46] Despite this,
reports regularly assured not just functionality but *perfection*. An article
on the Atlantic telegraph from the *London Times* and reprinted in the *New
York Herald* announced that the additional length of cable manufactured
to replace that which was lost undersea in the last attempt "is of precisely
the same kind of cable as the rest [made for the last, failed, attempt], which
we have already described—flexible, strong, small and light; it has been
tested and retested to insure its *perfect* insulation, and its completeness
being thus definitely ascertained."[47]

Perfection replaced the practical likelihood of failure with an impossible standard. It worked like a utopian shell game, hiding one impossibility under the fast-moving cups of another. The reprinted article stated,

> It is no exaggeration to say that there is one portion of the apparatus upon
> the fitness and proper management of which the success or non-success
> of the whole plan must ultimately depend, and that is upon the paying
> out machinery. That this machinery was bad last year, and that it was
> made still worse by the most absurd management, no one now denies;
> but *we trust and believe* that there is no chance of a repetition this year
> of great blunders. How the new machinery is constructed *we cannot at
> present say*, further than that a new self-acting brake has been devised,
> which is *said to be perfect*.[48]

The *Columbus Tri-Weekly Enquirer* noted the vast length of the cable (precisely what made it so fragile) and proclaimed perfection for the paying-out

Figure 3.2. "The Coiling of the Atlantic Telegraph Cable on Board the H.M.S. 'Agamemnon,'" *Illustrated London News*, August 1, 1857. (With special thanks to Bill Burns)

machinery in the same sentence: "More than two thousand miles of the cable have been coiled on board the ships, and machinery is completed and pronounced perfect."[49] Characterizations of the telegraphic venture as "perfect" provide a vital example of the imaginative work required to produce a coherent totality out of an experience of fracture and failure.

Perfection is a peculiar assurance against further failure, particularly with new technology. The only way to know if a technology is perfect is to see it function through all the unforeseen factors that inevitably besiege a new venture. Unprecedented technology bears unprecedented problems. A new technology can only be declared perfect in retrospect, once it has successfully survived the conditions that befall it. Perfection for new technology works through its absolutism because it is, by definition, unable to provide sufficient explanation or substantial evidence. No technology, particularly no new technology, is ever perfect.

The logic of subsuming failure within declarations of perfection was a mainstay of reporting on the cable, particularly as problems plagued it. In another article in the *New York Herald*, faulty wire actually strengthened the cable: "When a defective part [of the cable] is detected the process of coiling is suspended until the imperfect portion of the wire is cut away, and the whole is replaced in a manner that not only *secures the perfect* insulation of the conductor, but actually *adds to the strength* of the cable."[50] Regular failure became the condition for perfection, and perfection's impossibility was swept away under enthusiastic guarantees that this moment would realize new possibilities here and now.

Technological perfectionism echoed the logic of lived Oneidan perfectionism, troubled as both were with the challenges of everyday realities. The Oneidan affinity for the telegraph as a parallel experiment with perfection is particularly striking given that Oneidans took up the burgeoning promise that telegraph technology would unite the world despite the necessarily local nature of their shared lives. They described the telegraph as the key tool for the realization of global connection in a form that assimilated a popular idea to their particular theology and way of life.

In Space: Living in an Impossible World

The lived nature of US utopias in the nineteenth century broke from the pie-in-the-sky utopian tradition to establish new ways to live in the here and now that pushed past present realities. In that sense, these lived experiments were not fantasies but imaginaries. They emerged in experimental negotiation with the limits of the known world and extended aggressively into promises of an alternative existence. Oneidan utopia, understood as imaginative inhabitation, was already engaged in becoming. It was lived and negotiated in messy relationship with intractable realities. The Oneidans' imaginary of a perfect, telegraphically united world was not a rigid system of meaning; it was decidedly unsystematic and often sacrificed coherent meaning for the allure of living out the impossible.

The disjuncture between the lives Oneidans lived and what they envisioned as the imminent new reality for the world marks one of the most striking ways in which utopian logic established the impossible as a way of life. The telegraph exemplified Oneidan attempts to live outside the world they knew from experience. It also exemplified the broader US twists and turns of logic and common sense that attached unlikely fantasies to a faulty submarine wire. The Oneida Community's commitment to communal living necessitated a very *local* existence, and yet it became enchanted by visions of *global* Bible Communism. What is perhaps most notable is that the idea of global connection was mobile—appearing in all sorts of forms in the United States at the advent of the Atlantic cable—and dynamically adaptable to the particular context in which it was adopted. Whether by missionaries or politicians or Bible Communists, global telegraphic connection made sense. And in each setting it was inflected anew with diverse sets of Protestant and protestant values.

In both the Oneidans' religious project and what they imagined to be the effects of the transatlantic telegraph, they envisioned that global unity would emerge naturally from Bible Communism and communication technology. The redundancy (community, communism, communication) mattered to them: all good things led to sharing in common (the shared root, *communis*, means shared by all). Although their vision of global unity was particular to their religious commitments, the belief in an approaching unity empowered by communication technology was widespread in the nineteenth-century United States.

In Oneidan theology, selfishness was conflated with individualism and its modern counterparts in property ownership and domestic life organized around monogamous heterosexual marriage. Oneidans understood the divine promise to directly oppose this system such that the end of selfishness was also the eradication of the individual in favor of an infinite unity of human beings with each other and with God. The theme of global connection dominated the Oneidans' way of life. They adamantly imagined this unity not as a loose amalgamation of diverse organizations and religious sects but as the realization of absolute homogeneity in which Christ, by abolishing sin, would abolish any form of disunion.

According to the community's theology, sin was the expression of division. "The Age of Unity," which was reprinted three times over ten years, explained it this way: "The ages of the reign of sin have been ages of *Division*. Sin itself is centrifugal, driving away from God and unity." This division was expressed in six forms: "(1) death is an ordinance of division, (2) diversity of language, (3) dispersion of the race by distance, (4) the separation of Jews and Gentiles, (5) family exclusiveness, (6) property exclusiveness." The meaning of the comings of Christ and, specifically, the abolition of sin was equated with the abolition of division; the kingdom of God, the ultimate expression of the ideal world, was framed as the absolute unity of the world and the unity of that world to God. "Christ came to displace sin, and bring about *unity*." According to the article, evidence for the eradication of division could be found in the early organization of Christianity and was further supported by the spread of communism (which eliminated family and property exclusiveness), spirit manifestations (which eradicated division by death), and tools of communication such as the telegraph (which established a common language and abolished distance).[51]

Connection sat at the heart of Noyes's theology, governing both the form of salvation and the organization of the community. For Noyes, the Old Testament saints loved God but were not yet the "sons of God" that they became at Christ's incarnation; the promise of unity was made possible by the Second Coming of Christ and was visible in the early church. The difference among these epochs was one of salvation expressed in terms of connection. As Noyes wrote, "Did not the Old Testament saints *love* God? Answer. Yes; and so, many servants love and honor their masters, while yet there is no *vital union*, no *blood-relationships* between them. So there was no *vital union* between God and man, till Christ came in the flesh."[52] This emphasis on connection framed the very meaning of Christianity for Noyes, who wrote, "To *believe* in the gospel, is to credit and heartily embrace the truth that God is reconciled to man, and that Christ is in all flesh."[53] According to Noyes, the salvific effects of the first two comings of Christ were "fulfilled by believers by the energy of the *blood of Christ*, the spirit of the living God."[54] In other words, the work of Christ in humanity was realized through the kind of unification made possible by communion. The regeneration of humankind was, according to Noyes, a change in the spiritual condition of people such that they find a "junction with the Spirit of God."[55]

Noyes lamented the fracture of humanity into multiple nations and the separation of the state from the church. He was adamant that such division, while perhaps true to the fallen state of humanity, reflected nothing of God or the telos of the kingdom of God. Rather, the ultimate kingdom would be marked by the connection of the whole of humankind, whether in glory or damnation: "When that kingdom comes, a principle of unity will appear which will draw them [the nations and organizations] all into one organization, or sweep them away with the besom of destruction."[56] The arrival of the kingdom of God would eradicate the two "disunities" that concerned Noyes: the disunity of the nations from each other and the disunity of the state from the church.

Connection, as the ultimate aim for humankind, also served as the foundation for living life in expectation of that end: "The central doctrines of Perfectionism, one and all, draw with their whole face toward unity."[57] In fact, the very faith the Oneidans practiced was understood to be the execution of unity:

> *Faith*, which is the root of holiness, is an act of union. It joins the life of the believer to the life of Christ. It draws a man out of his individuality, and merges self in fellowship with another. It is directly opposed to isolation. And that which draws a man out of self into partnership with God, necessarily establishes in his spirit a social principle which draws him toward unity with his brother.[58]

The holiness produced by faith was a form of connection: "We aver that every branch of the doctrine of holiness tends to unity." Holiness was itself "essentially a uniting principle."[59] Because holiness was not merely the absence of sin but the positive energy of love, holiness was a principle of attraction that bound humans to each other and to God: "Its tendency is to make all who possess it, one in heart; and unity of heart is the earnest unity of mind and action." For Noyes, it was through this principle that holy people the world over shared "one heart, one mind and one voice."[60] Ultimately, the central principle and practices of the Oneida Community aimed toward a global unity so intimate that it rendered the whole world as one being.

Despite the centrality of unity as an inevitably arriving future, the kind of global connection that the Oneida Community proposed directly contradicted the obvious geographic limitations demanded by its community structure. The Oneida Community was a "family" governed by the law of complex marriage, which necessitated physical and emotional proximity. Likewise, since children were the shared responsibility of all of the adults, the community was geographically bound. The community managed these social and religious practices with carefully constructed protocols, all of which required an elaborate system of community decision-making and concentrated leadership. Expanding the community's system of Bible Communism, plural marriage, and stirpiculture to a global scale would have been unmanageable; all of these systems depended on geographic and social consolidation, voluntary participation by members, and collective adherence to a centralized system of community governance. Oneidans' imaginary of global perfectionism was impossible.

The complete global connection that the Oneida Community declared imminent was not one of an implemented system of worldwide Bible Communism but rather an impromptu global union that would echo the unity that Oneidans saw themselves forging in upstate New York. While Noyes imagined a world governed by a singular church-state in which the practices of Bible Communism would thrive, neither he nor anyone in the Oneida Community wrote about the logistics of implementing the keystones of their religious life worldwide.[61] Where one might expect to find guidelines for global governance, Noyes wrote that global unity was, simply, inevitable. For Noyes, this was not a process of joining independent entities into alliance but, rather, a final ontological melding: "All confederacies but one are destined to extinction."[62] The Oneidans' was a vision of the universalization of their spiritual project in general and inevitable terms; they expected to realize unlimited divine unity and did not concern themselves with producing a plan for expansion such as preoccupied Fourier.[63]

The Oneidans' organization around an imaginary of impossible unity was in part what made the telegraph so compelling for them. Widespread public excitement for global communicative connection amplified the enthusiasm for unity that was the mainstay of the Oneida Community. It realized in material form the Oneidans' uncharacteristically abstract dreams for divine global connection. The telegraph seemed to pave the way from their local lived experiment to a worldwide future of absolute unity, in which the collectivity they established would be written on a global scale. The Atlantic Telegraph Cable would, in no uncertain terms, unite the world:

It will be observed that the meaning of this latest time-wonder is UNITY. The merchant may see one use for it, the news-writer another, the statesman a third; the true heart of *man* recognizes in it the token and medium of a broader and better *unity* than has heretofore prevailed. Every flash that passes over those deep oceanic wires, will carry a shock into the bowels of old-time isolation and prejudice.[64]

The enemies of isolation and prejudice were here outdated by the transformation launched by the telegraph. The capacity for unity, however, preexisted the telegraph in the internalized "true heart" belonging to the universal "man" that would override the diversity of perspectives determined by different professions. The telegraph allowed that preexistent capacity for unity to be manifest.

For the Oneida Community, the telegraph appeared to erase mediation itself. In the community's writing, the telegraph produced immediacy in four critical ways: the telegraph abolished distance, produced a shared global language, unified all people to each other and to God, and physically bound the world. First, the telegraph's eradication of distance was a repeated theme, as in the hyperbolic announcement of the end of distance and war at the successful laying of the 1858 Atlantic cable and in "The Age of Unity."[65] Second, a global telegraph produced new forms of linguistic homogeneity necessary to realize divine unity. For Noyes and the Oneida Community, communication, even as an imperfect and mediated practice, could create the unity that marked the arriving perfect world by establishing a universal language. The telegraph was the technology par excellence to do so.[66] One article expressed this idea in its closing lines: "In forty years more the earth may be belted round with cables and wires, differences of time may be abolished, and diversities of speech all sunk in, or at any rate subordinated to, one universal language—that spoken by the quivering needles of the telegraph."[67] This universal language was understood not as an instrument to agreement but as a sign of unity in and of itself.

In fact, Noyes was suspicious of communication when understood as speaking together or sharing messages. Writing eleven years before the first successful transatlantic cable, during which time the community's tone on the matter became increasingly positive, Noyes referred to the dangers of communication for unity in *The Berean*. While discussing the ascendancy of the devil in the approach of the millennium, echoing the colonial bigotry that reigned in Western Christian discourse, Noyes wrote,

> The channels of communication between Europe and the East—which during the dark ages were closed—have been opened by the improvements of navigation, and the revival of commercial enterprise; and in all communications between good and evil, where fallen human nature alone is concerned, evil has the advantage. Instead of imagining that England by her eastern enterprises has civilized Asia, we apprehend that Asia has well nigh *paganized* the spirit of England.[68]

It was not speaking together that promised unity, and a theory of democratic agreement should not be read onto Oneidan theology. Noyes was clear that nations alone could not unify the globe, nor could conversation among practitioners of diverse religions. This unity would not be created through speech but through a divinely granted shared subjectivity with an irradicable Western Christian root.

The telegraph appeared to facilitate a different kind of communication closer to communion, a joining of subjects such that communication through speech would no longer be necessary. In a toast at the jubilee to celebrate the Atlantic cable, George Washington Noyes (John Humphrey Noyes's younger brother) offered these words of linguistic unity:

> The restoration of unity of language is one of the great things that may be foreseen among the effects of the International Telegraph. It will tend to bring the nations into a familiar group where they will talk directly together, and will gradually assume one form of language. Thus we shall retrace our steps and recover the ground that was lost by the dispersion of tongues. I would offer as my sentiment: The Electric Telegraph—may it send the Electricity of Heaven into the hearts of men, and so make the nations truly one.[69]

More than facilitate speech, the telegraph would secure the "mingling of the minds and hearts of the people" of the world.[70] The Oneidans imagined that this mode of electric communication would forge a collapsed subjectivity that would serve to unite—by which they meant utterly homogenize—the world, a striking reflection of the structure of their communal life at home.

The third way, then, that the telegraph facilitated global and cosmic unity was premised on an idea of unmediated communication as the collapse of individual subjects into a subsuming whole. In this frame, the Atlantic cable appeared as a friction-free mode of fusion and barely a medium at all. One report in the *Circular* described the way the two ships laying the cable would remain in contact with each other: "The wires will enable them during the entire process to telegraph each to the other at will, so that their combined movements will be as it were at the direction of one mind."[71] The telegraph may be most productively read in their discourse not as a medium per se but as a mode of communication that would overcome the mediation of space and time. The telegraph bound all nations together through communication and commerce such that "what takes place in one country must be of vital importance to all," with the ultimate end of "complete amalgamation."[72] The mediation of telegraphy was effaced by the union it would inevitably produce.

This understanding of telegraphic media paralleled what Noyes understood Christ to do as the unifier of God and humanity. As he wrote in *The Berean*, "Through Christ, under the Gospel, God and man are identified. The two parties of the former covenant flow together and become one *in the mediator*; so that he is no longer properly a mediator. God, and Christ, and man, are not three, but one; for the divine nature dwells in all, and 'God is one.' In fact, there is but one party to the new covenant; so that it might properly be called an unconditional promise."[73] Salvation took the form of absolute identity in which divine and human subjectivity were understood to be one and the same. Mediation, while necessary to the process of producing unity, was subsumed by it once unity emerged. In a poem by E. L. Blanchard, reprinted in the *Circular* from the English *Reynolds' Weekly Newspaper*, the unifying power of technology was made clear: "O! Would that some kindred communion / To man we could hope to impart, / That a bond of such magical union / Might link every heart unto heart!"[74] The power of unity secured by the telegraph was understood through the idea of unmediated communication as the identity of subjects with one another to produce a single subject: the teleological unity of humanity, God, and Christ as one.

In fact, Noyes identified unmediated communication as the absolute pinnacle of belief. There were, according to Noyes, four kinds of belief: imaginative belief (i.e., without correspondence to the world of the senses), belief of testimony (belief confirmed by the reports of others), belief of reason (belief arrived at through rationality), and belief of the senses (belief arrived at through observation). Against these, he posed a fifth kind of belief that he called "spiritual belief": "One spirit can present itself to the perception of another and communicate thoughts and persuasions, without the intervention of any verbal testimony, any process of reasoning, or any impression of the senses." Noyes went on to state that this form of belief "is proved by the phenomena of Mesmerism," a method in the late eighteenth and early nineteenth centuries of interacting through touch, electrical conduction, and eye contact with a magnetic fluid believed to be part of all animate beings.[75]

Despite this aspiration to erase mediation, the materiality of the cable became a critical trope in Oneidan imaginaries of global connection. The fourth way the telegraph ensured unity was as a material link that literally bound the world together with a unifying power that far exceeded that of rapid and long-distance communication. True to the hope for unmediated union, discourse on the telegraph for Oneidans and other US Americans did not attend to the communication and commerce that would pass over the cables.[76] But their disregard for the telegraph's transmissive capacities did not erase the importance they lent to the material, binding action of the cable itself. According to one Oneidan, "Telegraphs will wind their electric ways over all lands and under all oceans to the myriad homes of Communism. Then will come the fulfillment of the promise: 'The earth shall be filled with the knowledge of the glory of the Lord, as the waters cover the sea.'"[77]

The meanings the Oneida Community conferred on the telegraph used its materiality to imagine a world that defied such materiality. It served as a metaphor for the Oneidans' faith, which would accomplish the same fantastical feats they attributed to the cable: "We should twist the little fibers of our own faith into one cord, and the cords of all into one invincible cable. This condensation of faith will conquer the world" and, ultimately, "bring heaven and earth together."[78] The cable as a metaphor of strong connection in *faith* secured a meaning for *telegraphy* that far exceeded its actual technical power. In an article about meetings of

the community, the editors of the *Circular* directed the readers to attend
to the possibility of communication beyond physical proximity. They
named the telegraph and the railroad as foil modes of communication
bound to the physical world; in contrast, Christ acted as a medium for
union beyond the limits of the material: "If you know where to find
[Christ's] spirit, you have access to all that is *in* his spirit; i.e. you touch a
conductor that communicates with all believers, in heaven, in this world,
and in Hades."[79] Metaphor worked both ways. This attempt to envision
communication beyond the telegraph rendered earth-bound electric
communication as an immediate and universal connector. This excessive meaning for the cable was echoed in the hymn that serves as the
epigraph to this chapter, in which the "celestial wire" and "word-woven
cord" binds people to Heaven, to God, and to each other.[80] The materiality of the cable mattered in ways that exceeded materiality—here
it bound not just the earth but the cosmos, a site cables have not yet
reached. The cable became an impossible sign of pure connection.

The telegraph disregarded distance by crossing it. In an early report
of the plans to string a telegraph cable across the ocean, an article in
the *Circular* stated, "The line is intended to be used exclusively for the
direct transmission of *foreign intelligence*, and when completed, the only
unbroken link in telegraphic communication for many thousand miles,
will be the Atlantic Ocean."[81] The world buckled under the descriptive
demands; the Atlantic Ocean was made the site of absolute communicative proximity by virtue of its vast expanse. Space and its meaning were
reformulated so that distance itself became the condition for intimacy.

The Oneidan utopia's disfiguration of time and space, in which the
ocean became the most intimate site of connection because it was vast
and in which the present was already at the end of history, made the
modern Christian move of rendering the impossible uniquely accessible. Modern US utopias of global networks should not be characterized solely by spatial and temporal dislocation, nor should they be
remembered only as islands or futures. The Oneidan imagination of
the Atlantic telegraph illustrates that some modern utopias were able
to overcome the structural limitations of their own form. This is also
true for other US modern global imaginaries built around the Atlantic
telegraph that claimed the arriving perfection of the world well outside
a theology of perfectionism. For example, an August 1858 article in the

New York Herald, titled "The Atlantic Cable—The World Revolution Begun," stated,

> The magnetic telegraph ceases to be a local, and becomes an instrument of universal power. It grasps the thought of man, and carries it instantaneously to the utmost confines of civilization. Henceforth the whole world is to be moved simultaneously by the same thought, and action will be immeasurably quickened. . . . In science, art, literature, and every branch of knowledge, every event that will quicken the human intellect, every discovery that will open new paths of usefulness, every achievement that will confer new power on man, will be at once communicated to every wing of the great army of progress, and the march of the world will be incredibly hastened.[82]

Even without a grounding theology in perfection, public discourse about the cable in the United States echoed what resounded in the Oneida Community: the Atlantic cable refigured global space through absolute connection and heralded a new and better age.

In Time: Proximity and Progress

In a dialogue recorded just after the Atlantic telegraph was successfully laid, a community member identified as "G." offered a temporal formula for the Oneidan imaginary of the world that complicated the distance of the future. G. attested to a feeling that the proximity of God was affirmed by "signs of it in the success of the Atlantic Telegraph. These are footsteps of his advancing presence."[83] Here the promise of presence had already marked the earth, leaving a trace of its own future arrival. G. went on to say,

> It was necessary that communication should first be established between heaven and this world—that there should be a line of connection for the transmission of the spirit of the Primitive Church into this world, in order that such a means of communication as the Atlantic Telegraph should be put to its proper use. A line connecting this world and heaven has been established, we are perfectly sure, and see in it a fitness and preparation for the event that we are all so much interested in.[84]

In this construction, a previous spiritual telegraph prepared the way for the Atlantic telegraph, and the Atlantic telegraph fulfilled the cosmic connection inaugurated by the first Christians. The culminating future was already arriving. In the words, of G., "God is approaching the world."[85]

The utopian perspectives of the religious groups that emerged from the Second Great Awakening adopted a temporality of unfolding: a new world had already begun but had not yet been fully realized. Their sense of the present and future was oriented to a strong sense of ongoing arrival and thus required a less absolute approach to the distance between the society they knew and the society they wanted. They did not imagine an absolutely impassable division between the familiar and the ideal or between the present and the future.

Utopia, particularly in its original coinage by More, is ideal and inaccessible. In both its perfection and its distance, the utopia we inherit from fiction promises a radical rupture with life as we know it. The value of utopia, then, is its distance from the status quo.[86] However, this value is also utopia's primary challenge: How can people invent a society utterly different from their own when they are limited to creating it out of the materials at hand? Constrained by local construction, utopia emerges from and responds to the present conditions, which calls into question whether utopia can really provide the radical rupture it promises. Utopia always courts the danger of being nothing more than a feeble restructuring of contemporary failures; it is suspended between absolute alterity and potentially useless familiarity. By definition, utopia cannot make any legitimate appearance.

The necessary failure of utopia is an essential instance of the integral nature of fracture to networks, which have come into being through imaginaries of outrageous optimism. Three of the great thinkers of utopia, Fredric Jameson, Gilles Deleuze, and Félix Guattari, offer critical considerations of utopia as present, and all three consider imagination to be a vital part of that impossible possibility. Jameson understands utopia's very impossibility to motivate a radical politics toward a new future. For Jameson, we are restricted to create utopia out of the limited resources we find in the present. The primary condition of utopia is its restriction to familiar terms, such that "even our wildest imaginings are all collages of experience, constructs made up of bits and pieces of the here and now."[87] As imaginative bricolage, utopias respond to the failures of the status quo.[88] Our "incapacity to imagine the future," specifically a future that escapes the determination of the present, becomes the only thing that utopia can demonstrate: "[The utopian genre]'s deepest vocation is to bring home, in local and determinate ways, and with a fullness of concrete detail, our constitutional inability to imagine Utopia itself, and this, not owing to any individual failure of imagination but as the result of the systemic, cultural, and ideological closure of which we are all in one way or another prisoners."[89] Faced with the unbreachable boundary of the present, utopia's only possibility is "to succeed by failure."[90] This refrain of utopia's failure in Jameson's thought demands that the only authentic utopia—viable or not—is the one we cannot imagine, or, in his words, the best utopias are those that "fail the most comprehensively."[91]

While utopia always succumbs to this constitutive failure, investment in utopian impossibility is necessary for any possible escape from present politics. In Jameson's words, "This clearly does not mean that, even if we succeed in reviving Utopia itself, the outlines of a new and effective practical politics for the era of globalization will at once become visible; but only that we will never come to one without it."[92] Impossibility here serves as a condition for utopia's success. If utopia were not impossible—that is, outside the possibilities presented by the present politics—it would serve no purpose at all.

This thinking of the possibilities offered by impossibility owes a great deal to the work of Jacques Derrida on the impossible figure of the trace. The "trace" for Derrida is a mark of absence, such as the marked absence of the past in the present. In a footnote to the introduction to *Archaeologies of the Future*, Jameson flips this temporally as a way to think about the effective presence of an impossible future:

The presumption is that Utopia, whose business is the future, or not-being, exists only in the present, where it leads the relatively feeble life of desire and fantasy. But this is to reckon without the amphibiousness of being and its temporality: in respect of which Utopia is philosophically analogous to the trace, only from the other end of time. The aporia of the trace is to belong to past and present all at once, and thus to constitute a

mixture of being and not-being quite different from the traditional category of Becoming and thereby mildly scandalous for analytical Reason.
Utopia, which combines the not-yet-being of the future with a textual
existence in the present is no less worthy of the archaeologies we are willing to grant to the trace.[93]

For utopia, the present can be marked by the absence of the future we
cannot imagine. Or, in Oneidan terms, the present can be marked by the
"footsteps of his advancing presence." Taking seriously Jameson's indication of what we might produce if we were willing to "scandalize" reason
opens a possibility for understanding the refiguration of nineteenth-
century utopias as present.

Whereas Jameson preserves utopia's constitutive impossibility through
the trace—utopia is only present in its absence—Deleuze and Guattari
open a way to think of utopia as both radically different (impossible) and
proximate. For them, like Jameson, utopia answers a need for imagining
the world otherwise. Their utopia is a call for productive rupture with the
known world outside the logic of absolutes: "We lack creation. *We lack
resistance to the present.* The creation of concepts in itself calls for a future
form, for a new earth and people that do not exist."[94] For Deleuze and
Guattari, as for Jameson, the creation of concepts is resistance. However,
because Deleuze and Guattari turn to becoming as temporally situated
ontology that does not distinguish absolutely between the present and
future (and because their imminentism holds little interest in not-being),
they offer a stronger emphasis on the way that this mode of creation can
intervene here and now. To engage in this kind of creation is to resist the
present without collapsing the power of utopia's difference from the present into an absolute, and therefore unreachable, alterity. In their words,
"It is not that the actual is the utopian prefiguration of a future that is
still part of our history. Rather it is the now of our becoming."[95] Utopia is
thus understood as a future unfolding at the cusp of our present through
our imaginative action. In this way, utopia can be arriving without a
static future telos—what Jameson would call the "attempt to colonize the
future"—and exist in a productive suspension between radical difference
from and negotiation with the present reality.[96]

The concept of utopia at work among the pioneers of new ways of
life in the nineteenth century presented a desired ideal as uniquely

accessible; in this religious discourse, utopia's tense place between distinction and familiarity was productive, dynamic, and imminent. In the context of the nineteenth-century United States, understandings of utopia turned from absolutism; utopia's necessary intelligibility did not appear to be too local and too familiar to rupture the status quo, nor did its necessary alterity render it too distant to be grasped. Utopia's suspension between the known and the strange in this context became an empowering mode for life in the present. Members of the Oneida Community understood their present to reach into a future that came rushing toward them, swallowing oceans of distance in its approach.

The Oneidan utopian future took on the already-not-yet of Christian salvation and amplified it to the already-becoming of perfectionism. According to John Humphrey Noyes and his Oneidan followers, the Second Coming of Christ made a certain kind of redemption possible but did not secure perfection permanently. In Noyes's exuberantly italicized words, the Second Coming meant Christ's "coming in the power of judgment, to *reckon with, reward, and punish, those to whom he delivered the gospel at his first coming*—we mean *the day of judgment for the primitive church and the Jewish nation.*" Noyes was adamant that the Second Coming was not Christ's final appearance: "*We do* NOT *mean by the second coming of Christ, the* FINAL AND GENERAL JUDGMENT."[97] Noyes predicted a third coming of Christ that would provide a parallel judgment of Christians.[98] For the Oneida Community, therefore, the Second Coming of Christ enabled moral perfection but did not signal the end of time. That date still lay ahead.

This constitutive suspension between the second and third coming of Christ in Oneidan theology, paired with Oneidans' excitement for the telegraph as a sign of the "advancing presence" of God, signaled the proximity of US technological utopias. For them, the impossible future was being realized in the present while remaining incomplete. Its arrival was underway, but its closure still stretched ahead. Noyes used a germinal metaphor to describe the arriving future: "The truth is, in both of these events—viz., the resurrection of Christ, and his second coming—the great last victory over the powers of death and hell, was achieved *in the seed.*"[99]

Undergirding the promise of present utopia was a specific, urgent sense of suspension. Suspension was the necessary helpmate to evangelical claims of Christ's imminent return. Where progress charged forward with electric momentum, deferral held back, digging in its heels, and responding to progress's urgent cry of "Now!" with a stubborn "Not yet." Progress appeared to have opened radically new possibilities for the world, while deferral set those possibilities just out of reach in the near future. Deferral initially seems straightforward; it is creating an object (in this case, the connected cosmos) and setting it in the future. However, in this nineteenth-century religious formulation, deferral was urgent, framed by the sense that this object would arrive any minute now or, for the Oneidans, had already begun to appear.

Techno-Utopian Thought beyond Utopian Communities

The keen expectation of Christ's imminent always-future return was conventional in nineteenth-century religious utopias and other religious movements that made no formal claims to utopianism. Mapping the widespread emergence of utopian discourse beyond the boundaries of intentional utopian communities in the United States—among other new religious movements and in missionary discourse—allows us to follow the spread of this religious language into what was becoming US public culture. According to historian Paul Boyer, apocalyptic belief was ubiquitous in the mid-nineteenth century.[100]

One new religious movement, the Millerites, predicted the return of Christ between 1843 and 1844. In the midst of that period of profound expectancy, the leading Millerite newspaper urged readers to live in the suspension of already-not-yet: "It is not safe, therefore, for us to defer in our minds the event for an hour, but to live in constant expectation, and readiness to meet our Judge."[101] This rejection of deferral ironically provided a clear guideline for *waiting* for an imminent future that was always about to arrive. William Miller, founder of the Millerites, repeatedly had to revise his prediction of Christ's return as the expected dates came and went. His revised time made use of what was becoming a familiar mix of urgency and deferral: "I have fixed my mind upon another time, and here I mean to stand until God gives me more light.—And that is *Today*, TODAY, and TODAY, until He comes."[102] Predictions of the end-times marked many of the most influential religious movements to emerge out of revival culture, including the Mormons and Jehovah's Witnesses alongside the Oneida Community and the Millerites (which gave rise to the Seventh-day Adventists). According to Adventist historian Jonathan M. Butler, those religions that survived the nineteenth century did so by ultimately favoring deferral over urgency: "The key to transforming an effervescent apocalypticism into an established, complex religious system includes, above all, an elongation of the eschatological timetable."[103]

The emergent links between technology and an approaching perfect future became a hallmark of confluent discourses: global Protestant mission, transatlantic religious innovation, nascent US nationalism, local US utopian communities, and new networks. To return to the missionary discourse of chapter 1, US utopianism can help make sense of Cyrus Hamlin's emphatic distinction between his prediction of a good future and what he called the "fatalism" of Muslims. Hamlin critiqued Muslims' resignation to the future as a religious and national apathy, which, he insisted, rendered Turks unable to fight in war or fight off disease.[104] He frequently described death due to diseases he considered preventable as suicide, lamenting that people with cholera would wait for death rather than take his sure cure: laudanum, spirit of camphor, and tincture of rhubarb on a lump of sugar.[105] For Hamlin, acceptance of a known future was a significant marker of religious difference: "As in the plague, so in the cholera the Moslems and Jews were the greatest sufferers; the latter for their filth, the former for their fatalism. Filth and fatalism are the grand aid[e]s-de-camp of the enemy."[106] Yet, in nearly the same prejudiced breath, he celebrated the inevitable arrival of a new and better future that he saw unfolding in the increase in Protestant converts, technological progress, and the constitutional governments of emerging nation-states: "Whoever will look over Labeau's, or any other history of the Byzantine empire, will only wonder that it endured so long. If its government was demoralized, its religion was paganized. *The time was approaching when it must pass away.*"[107] Hamlin harnessed the old aligned binaries of western colonialism (Christian/Muslim and Jewish, active/passive, civilized/savage, triumphant/expiring) to forge a difference between his entropic teleology and the fatalism of which he accused the Turks: he understood the Turks to accept guaranteed death while he envisioned an inevitable triumph for his white US Protestantism that required his active labor.

Missionary writing at the time rang with the ambitious refrain of imminent utopia: all this and soon. The ABCFM, with enthusiastic urgency, predicted the "immediate" or "speedy" conversion of the whole world to Christianity throughout its history.[108] The thirty-fifth annual report closed with Rufus Anderson's announcement that "'[Christian missionaries] can evangelize the whole world in less than half a century.' In other words, the laborers who may go forth from Christian lands, can with the aid which they may hope to receive from native helpers, carry the gospel to every part of the earth, in less than fifty years."[109] Forty-two years later, ABCFM members were still predicting that the completion of the project to Christianize the world would arrive within the present generation.[110]

Deferral justified the work of various religious groups, from the Oneida Community to US missionaries, as an urgent and yet perennial cause. Rallying cries promised that such labor would bring a united Christian world soon and thus put deferral at the heart of the modern global imaginary of a networked whole. Common sense might lead one to think that US Americans who participated in this imaginary *first* desired a unified communicating Christian world but *then* encountered a world of fracture, power plays, war, and endless miscommunication. Optimistic utopians met a recalcitrant reality and resigned themselves to faithful patience. But this timeline should be inverted. Deferral was not tertiary to the religious imaginary of a networked world but foundational. The not-yet arose in tandem with the now-here. Deferral's disconnection from the present was productive for these religious actors: an end that constantly slipped just out of reach opened the opportunity for creative labor in the production of global Christianity united to the divine cosmos. If global Christianity were achieved, the window for action would be closed. The connection to the future required the disconnection of delay.

For all these diverse nineteenth-century techno-utopianists' sense of becoming, they were, in Jamesonian terms, colonizing the future. *Progress* offered a successful resolution to the contradiction between the proximity and suspension of utopia. The tense temporality of deferral could be stabilized with a specific teleology and assured forward movement.[111] To the indeterminacy of a new world, these techno-utopians responded: the new world will be *this*. The networked cosmos was not expected to be the site of an unimagined future. Rather, the enthusiasm for its novelty, particularly the cutting edge of religious possibility and technological change, was grounded in the widely held belief that it would offer one fixed future. Technologically empowered US Christians would—in their imaginings—lead the world in progress toward a predetermined end: the global religious unity of a totality bound by cabled networks.

This teleological logic became true to the emerging logic of networks themselves. As the concept of the network moved among diverse discursive sites, it promised a webbed structure regardless of its composition, whether nerves, wires, rail, or social relationships.[112] Networks, wherever they were, whatever they contained, took the same sort of shape and could always—in ominous assurance—add a node. In this way, networks came to promise the infinite possibility of expansion and a fixed form for that future growth. The definitional sedimentation that occurred during this period—as network became an adaptable descriptor for various forms of relationship, transportation, and communication—cemented connection into technological and social forms as a given end, no matter the reality of this promise. The network in its many metaphorical-material appearances was already entangled in tropes of teleological progress.

The inevitability of progress sustained the assurance of the Oneida Community that it was part of the realization of perfection, a sentiment that an article in the *Circular*, aptly titled "The Method of Progress," expressed in telegraphic terms. It ties together the themes of this chapter—perfection, unity, progress, and telegraphy—and so is worth quoting at length:

> There is a connected chain of assimilating action going on throughout the whole series [of nations], from the highest and most advanced to the most rude and backward—from the United States to Japan—tending to establish spiritual equilibrium and perfect them in a common unity. Any movement here, any new birth of truth, tells on the whole line; it runs electrically in the first place along the channel of our relations with England, and thence is diffused with lessening power perhaps, but still with sensible effect, throughout the whole circle of her connection in Turkey, India, China, and throughout the East. . . . The practical consideration that accompanies this view is, that each one should be willing to stand as a link in the chain of communication by which God distributes his spirit to the race—not aspire to a solitary salvation, but recognize all good spirits above as mediums of progress to him, and himself as a

connecting channel of influence to others beyond him. So shall all be
made perfect in one.[113]

The colonial logics through which the Oneida Community imagined
an inevitable good future of global connection echoed missionary and
other public discourses.

The theme of progress was a vital linchpin of missionaries' understanding of their endeavors in an age of burgeoning industry. Progress
offered the power of inevitability to the vexed articulation of religion,
technology, and culture to which US missionaries were so committed. Judson Smith used progress as the very thing that linked Christian
conversion and technological change in a paper on mission in China
that he read at the annual meeting of the ABCFM in 1881, which offered a celebratory catalogue of change he claimed was wrought by new
technologies and techniques. Commerce, telegraphy, mining, and the
railroad, according to Smith, collapsed "old customs" and toppled "old
faiths" while spreading "new life" and developing wealth. Innovation,
he declared, opened China to Christianity in a "revolution" akin to
Augustine's conversion of the pagan Anglo-Saxons at the turn of the
sixth century. "As the English had lost faith in Woden and Thor when
Augustine and his monks preached Christ to them and in a single century won the whole island to the gospel, so God has here prepared the
way of his truth, and the messages of Christian love will to-day fall on
countless ears providentially open to perceive its sweetness and welcome its life."[114] While some readers might shudder at the thought that
mining was the nineteenth century's Augustine, Smith's understanding
that commerce and mechanic arts would lead to the realization of God's
kingdom on earth ekes its tenuous grasp on sense out of the widespread
understanding that technological development led toward a predetermined Christian end.

For many missionaries, innovations in the machines of communication served as a sure sign that the world was moving toward a fixed
future of divine global connection, specifically one built through an
extension of an imagined Anglo culture. Indeed, Cyrus Hamlin's understanding of his technological evangelism, in a rhetorically typical
humblebrag, is grounded in his participation in the forward march of

history toward a US end: "My connection with these two efforts to introduce the American telegraph into Turkey was incidental and unimportant; but there is always an interest in looking back to the beginning of things which have fought their way up from weakness to power. The customs of the Ottoman court, and indeed every thing peculiarly oriental, are so rapidly changing, that the above record will not be without some historic interest."[115] Hamlin understood the present he participated in as the past to a future he could already see: one empowered by US technology and rid of its "peculiarly oriental" weakness.

Progress organized an imaginary of the world around linked elements of cultural imperialism, Christianity, and technological innovation and held their relationship to each other to be given and unbreakable. After an occasion in which a convert from Islam to Protestantism was treated cordially by Ottoman officials, Hamlin wrote, "However interpreted, it was a proof of progress. The ignorant multitude are still fanatical and bigoted, but the governing class has wonderfully changed. Such a scene would have been impossible a dozen years before. The Scriptures, newspapers, books, education, and the course of things are working slowly down into the mass, and religious freedom is coming in slowly, and in the only way possible, by enlightenment."[116]

According to Hamlin, the coincidence of the fall of Constantinople and the "invention" of printing in Europe produced a significant change in the organization of global power and paved the way for what we would today call globalization:

> While the East held the sword, and cultivated the arts of war, the West gave itself to intellectual and industrial pursuits. Printing, Navigation, Commerce, Architecture, Painting, and finally, the Reformation, lifted the West out of its barbarism and ignorance; and its progress in arts and arms has left the East centuries in the rear. Four centuries ago it led the world in arts and arms. Now it gets its cannon from Krupp in Germany, its Martini-Henry rifles from Providence, Rhode Island, and its ammunition from New Haven, Connecticut! The press has proved itself mightier than cannon, and the arts of peace mightier than the arts of war.[117]

The technologies of communication developed in Europe refigured global commerce, inter-empire war, and world powers and thereby (somehow) spread Western culture by selling arms under the banner of peace.

This notion of progress was emphatically teleological; it moved determinately toward the universalism of US culture. Progress and destiny marched hand in hand in much of these missionary writings and particularly so in Hamlin's. For example, a future of Christian dominance was "irresistible" even in the largely Muslim Ottoman Empire: "It has also attracted government attention, that their 'rayahs' or Christian and Jewish subjects, the Armenians, Greeks, Bulgarians, and Jews, have nearly doubled within this half century, while the Moslem population is stationary. *Irresistible* forces would change eventually the balance of power without foreign interference."[118] The Christian future, for Hamlin, was a given.

Similarly, many of the news reports on the Atlantic telegraph couched the failures of the present in a longer forward-looking story in which the promises of instant communication would surely be realized. Progress, particularly when presented as a given, external force that worked like a natural law, made success appear inevitable no matter what failures it encountered along the way. What seemed impossible would be overcome through the innovation that was already in motion. Such inevitability subsumed the shortcomings that were part of this early telegraphic venture and recapitulated them as signs of success. Each attempt that ended in a no was understood as a step that defined the path to yes.

Therefore, doubts about the cable's capacity were expressed as evidence *for* the cable's preordained effectiveness at linking North America and Europe. The *London Times* reported on the limits of transmission within a frame of certain triumph (reprinted in the *New York Herald*):

To many of our readers unacquainted with the practical working of submarine lines only eight words per minute may appear to be but poor result after all, though we can assure them that, if ever attained, it is such an improvement in the rate of transmission as not many ventured to anticipate who saw the cable worked for the first time last summer. At the same time such a result seems to show with most convincing clearness that, though 480 words per hour through this line, if it is successfully laid down, might doubtless amply remunerate the company, it would still be almost as far as ever from accommodating the business messages between Europe and the New World. If, therefore, this line is submerged this summer it will *follow as a matter of course* that three or four others *must* be laid as well, and there seems no reason why if one can be laid down there should not be as many telegraphs under the Atlantic as there are now under the Channel.[119]

At work in these reports is a logic of scientific innovation, in which the new is understood as inevitably better. Indeed, 1858 marked a year in which US Americans stood on the cusp of a capacity for communication that would far exceed what had been possible. Science came to stand in as the embodiment of the momentum of progress such that science became an authority that no longer required substantiation. In one radical declaration that exemplifies this pattern of subsuming failure under the given authority of science, the *San Antonio Ledger* reported, "The gentlemen having charge of the operations, have recently reported that no element of failure beyond the control of science has been developed."[120] Here, unforeseeable setbacks are assimilated within a discourse in which science-as-progress always and inevitably wins.

* * *

The Oneida Community did not successfully herald the eradication of distance and war. The community itself disbanded just twelve years after its declaration of a new age of peace and proximity. Rather than understand both the Oneida Community and the global imaginary it authored at the advent of ocean telegraphy as missteps of history, we should read these inhabitations of an impossible world as productive and enabling practices that never premised themselves on an adherence to factuality. Understanding this imaginary as utopian encourages us to see that the ideals that Oneidans presented may have offered little recourse to reality—in fact, were envisioned as practices of breaching impossibility itself—but, all the same, provided powerful visions of the world that were embodied in lived practice. I am not arguing that the communism to which the Oneidans aspired or the global imaginary they declared really existed in the world. Rather, I am pointing to a site of human intellectual and material activity that not only disregarded association with what we might think of as reality but also made use of the disconnection from reality in a particular religious logic. As these lived utopian experiments circulated with broader US techno-utopianism, the network imaginaries they produced served as the announcement of a proximate ideal future in the present continuous.

The Oneidans understood the Atlantic Telegraph Cable to relate to their own endeavors precisely because stringing a telegraph cable across the ocean appeared to be an impossible feat. A central element of this utopia—one that is echoed by the missionary discourse addressed in chapter 1 and the nationalism addressed in chapter 2—is the imaginary of the world as connected by communication *technology* but not through communication itself. Perhaps there is a prescient wisdom to their imaginaries of powerful cables and impotent talk: the telegrams sent on the 1858 cable reveal more stuttering than speech. Chapter 4 examines what the cable served to communicate and makes the rather Oneidan argument that the communication of the cable was less determined by the transmission of meaning than by the infrastructure at stake. The material, social, and imaginative disconnections of this network emerged in communicative signals of disruption, expressed by the frustrated dispatch of the Atlantic telegraphers: "Received, but not intelligible."

4

"Received but Not Intelligible"

Signals and Infrastructuralist Meaning

The vocal organs are as external to language as are the electrical devices used in transmitting the Morse code to the code itself; and phonation, i.e., the execution of sound-images, in no way affects the system itself.
—Ferdinand de Saussure, *Course in General Linguistics*

The telegraph brought about changes in the nature of language, of ordinary knowledge, of the very structures of awareness.
—James Carey, *Communication as Culture*

The process for laying the 1858 cable across the Atlantic involved two large ships, the USS *Niagara* and HMS *Agamemnon*, each bearing half of the cable, meeting midocean, splicing the cable together, and then heading back home while "paying out" the cable on the way. To ensure that the cable had not broken, the ships kept up a running stream of simple electrical pulses. John Mullaly, special correspondent to the *New York Herald* who rode on the *Niagara* during the cable-laying voyage, termed these pulses "electrical communication."[1] The apparatus for transmitting these vital signals was, Mullaly clarified, "wholly different from those to be used for the *transmission of messages* when the ends of the cable shall be landed" and, in fact, could not even send the simplest of Morse code.[2] The committee investigating the cable failure—a joint venture of the British Board of Trade and the Atlantic Telegraph Company—asked Wildman Whitehouse, the chief electrician of the 1858 cable, how the viability of the endeavor was assessed before and during the journey. He explained that to test predecessor cables, the current was simply reversed, which "was merely enough to work a Morse instrument" but not to transmit even a letter. When they asked Whitehouse, "What was the form of signals used [in your experiments]?" he responded, "Mere dots."[3]

Yet, this simple signaling, incapable of messages, was able to bear the heavy weight of the imaginary of unprecedented global unity. Mullaly described the reverence the crew and engineers held for these "mere dots" in words that evoked that imaginary: "It would seem like a dream, were it not for the visible, palpable evidence which we now hold in our hands, the electric chain which binds the two worlds together. . . . The continuity, without which the cable would be utterly valueless, is as perfect now as it ever was."[4] Signals alone sufficed for a grand imaginary of global connection, and a world of meaning rode on that meaningless electrical communication. The affective charge of this continuous signaling overwhelmed the emotions of the crew and the modes of expertise that resided in the imminent world: "That word 'continuity' has created more uneasiness and anxiety than any thing connected with the work, simply because it is seemingly beyond the control of scientific skill, and, once gone, cannot be restored by human ingenuity. At any moment we may hear that it has parted, and sleeping or waking, the fear that it will haunts us like a nightmare."[5] The signals, in their complicated pairing of straightforward meaninglessness and excessive cultural meaning, forced a turn to emotive experience and a haunting sense that there were forces far beyond human control and sense making at work.

Scholarship on religion and media has often looked to media content or media practices (e.g., representations of a religious group in media, religious use or restrictions of a medium) to find religion at work. This book is, in the end, an attempt to show religion vitally active in the most technological and material aspects of a medium. While content and practice have traditionally been considered the sites of meaning, the telegraph, as James Carey insists in the epigraph to this chapter, fundamentally shifted how language worked. The telegraph relocated meaning from content to technology in a brief epoch in which signals, radially divorced from messages, sparked enthusiastic imaginaries of global connection. These signals did not pave the way for immediately following messages (as in phatic communication), establish contexts for interpretation (as in metacommunication), or encode meaningful messages (as in later theories of digital signals); they were signals and signals alone.[6]

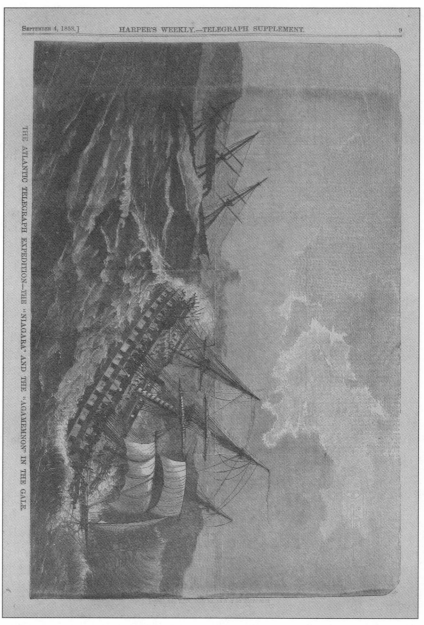

Figure 4.1. *Agamemnon* and *Niagara* in Atlantic storm, *Harper's Weekly: Telegraph Supplement*, September 5, 1858. (American Antiquarian Society)

This chapter argues that religiously charged affective investment in the divinity of the telegraph forged a vital meaningfulness for essentially meaningless signals.

Looking to the content and practice of Atlantic telegraphy demonstrates their irredeemable entanglement with technology and how protestantism, in its most subtle and pervasive forms, secured enthusiastic public value for this assemblage. Religion was a profoundly important source of cultural meaning. And while it appeared in forms unsurprising for the time, such as in telegrams sent on the cable, public prayers, and accounts of the cable laying, the role of religion to make signaling meaningful *before* messages could be sent, *before* signals even guaranteed a working cable, suggests that protestantism was more than merely a conventional trope in public discourse. Religion's creative force in the United States in the nineteenth century compensated for the emptiness of these signals, making the cable matter before it worked.

Public protestantism also sustained enthusiastic commitment to an imaginary of global connection through the cable's ultimate ruin and its final garbled transmissions. Those transmissions consisted of a series of incomprehensible fragments, free of meaning but full of lament in their very indecipherability.[7] But, more important, protestantism sustained the imaginary of global connection during the period of the cable's highest functionality, which was, on closer examination, quite *dys*functional. While the gibberish of the cable's early signals of continuity and its final death rattle are important, they imply that the communication between them was what we would expect: clear, coherent, encoded speech conveying meaning. But the cable's "successful" transmissions often were equally nonsensical. The transcript of some of the telegrams on the seventh day of the cable's *functional* operation, August 16, 1858, exemplified this:

Newfoundland to Valentia.
Sent 12.40 a.m.—"Send V's."

Valentia to Newfoundland.
Sent 12.20 a.m.—"Sent V's."

Newfoundland to Valentia.
Sent 12.34 [a.m.]—"Please send alphabet."

Valentia to Newfoundland.
Sent 2.27 [a.m.]—"Sent alphabet."

Newfoundland to Valentia.
Sent 2.57 [a.m.]—"All right but three letters. Please ask some question, but much faster."

Valentia to Newfoundland.
Sent 3.35 a.m.—"Understand. Can . . ." [The rest of the message, which was unintelligible: —"You take a message?" These words came afterwards, forming the twentieth message.].

Newfoundland to Valentia.
Sent 3.36 a.m.—"Please after care. Yes, at same rate."

Valentia to Newfoundland.
Sent 4.56 a.m.—"You must repeat each sentence in full."

Newfoundland to Valentia.
Sent 5.15 a.m.—"Repeat word before 'in.'"

Valentia to Newfoundland.
Sent 5.40 a.m.—"Sentence."

Newfoundland to Valentia.
Sent 5.55 a.m.—"I said—'send your message.'"
Sent 6.40 a.m.—"Received but not intelligible. Try again, commencing with four V's."[8]

It took six hours to transmit this correspondence, of which the only successful transmissions were Vs, an incomplete alphabet, and requests to send. More substantive messages fared little better; two short messages sent from England to Canada regarding troop movements took twelve hours to transmit and largely consisted of requests for the operator to resend the message.[9] The technology that would unite the world amounted to two telegraph operators sending "sentence" across the ocean.

More than anything else, the 1858 Atlantic cable transmitted signs of disconnection. Epitomizing the everyday disconnection that was (and is) integral to networks, the cable was primarily a medium for the failure of communication. Its transmissions were dominated by a kind of babble much like the repetitive stuttering of a child who makes the sounds of speech before ever communicating content: *V, V, V.* Transatlantic telegraphic communication in 1858 presented a form of language that made no sense. It also presented a form of religious activity that made such nonsense profoundly meaningful.

The repetition of *V*—a Beethovenian dot-dot-dot-dash in Morse code—returns us to the fundamental issue that haunted the 1858 telegraph cable and has haunted networks since: the constitutive disconnection that has undergirded imaginaries of connection.[10] The stuttering and spluttering of the 1858 cable were expressive of and constituted by disconnection on a massive sweep of scale, from grand oceanic ruptures to tiny mis-twitches in the mirror that received the currents from across the Atlantic. While many of the mechanical and technological failures that contributed to the ultimate failure of the 1858 cable were resolved with the next attempt, certain kinds of disconnection became part of network protocol at this originary moment. Pinging, the constant foundational signaling on which networked communication technology depends, is evidence for the regularity of disconnection. In other words, network media never overcame failure and disconnection, as the popular myth goes; they just learned to live with it.

In some ways, the centrality of disconnection for communication is not unique to networks at all; as John Durham Peters tells us, "The gaps at the heart of communication are not its ruin, but its distinctive feature."[11] We know from structural and poststructural theories of language that, despite our habituated trust in language to represent the world in words, it always fails on some level to make anything other than itself present. From text or conversation, no matter the force of our desire, we only ever get the words *ice cream*, never the real thing. Language's reach outside of itself as the precondition of meaning is necessarily doomed to failure.

The telegraph signals serve as an interesting site of inquiry about language because they not only defy the colloquial assumption that language transmits meaning by referencing the world but also defy the structural assertion that language transmits meaning by referencing concepts and the poststructural account that language makes meaning as words refer to other words. The simple electrical pulses and even the more developed signals of Vs stand in for nothing else; they are language outside of representation and language outside of referentiality. The signals are not part of a system of signs. They did not clarify messages, encode messages, or pave the way for messages; often they were the only telegraphic communication available. In fact, much of the signaling on the 1858 cable was done without the technological possibility of messages at all.

And yet, such telegraphic text composed most of what was sent on the 1858 cable and was necessary for any network communication to take place. As Colonel Tagliaferro Preston Shaffner reported to the committee that investigated the cable's failure,

> I have always found that in a bad working line (a five-word [per minute] line would be a bad working line) there is a large per-centage of the time required for the offices asking each other to repeat—they do not get what is sent, and for the correction of what they do send, so that a great amount of the five words that are sent per minute are words used for ascertaining what is sent.[12]

In other words, Vs were the norm; messages were the exception. Yet, without bearing meaningful content, this meaningless telegraphic language bore profoundly meaningful effects. The telegraph shifted the location of meaning from referentiality to affectively charged infrastructure; the Vs signaled the medium, not the message.

Let us not assume that the turn to signals or the infrastructure that called them into being necessarily places us beyond the boundaries of religion. Here, especially, religion should not be relegated to the immaterial and abstract, despite the imaginaries of immateriality that characterized both telegraphy and Protestantism in the nineteenth century. Telegraphy and Protestantism entangled in declarations of immediate communication, the erasure of space, and the eclipse of time. However, Protestant-inflected discourses declared the telegraph's triumph over the material world *through all sorts of material practices*. There is a paradox at the heart of Protestantism. If anything has been its hallmark, it is the emphatic priority of *immaterial* elements (transcendence, textuality, belief) that has been made possible by a vast gamut of *material* things and activities. A now-classic example: the retroactively conferred motto of the Reformation was "Scripture alone, grace alone, faith alone," orientations that spread through the undeniable mutual dependence of emergent Protestantism and the printing press in Europe.[13]

Religion was adamantly woven into the warp and weft of these webs of cables: it pushed Morse's machine around the world, fueled and framed nationalist enthusiasm for global communication, and crafted telegraphy as the herald of a perfect future. Religion also suffused the widely held idea that telegraphy would unite the world in friction-free communication at the direction of God by contributing potent affective, imaginative, and discursive supplements to the telegraph's linguistic failures. After six days of signaling, the first message to be sent and received on the 1858 cable was, "Europe and America are united by telegraph. Glory to God in the highest; on earth, peace, good will toward men."[14] The hymn singing of Inuit people under British rule was entered into a report as formal evidence of the likelihood of the future success of oceanic telegraphy. Mullaly included a transcript of the solemn prayer offered after the cable was landed in Newfoundland and made a point to note that "the 'Amen' which followed the conclusion of this prayer showed what a sincere response it received from the hearts of all present, and the depth of feeling it excited."[15] The celebratory message from Captain Hudson of the *Niagara* on the occasion of the cable's landing (but long before any messages were sent) was, "God has been with us. The Telegraph Cable is laid without accident, and to Him be all the glory."[16]

The infrastructure of the telegraph demanded new forms of language outside of representation and referentiality. Peters proposes—tongue in cheek—infrastructuralism as a response to structuralism and poststructuralism.[17] At the risk of providing gratuitous evidence for the humorlessness of academia, I would like to take his joke seriously. While structuralism concerns itself with social constructions of coherent systems of internally referential meaning and poststructuralism celebrates the gaps, breaks, and aporias that disrupt social systems of meaning, infrastructuralism attends to the social, material, and energetic installations that make modern life possible. This chapter thus turns to the role of infrastructure guided by the contention that making sense of how communication works always requires attention to the media at stake and the (here religious) modes by which those media come to matter. That is, a viable theory of language must also be a theory of media and affect.

An infrastructural analysis of telegraphy needs the rejection of representationalism that we inherit from structuralism (via Ferdinand de Saussure) and the embrace of disconnective communication that we inherit from poststructuralism (via Jacques Lacan). But telegraphy also requires a supplement: a robust consideration of the meaning constituted by the infrastructural form of the medium and the ways that infrastructural form was imagined as meaningful. In this case, religion fueled the latter, rendering network infrastructure both the message and the mission. James Carey, whose work granted the telegraph its fame in communication studies, offers rich (if often ambiguous) attention to the impact of telegraphic infrastructure on communication. By taking up Saussure, Lacan, and Carey in turn, we can see how these lineages shape the proposition that meaning in network communication is always also infrastructural and affective and was originally religious. In this case, given the particular nineteenth-century US context, this infrastructural meaning was empowered through specifically protestant techniques of enthusiastic imagination. Among the surprising coincidences of Jacques Lacan and James Carey—strange bedfellows that they are—is their shared understanding of religion at the root of meaning.

The Structure of the Sign

In the one extant transcript of the 1858 Atlantic Telegraph Cable, provided by Colonel Shaffner to the Joint Committee investigating the failure of the venture, 403 messages were sent. Of these messages, 367 were communications between operators trying to get a handle on telegraphing across the ocean and managing the recurring disconnections (e.g., requests to repeat). Of the remaining 36 messages, 20 were about the funding, supplies, and engineering of the cable, and only 16 messages were sent by people not directly involved in the everyday working of the cable itself. Of these, 10 were congratulatory notes on the success of the cable. That is to say, for the life of the 1858 Atlantic cable, just

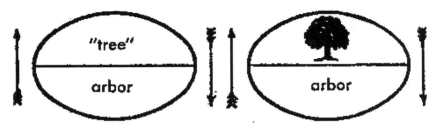

Figure 4.2. Diagram of the sign. (Ferdinand de Saussure, *Course in General Linguistics*, ed. Charles Bally and Albert Sechehaye, trans. Wade Baskin [New York: Philosophical Society, 1959], 67)

6 messages conformed to what we expect of cabled communication—news of current events or military orders.

While the transcript includes *requests* for the other station to send the alphabet or even just single letters, it does not include the alphabet or letters themselves, let alone the preceding pulses. This tells us two things. First, signals and messages that were sent to establish the ability to send and receive messages composed significantly more than the recorded 91 percent of cabled communication. And, second, that there was something qualitatively different in the eyes of Colonel Shaffner about those messages that did not warrant their inclusion—this, despite the fact that he was attempting to run a competing line between Europe and North America through Greenland and had every motivation to amply illustrate the cable's faults. Ultimately, the primary use of the Atlantic Telegraph Cable was not to speak but to signal, and signaling is fundamentally different from other sorts of language. The root of why lies with a lineage of thinkers, starting with Ferdinand de Saussure, who provide a pathway to understanding the working of language outside of representation.

Saussure's structural linguistics effectively upends the notion that language works by representing the world. For Saussure, language is a system of signs in which each sign is composed of the one-to-one correspondence of a sound-image (such as the Latin *arbor*) with a concept (the category that holds oaks, maples, and sycamores apart from shrubbery).[18]

Saussure's sense that these pairings are arbitrary (there is nothing about oaks and maples that makes them best expressed through the particular sound-image, /'ärbər/) indicates that meaning is not made by any inherent relationship between a word and the concept it refers to. We understand a word not because it naturally evokes its referent (as an unfamiliar word can make clear) but, rather, by distinguishing it from other words (e.g., tree from bee, track, bush).[19] In this way, the relationships between words and concepts function through words' relationships with other words. Thus, the primary site of meaning is the structural relations internal to the system of language itself.

On this point, Saussure is emphatic. Language, he tells us, is not a process of naming what we encounter in the world. Signs pair sound-images with *concepts*; they have nothing at all to do with things.[20] The distinction of language from matter is so important for Saussure that he goes to great lengths to ensure that language is carefully secluded in the adamantly immaterial realm of the mind. Even the sound-image, which holds open the possibility of eardrums vibrating to sound, is immaterial for Saussure: "The [sound-image] is not the material sound, a purely physical thing, but the psychological imprint of the sound, the impression that it makes on our senses."[21] The sign, this correspondence forged between concept and sound-image that acts as the basic building block of language, is thus a purely "psychological" entity, existing as an abstraction in a carefully secured immateriality.

Saussurean linguistics thus insists that language is a system of meaning that exists and is fully functional in absolute distinction from matter and medium: "language . . . is a self-contained whole and a principle of classification," and naturally so.[22] As Saussure set out to define the field of linguistics, he offered a foundational distinction between speech and language. Speech is the human faculty of articulating language—meaning *and* medium—and, as such, is unwieldy as an object of study. Speech is composed of the interrelation among sounds as they are spoken and heard; ideas expressed and interpreted through such sounds; individuals thinking, speaking, listening, and interpreting; social practices of establishing meanings; and the tension between tradition and evolution. All of these aspects of speech affect the others, preventing any scholarly disentanglement in the service of clarity: "We are left inside the vicious circle."[23] Speech refuses to separate meaning and medium or to prioritize one over the other.

But language is a far more straightforward object of study: "a system of distinct signs corresponding to distinct ideas."[24] Or, in Saussure's helpful formula, "Language is speech less speaking."[25] Whereas speech is "heterogeneous," language is "homogeneous."[26] Whereas speech is physical (sound waves), physiological (as vocal muscles flex), and psychological (requiring the brain to associate sound-images and their concepts), language is purely psychological.[27] And whereas speech is individual (in the unique activity of phonation and hearing) and social (in the establishment of a shared corpus of sound-images with durable relationships to concepts), language is purely social.[28] In all things, language offers the alluring advantage of being an abstract immaterial system, clear and contained. As such, language initiates order out of the chaos of speech, confirming its right place at the head of the beast: "As soon as we give language first place among the facts of speech, we introduce a natural order into a mass that lends itself to no other classification."[29] Here, meaning precedes media, and media are merely an accessory. A Saussurean reading of Shaffner's transcript would tell us that the Vs were the unfortunate noise of the vehicle but had no bearing on the messages, let alone the system of meaning that sustained them.

Because Saussure separates language from matter and media, the signals and the religion at work in them—which are material and affective—are necessarily excluded from a structuralist analysis of ocean telegraphy. But we know from the repeated struggle of the telegraphers and their need for Vs to make any other message possible that matter, medium, and affective investment bore heavily on messages and meaning. In an unfailingly polite exchange between Cyrus Field and President James Buchanan upon the landing of the cable, Field assured the president that the first messages would be an exchange between the president and Queen Victoria. The president, perhaps anxious about missing such a vital message, sent word to Field that he had not yet received the awaited telegram from the queen. Field's response clarified that signaling was the necessary groundwork for messages; the latter was impossible without the former: "Until the telegraph instruments are all perfectly adjusted, no message can be recorded over the Cable. You shall have the earliest information, but some days may elapse before all is effected."[30] Twelve days of signals and test messages ultimately

Figure 4.3. Circuit of communication. (Ferdinand de Saussure, *Course in General Linguistics*, ed. Charles Bally and Albert Sechehaye, trans. Wade Baskin [New York: Philosophical Society, 1959], 11)

passed from the landing of the cable until the queen's message was successfully received (which itself took sixteen hours to transmit) and another two days before the president's response could successfully be sent.[31] The impact of the *V*s requires heterogeneous attention to media in ways that disorder Saussure's neat separation of language from what he considers its material vehicles. Most important, the *V*s also seem to disorder the logic of language itself: that meaning takes place in language through a correspondence between concept and sound-image alone. Here we have a sound-image with no concept, a signal without a sign. Di-di-di-dah.

The telegraph makes two important appearances in Saussure's work. First, as Peters notes, Saussure uses circuitry as a model for communication.[32] For Saussure, all communication is a reciprocal exchange of meaning between a speaker and a listener. That is, communication is an interpersonal circuit in which concepts are translated to words, vocalized, received, and retranslated back into concepts. Language is that part of the circuit in which meaning resides; the rest of the circuitry is merely an external vehicle.

Unsurprisingly, then, the second appearance of the telegraph in Saussure's work is as a metaphor for the separation of meaning and media, as can be seen in the epigraph to this chapter.[33] Language's ontological definitiveness as psychological and social and its containment as a system of signs effect a critical distinction between meaning and media. For Saussure, language is a system of meaning, pure and simple, and thus media—so inextricably material and important only in their transmissive function—are absolutely external and secondary to the system of signs they transport. Even the telegraph, which proved such a helpful analogy for the circuitry of language, ultimately stands as an illustration of the meaninglessness of the medium to meaning itself. For Saussure, the telegraph has no more power to change language than a train might have to change its passengers.

Of course, trains *do* change their passengers, exposing them to certain movements, chemicals, sights, and experiences. Indeed, as James Carey tells us in the second epigraph to this chapter, the telegraph changed language itself. On the Atlantic voyage of the 1858 telegraph cable and then once it was secured to its landing posts in Ireland and Newfoundland, the medium determined to a large degree the sort of speech that could happen. The cable midocean could send nothing more than signals (i.e., not even *V*s). As the apparatuses and relays were adjusted in the first days after landing the cable, a director of the Atlantic Telegraph Company attested, "I do not make out any one single word completely and correct, and no one sentence that could be even read at all from the indication of the relay. I find altogether two or three words and a few more letters that were legible, but the longest word which I find correctly given is the word, 'be.'"[34] And yet it was this babble that spurred praises to God and mechanical ingenuity for this marvelous evidence of the cable's precious "continuity." The telegraph upended the referential logic of the sign not by a mechanism internal to the system of signification but through its articulation. Making sense of the signals and even the *V*s requires Saussure's concept of nonrepresentational communication, but the *V*s also induce a chaotic rupture in the logic of the sign that Saussure secures in place of representation. The *V*s stuttered across the ocean illustrate that the failures of the processes and technologies of communication are also failures in the structure of the sign and that such failures required an affective supplement—in this case supplied by religious imaginaries of global connection—to make any meaning at all. Which is to say, these signals are another site where imaginaries of network connection were undergirded by mundane practices of disconnection.

The Failure of the Sign

Unlike Saussure, Jacques Lacan (and Carey, as we will see later) invests religion with a unique and ubiquitous capacity to make meaning. Religion, Lacan once wryly declared, will triumph over psychoanalysis and "lots of other things too."[35] His enigmatic pronouncements on religion form one thread of a tangled conversation about psychoanalysis between Lacan and a group of increasingly frustrated journalists in Rome in 1974. (If one can sidestep empathy for the journalists, it's quite a funny read.) Lacan claims that religion (Roman Catholicism, in particular) will emerge victorious because of its power to give meaning to distressing discoveries.[36] Religion and its agents become, in Lacan's rendering, a meaning engine on overdrive humming energetically through the challenges posed by science:

> They can give meaning to absolutely anything whatsoever. A meaning to human life, for example. They are trained to do that. Since the beginning, religion has been all about giving meaning to things that previously were natural. It is not because things are going to become less natural, thanks to the real, that people will stop secreting meaning for all that. Religion is going to give meanings to the oddest experiments, the very ones that scientists themselves are just beginning to become anxious about. Religion will find colorful meaning for those.[37]

Religion serves for Lacan as a quintessential instantiation of our robust capacity to make meaning in the absence of representation. Lacan's work is always, on some level, concerned with absences, lack, and failure. (As the Lacanian scholar, psychoanalyst, and translator Bruce Fink quips, "You can't take the lack out of Lacan.")[38] And it is at the site of failure that religion makes its most meaningful contribution to the signals at hand.

The ontological distinction that Saussure proposes between language and the world it represents becomes a critical resource for many poststructuralist thinkers. Lacan, who in typical fashion extends, critiques, and supplements Saussure's thinking without any explicit distinction among these moves, retains an emphasis on Saussure's primary logic: that language makes meaning in and of itself without any referential reach into the world it represents. Yet Lacan also offers us a particularly useful way to think about the radical shift in language demanded by network infrastructure, for he describes a way in which meaning can be understood as an effect of failure.

Centering failure as integral to network function is critically important in any consideration of the telegraph. Telegraph networks comprised failures in manifold forms, from broken cables to missed signals. The transcript of the 1858 cable illustrates how such failures were necessary to establish functional connection and how the insufficiency of signals made space for religion to do its most effective (and affective) work: to invest profound cultural meaning in an ambiguous technological event that barely and briefly touched success. More than 367 communications negotiated failure in one form or another, and their negotiation was necessary to successfully send and receive 36 messages. The only way to make sense of telegraphic communication is to see the failure at its heart and the religious imaginaries that supplemented it.

For Lacan, language, for all its purported representative work, is incapable of re-presenting anything but itself. Language makes meaning not despite such incapacity but because of it: "I always speak the truth. Not the whole truth, because there's no way, to say it all. Saying it all is literally impossible: words fail. Yet it's through this very impossibility that the truth holds onto the real."[39] The deep division between words and the world is represented for Lacan by the ontological separation of the symbolic (the domain of language) and the real (the embodied, natural, material, and libidinous condition of life). This separation defines the real; Fink's lucid description of the real is "that which has not yet been symbolized, remains to be symbolized, or even resists symbolization."[40] Language, in Lacan's understanding, works by virtue of its *necessarily* failed attempts to categorize and express experience. For Lacan, the failure of communication is its very condition of possibility. Or, in Fink's rendering, "The essence of communication is miscommunication."[41]

Lacan elaborates his argument for language's productive failure in his attention to the fundamental unit of Saussurean linguistics: the relationship between signifier and signified. Lacan affirms Saussure's argument that the signifier bears no inherent relationship to the signified. However, Lacan is dissatisfied with Saussure's characterization of the relationship between the signifier and the signified as arbitrary. That is not enough, Lacan insists: "What passes for arbitrary is the fact that meaning effects seem not to bear any relationship to what causes them."[42] An example Fink provides is a rather perfect illustration: "How do you like them apples!"[43]

The mutual exclusivity between symbolization and the real is central to Lacan's work but also appears faintly in Saussure's. The critical difference Saussure proposes between the referent (the real, living, photosynthesizing oak) and the signified (the concept of a tree) provides evidence to Lacan that Saussure must have known there was an unbreachable boundary far more substantial than mere arbitrariness between signifiers and signifieds, let alone the real thing they purportedly represent.[44] The signified may appear to mediate between the real and the signifier for Saussure, but for Lacan signifieds signal the definitive gap between the symbolic and the real: "At the level of the signifier/signified distinction, what characterizes the relationship between the signified and what serves as the indispensable third party, namely the referent, is precisely that the signified misses the referent. The joiner doesn't work."[45] The relationship between signifier and signified is actually a relationship among those two and the *absence* of the real. The bar in Saussure's diagram for the sign thus remains fixed in place in Lacan's revisions to the diagram of the sign to S/s (signifier over signified, with the bar between). The bar characterizes the relationship between signifier and signified: it stands in for the absence of the real. Once a signifier is in place, the referent is "barred" from presence, and this fundamental failure is "quite essential to the function of language."[46]

Rhetorician Christian Lundberg clarifies, however, that this exclusivity does not prevent the mutual influence of the symbolic and the real. The real affects the symbolic, and the symbolic affects the real; but the symbolic "cannot internalize" the real.[47] Indeed, the signals seem to have abided by this principle of the simultaneous exclusion and influence of the real. The pulses of electricity persisted, offering the appearance of a working line, all the while passing through what the Joint Committee ultimately determined to be a complete break in the internal wire:

> On [one] occasion a sudden cessation of the current was perceived, but the insulation was good, and after a time the currents came again as strong as before. This could only be accounted for on the supposition that the internal copper wire had broken from the strain, and that when

the cable in which it was had reached the bottom the two ends had been brought together again by the elasticity of the sheath.[48]

If the signals of electrical communication between the *Niagara* and the *Agamemnon* represented anything at all, they appeared to represent continuous electrical connection. While the matter at stake offered something quite different—disconnection embedded in a tenuous joint—the signals produced an experience of connection for an expectant public anxious for continuity. Taking our cue from Lacan, we can understand the signals to have produced a "reality" of connection between continents—indeed, a reality of a divine connected world—that many US Americans experienced as more real than the broken cables, faulty pulses, and missed signals.[49] The religious imaginary barred these failures, forging a united, communicating world through the reinforced absence of real ruptures.

Given that the real is always excluded in a Lacanian frame, how does meaning making happen? Lundberg centers affective investment as a primary mode of meaning production at the site of this fundamental failure.[50] While Lacan maintains Saussure's bar between the signifier and signified and extends the bar's meaning to represent the fundamental exclusion of the real, he makes some other much more overt revisions to Saussure's diagram of the sign that help to situate affect as vital for meaning making. In particular, his refusal of the coherence of the sign as a bound entity provides an important contribution to understanding the signals on the Atlantic cable as meaning a great deal while referring to nothing. For Saussure, *signs* are interdependent in the system of language: once the "bond" between signifier and signified is socially secured, the pairing can be treated as a unit: "The [concept and sound-image] are intimately united, and each recall each other."[51] Safely ensconced in monogamous enclosure, each sign forms part of the web of language, where it is made meaningful by other equally stable signs. In this way, language functions through a system by which the "value of each term [sign] results solely from the simultaneous presence of the others."[52]

For Lacan, however, signs prove to be promiscuous and unreliable; thus, he removes the circle from around the sign. As in "How do you like them apples!" none of the signs serves as a fundamental unit of meaning.[53] In fact, any meaning is generated despite or in direct defiance of the supposed relationship between each word and its signified. The signs don't matter to meaning. Rather, the meaning effect is produced from a "signifierness" that has little to do with the signs themselves—let alone a reference to the real—and everything to do with the ways signifiers relate to other signifiers.[54] In contradistinction to Saussure's sense that language is a system of interdependent signs, Lacan understands language to be a system of interdependent signifiers. Meaning can only be made when the signifier is released from the closed cage of the sign; the signifier makes meaning not out of a pairing to a concept but in relationships—serial, multiple (nearly Oneidan) relationships—to other signifiers.

The relationships among signifiers—what Lacan calls the "signifying chain"—are the primary site of meaning making and overturn the referential logic of the sign.[55] For Lacan, "It is in the chain of the signifier that meaning *insists*, but that none of the chain's elements *consists* in the signification it can provide at that very moment."[56] Signifiers are meaningful only in the absence of a relationship to any referent—thing or concept—and this radical, doubled disconnection between the symbolic and the real is the precondition for communication. If meaning is understood through reference—for a sign to *consist* of meaning—then all language is meaningless. But if we take seriously the idea that language *insists* on meaning, we open the possibility of a function for language outside of referentiality of any kind and, in particular, for the determining power of affective investment to make meaning in place of language's essential failure.

Lacan offers a way to understand the stutters of telegraphic signals as a *productive* babble in the absence of meaning. The V, V, V referred to nothing but itself.[57] The Vs, disconnected from any possible referent, may not have *consisted* in meaning. But their incessant di-di-di-dah *insisted* on attention to their unprecedented presence as meaningful, if nothing else. For Lundberg, it is the power of affective investment that enables the production of powerful meanings at the site of referential failure. The affiliation of one signifier with another in particularly powerful pairings—what Lacan calls metaphor—is secured by affective investment that offers these pairings "substantial gravity."[58] Insistence is fueled by an affective charge that emerges at the site of that persistent bar: the friction between the symbolic that fails to consist in meaning and the real it thus excludes.

In Lacan's comparison of religion and psychoanalysis, he describes religion as bearing an unfathomable power because of its ability to affiliate elements: "[Religion] will find correspondences between everything and everything else. That's its very function."[59] Religion's power rests in its ability to churn out infinite chains of connection and multiply meaning with irrepressible creativity. As an unstoppable generator of sense, religion is language run amok: it may just "secrete meaning to such an extent that we will truly drown in it."[60] While Lacan seldom addresses religion, he here ascribes ubiquity to it ("the place is crawling with it") and its attendant power to make meaning.[61]

The insistent signals on the Atlantic Telegraph Cable were charged with meaning, not by referencing a concept or by referencing another signifier but by becoming a site of affective investment through these failures to refer to anything at all. Mullaly's description of the landing of the cable in Trinity Bay, Newfoundland, on August 5 (eleven days before the transmission of the queen's message) evokes the mobility of this meaningfulness among matter, imagination, and emotion. To fully quote the passage mentioned earlier,

> Never was such a remarkable scene presented since the world began. Even now, at the very point of its realization, it does not seem as if the work in which we have been engaged has been accomplished. Looking back on the past, the seven long days of anxiety and suspense appear but as one, and it is almost impossible for the mind to comprehend the great fact that the cable is really laid. It would seem like a dream, were it not for the visible, palpable evidence which we now hold in our hands, the electric chain which binds the two worlds together. No, it is not a dream, but a great reality, the announcement of which will startle the incredulous and unbelieving of both continents.[62]

Mullaly's performance of profound feeling was more than echoed by the sailors and engineers who surrounded him. After the fervent prayer led by Captain Hudson and the heartfelt amen by the crew, the scene erupted into the wild enthusiasm that distinguished the "great fizzle" of the 1858 cable:

Oh, had the people of New York—of the United States—of the two worlds, heard the wild huzza that went ringing over the hills, chasing the deer from their coverts, sending thousands of startled sea birds out upon the ocean, as if the land no longer afforded them a place of security—had they seen the faces of these men, they would understand what enthusiasm is, and how unjust the suspicion that denied them the possession of an attribute only second to hope itself. A cheer it could hardly be called; it was one wild, prolonged shout of delirious joy, such as might welcome the disenthralment of a nation, or the union of two worlds—a union in which we all participate, you and I and every one of us, and the remembrance of which will live with us to the end.[63]

The signals represented nothing and yet, charged by the fundamental nature of modern public protestantism and its affective power, sparked the inhabitation of a durable imaginary of national and global network connection. A vital meaningfulness emerged through religious affect for the cable that could yet transmit no meaning at all.

Rituals of Communications

Both Lacan and Saussure assume that the function of communication is to transmit messages, whether or not it succeeds at doing so. James Carey offers an alternative: that communication works through repetitive action (and not necessarily content) to establish relationships (not necessarily send information). He calls this kind of communication "ritual communication" and relates it to particular forms of religion; he gives prayers, chants, and ceremonies as representative examples.[64] His work is thus a critical resource for considering how religious practice in particular makes communication meaningful when transmitting little meaning per se.

For Carey, the arrival of telegraphy lent dominance to the idea that communication is the transmission of messages across distance. But, he argues in his landmark essay "A Cultural Approach to Communication," the ritual model of communication—that is, the old and long-overshadowed model of communication as the foundation of all social life—is also at work. The ritual model of communication emphasizes communication's maintenance of a cultural world in time, sharing conceptual and etymological ties to communion and community.[65] Rather than focusing on sending information, the ritual view looks to those communicative acts that establish relationship and represent shared beliefs, as in greetings, liturgies, or the Pledge of Allegiance. Ritual communication is "the sacred ceremony that draws persons together in fellowship and commonality."[66]

With few other points of intersection, Carey, like Lacan, thus understands religion as a rich generator of meaning. Carey locates the origins of both ritual and transmission communication in religion. These models, he states, "derive, as with much in secular culture, from religious origins, though they refer to somewhat different regions of religious experience."[67] The transmission model's attention to movement across space finds its roots in the onset of modernity, particularly in European colonial expansion and its Christian missionary commitments: "The vast and, for the first time, democratic migration in space was above all an attempt to trade an old world for a new and represented the profound belief that movement in space could be in itself a redemptive act."[68] Modern missionary travel provided the primary mode by which communication was understood to be an "extension of God's kingdom on earth."[69] Indeed, the activities of Cyrus Hamlin and his fellow missionaries of the ABCFM illustrate this point in spades.

The ritual model stems from older religious origins, and Carey associates it with a sense of primordial religion in line with the anthropological views he draws on.[70] This deeper tie is expressed in the explicit reference to religion in the name itself:

> It derives from a view of religion that downplays the role of the sermon, the instruction and admonition, in order to highlight the role of the prayer, the chant, and the ceremony. It sees the original or highest manifestation of communication not in the transmission of intelligent information but in the construction and maintenance of an ordered, meaningful cultural world that can serve as a control and container of human action.[71]

Carey thus locates religion at the foundation not just of communication but also of culture, where it is less explicit but much more powerful.

Indeed, the Atlantic cable transmitted little other than signals that established relationship. This was what these signals were meant to do and nothing more: create and demonstrate electrical "continuity" along the cable. The rupture of continuity revealed a break in the cable and could, if not resolved, doom the venture completely. The people on board spoke of it so often with such concern that one frustrated sailor remarked, "Darn the continuity; I wish they would get rid of it altogether. It has caused a darned sight more trouble than the hull thing is worth."[72] It was the ability to signal, and the ability to signal alone, that established the vital relationship between the *Niagara* and the *Agamemnon* as they sailed their respective ways to land. Everything rode on that repetitive ritual action of meaningless electrical pulses.

Continuity epitomizes ritual communication: it established relationship and created a social foundation of shared belief, in this case, of the marvelousness of the cable as blessed unifier of the world. It is tempting to claim the continuity of the cable as not just ritualistic but, by extension, religious. However, such an analysis points too heartily to religion as the establishment of community through shared beliefs and actions, a view now rightfully considered by many scholars of religion to be outdated and to often reflect the problematic political orientations of the modern anthropological lineages from which it stems. Religion in lived experience is much more often the site of fracture, diversely negotiated beliefs, and divergent, incoherent actions. I propose that we use the analysis of ritual communication without succumbing to the temptation to consider ritual to be de facto religious. Rather, the religion at work in this ritual communication is not the religious roots of ritual in general; it is the historically specific social practice of US Americans investing religiously fueled affect in these signals, rendering them meaningful through religious actions and discourse, and thus producing a religious imaginary of a divine connected world. Continuity, as abstract and precarious as it could seem to those who were involved in its daily maintenance, held concrete electrical *and* affective charges and marshaled a historically specific, religiously formed emotive behavior. On an earlier failed attempt to lay a cable, the restoration of continuity after a momentary loss was met with "tears standing in the eyes of some as they almost cried for joy."[73] These forms of emotive comportment were steeped in the passions of revival culture.

While the transmission model requires meaningful content, ritual communication bears a much more ambivalent relationship to meaning and, thus, is a useful way to think about the insistent, redundant *V*s of our persistent transatlantic telegraphers. Ritual communication includes those modes of communication whose social functions rely on action and context over representative or referential meaning. Ritual communication prompts the relationship established by the essentially unanswerable "What's up?" or the power of a prayer recited without thinking. These communicative acts are, on the one hand, profoundly meaningful in the sense of their importance in establishing sociality. On the other hand, they are essentially meaningless; their content barely matters.

Carey's minimization of content in ritual communication is not meaninglessness per se; ritual still relies on a representational function to portray society to itself through a formal symbolism of shared culture.[74] That symbolism can be, for Carey, embodied and material; he offers architecture as one example, which could easily be extended to the Atlantic Telegraph Cable as a spectacle of "community ideals."[75] The idea that rituals *represent* something that a culture holds in common— Carey emphasizes shared beliefs—grounds ritual communication in that old priority of the resurgent relationship of sign and concept.[76] Yet there is in Carey a productive ambiguity about the site of meaning. While he describes ritual as a "representation of shared beliefs," his commitment to constructivism shines through when he notes that ritual "induces the dispositions it pretends merely to portray."[77] Ritual uses representationalism as a cover for its creative action; it appears to represent something that it is actually bringing into being.

The creativity of these signals matters and is the site where religion did its vital work. These signals did more than simply establish contact or prepare listeners for forthcoming meaningful communication, as in phatic communication (e.g., "Lend me your ears!").[78] While there was certainly an expectation that the Atlantic cable would transmit meaningful communication—this was, indeed, its purpose—something else happened in the moment. Days before meaningful communication proved possible (let alone actually happened), celebration erupted for a global connection established by signaling *alone*. That is, public, religious enthusiasm erupted before any message was sent, before any message *could* be sent—hence the prayer at the cable's landing, the "sincerity" of the amen offered by the sailors, and the "depth of feeling" it elicited.[79] With apologies to the frustrated sailor on the *Niagara*, "continuity" is a rather apt expression of this purely technical electrical flow—the simple passage of electricity without the remotest ability for speech per se, which sparked charged imaginaries of grand national, global, and divine *connection* that were and are quintessential to networks.

While Carey sees a religious origin for both models of communication, he assumes that the influence of religion falls sway to the power of secularization: "Soon, as the forces of science and secularization gained ground, the obvious religious metaphors fell away and the technology of communication itself moved to the center of thought."[80] With the advent of the telegraph, Carey claims, the ties between transportation and communication were broken, and religious thinking of the era insisted that the goals to which transportation was previously aimed could now be accomplished by communication alone. Yet both models retain some tie to their origins in religion, if only as a bind that "Americans have never escaped."[81] Religious roots reappeared for Carey in the language that attended this period of technological change, a descriptive storehouse that firmly situated new technology in the "rhetoric of the electrical sublime."[82] The telegraph was couched in religious dreams, "cloaked . . . in religious metaphor," and "mediated through religious language."[83] Even as Carey sees religion's impact dim with secularization, religion served as a medium through which the telegraph became meaningful.

Religion, even under what Lacan and Carey both identify as the rise of science, retains a potent meaning-making function in the absence of representation. Religion did not fade with the rise of science, as the old modern myth claims, but became more fundamental. Lacan and Carey turn to expansive definitions of religion that emphasize religious capacities that exceed institutions, systems of belief, modes of practice, or everyday activity. Religion becomes, in these renderings, a governing set of practices that organize language's existence in space, time, and social life and determine what meanings can emerge and how. Thus, both Lacan and Carey locate religion at the heart of the modes of communication that thwart denotative discourse. For both, religious logic undergirds the ways we live in and make sense of the world. That is, even in the case of these meaningless signals, which consisted of nothing but their own presence, religion and its attendant affective power made them profoundly meaningful.

The *V*s of oceanic telegraphy represented little but brought much into being. They were the chords of a chorus of new communication, and through their symphonic articulation a new submarine cable infrastructure emerged. They were a ritual of disconnection: signaling the persistent cycle of loss and recovery, consisting of nothing, and creatively insisting on new modes of communicative and imaginary action. As ritual communication, the *V*s stuttered a particular relationship between telegraphers, telegraph stations, cables, electricity, and nations into being in particular ways, inscribing these infrastructural entities into a communicating world wrestling with disconnection.

Infrastructures of Communication

The massive infrastructural project of developing a global telegraph network with a transatlantic cable sent mostly nothing more than empty electrical signals crashing against the shores. Infrastructuralism helps us to see the way that media are more than modes of content delivery; infrastructural media are matter and processes that order space and time in ways both intimate and grand, from the vast material networks of cables to the tapping of fingers on telegraph keys, from the great ships spooling cable into the ocean to the financial currents that carried them there, from the religious imaginaries that invested the movement of electricity with divine power to the inner workings of language. While submarine infrastructure is often invisible to us, lifting telegraphic communication into view makes the case for the fundamental entanglement of media infrastructure and religious meaning in forms that defy traditional attention to media content.[84]

The attention this chapter has paid to the repetition of a pulse of electricity or to the repetition of a single letter in Morse code is a sort of content analysis, but an admittedly strange one: an infrastructural content analysis. In this case, the content—largely telegraphic babble—does not offer great insights into the meanings circulating in culture. Instead, the content points us to a circulating meaninglessness. And, as such, it illuminates the way that the intimacy of religion and media matter not just to the content of language but to the very structure of language and its capacity to make meaning and also to the meaningfulness that can arise in conditions where meaningful content simply cannot appear. Attention to the signals of the 1858 cable is not meant to be myopic. Paul Edwards, who studies knowledge infrastructures, warns that the study of infrastructure always demands nimble movement among the macro, meso, and micro scales that infrastructures comprise: "To be modern is to lie within and by means of infrastructures, and therefore to inhabit, uneasily, the intersection of these multiple scales."[85] Paying attention to the Vs is always also about the cable, the ocean, and the grand affective, imaginative, and discursive demands that public protestantism made on those empty signals. This analysis highlights the negotiation of micro protocols (V, V, V) and macro religious logics (divine, divine, divine).

We have already seen the ways in which religion shaped the imaginary of networks as connective in the ways religious people spread network technology for the sake of global unity, religious discourses and affects located networks at the foundation of nationalism, and religious movements affiliated networks with utopias. By addressing the infrastructural role of religion in the making and unmaking of structures of meaning under the promise of communication as perfect communion, we can see that religious affective investment in the divinity of the cable forged a culturally important meaning for what was, essentially, a meaningless signal. The electrical pulses that were celebrated, claimed as evidence of divine attention, and prayed over in solemn gratitude did not even signal the success of the venture, let alone legible messages. At this scale, religion is at its most diffuse but also its most powerful. It is worth remembering Peters's caution: "Logistical media pretend to be neutral and abstract, but they often encode a subtle and deep political or religious partisanship."[86]

In ways that structuralist and poststructuralist accounts cannot, an infrastructural perspective on the telegraph network reveals that the Vs' most important work was to secure a particular sort of relationship among diverse participants, human and nonhuman, abstract and concrete. This is true to the nature of infrastructure in general, which is never something so stable as pipes or cables alone. Infrastructure always involves social protocols, environmental affordances, and negotiation with the "slight surprise of action."[87] The scholar of queer and environmental humanities E Cram argues that "what is categorically determined as infrastructure depends on regimes of value."[88] The mid-nineteenth-century context of networks' emergence established an infrastructure that was wildly expansive. The index to evidence in the Joint Committee's report is illuminating, including such categories as earth currents, hemp, lightning, shellfish and worms, static electricity, submarine glue, the temperature of the sea, and vulcanite.[89] Those who provided evidence discussed, among this wide array of topics, the religious lives of locals at potential cable landing sites.[90] In an obvious way, the Vs established and reestablished connection among telegraph stations and operators. But they also, thus, served as a ritual enactment of what networks were: a new circulation of nonreferential communication among a new expansive set of participants that produced an enthusiastic protestant imaginary of global connection sustained by an everyday environment of malfunction.

While the Vs themselves did not appear in transcripts of the telegraph cable's operation, they haunted the records of the cable's life. The Vs did not function as signs or signifiers or even, really, as letters; they were signals of the cable's constitutive cycle of connection and disconnection and the cable's involvement in social—particularly religious—processes that far exceeded the technological. The Vs are not alone; signs are not structures of symbolic action safely separate from the material apparatus on which they are sent or the social processes they engage. Carey understands the telegraph to have urged communication toward denotation and transmission in its most representative function:

> The wire services . . . demanded something closer to a "scientific" language, a language of strict denotation in which the connotative features of utterance were under rigid control. . . . The telegraph, therefore, led to the disappearance of forms of speech and styles of journalism and story telling—the tall story, the hoax, much humor, irony, and satire—that depended on a more traditional use of the symbolic, a use I earlier called the fiduciary.[91]

But while formal telegrams confirmed this account, the telegraphic signaling that made such messages possible diverged from it. It was language in its most abstract, a far cry from denotation. Telegraphic infrastructure—that is, networks—changed the logic of language, making signaling common, quiet, and utterly necessary to any other form of cabled communication. Few messages were sent without some preceding and interspersed alphabetic babble. The first formal message was sent and received on the Atlantic cable of 1858 on its *seventh* day of operation.[92]

It may seem foolish to enlist James Carey to make the argument that cabled networks relocated meaning from language to infrastructure. It was Carey's iconic study of the telegraph that granted it disciplinary fame as the technology that severed the relationship between communication and infrastructures of transportation: "The telegraph, by ending the identity [of communication and transportation], allowed symbols to move independently of and faster than transportation. To put it in a slightly different way, the telegraph freed communication from the constraints of geography."[93] But it was this same essay that also conferred fame on the telegraph as the agent of radical changes in how communication took place and how we understood it. For Carey, the telegraph altered language, knowledge, and even the structures of awareness, as the epigraph to this chapter attests.[94] In the double sense of the word, Carey *cleaves* communication and infrastructure. In the first breath, the telegraph freed symbols from material constraint. In the second, the telegraphic apparatus irrevocably shaped symbolic action.

This ambiguity in Carey's essay is persistent. Even Carey's direct assertion of the telegraph's landmark separation—the telegraph "provided the decisive and cumulative break of the identity of communication and transportation"—introduces a discussion of the development of the telegraph *alongside* the railroad.[95] While communication is no longer dependent on the transportation of people, Carey effectively claims that communication and geography are indelibly linked: "The telegraph twisted and altered but did not displace patterns of connection formed by natural geography: by the river and primitive foot and horse paths and later by the wooden turnpike and canal."[96] The telegraph's relationship with geography may have eschewed the need for a moving human, but this should not obscure the important material relationships the telegraph had with land and sea, train and ship.

In other words, despite disciplinary efforts to separate symbolic action and infrastructure, communication and communications are always already linked. As the scholar of culture and technology Jonathan Sterne asserts in his reading of Carey, communication is more than symbolic action; it is also the constitutive action of material movement in space and time.[97] Even the etymology of communication bears this indelible intimacy of communication and transportation, as Carey himself notes: communication in the nineteenth century meant both.[98] The rich entanglement of symbolic communication and kinetic transportation, between ideas and matter, opens the possibility of infrastructural analysis.

Transportation has always been symbolic, whether because certain vehicles (e.g., a steam train chugging through the pastoral landscape) bear profound cultural meanings or because certain forms of transportation rely on symbolic action (e.g., the Underground Railroad).[99] And the inverse is easily seen in the case of the telegraph, in which the immateriality of symbolic communication remained tethered to the transportation of pulses of electricity dependent on a highly material network of cables and stations. While Carey describes the work of the telegraph as an instance of communication controlling transportation, the telegraph's wily location between transportation and communication makes a neat causality impossible. Transportation and communication were mutually constitutive and profoundly mutually dependent. Sterne's extrapolation from Carey puts it this way: "It is therefore true that in *use* the early telegraph governed the movement of the trains because the electrical signals contained instructions for the movement of trains. But it is also true that in material form—in infrastructure—the physicality of the train tracks governed the geographic movement of the telegraph signals."[100] Carey invites us to think about communication in infrastructural terms, even while encouraging us to consider their separation; his declarations of distinction between transportation and communication amply illustrate their profound interconnection.

When the fundamental relationship between symbolic and kinetic communication is restored, the *V*s make a tremendous amount of sense. They are not extraneous babble, unfortunate noise, or simply the material trace of the mode of articulation. Nor do they represent a particular meaning. They signal the infrastructure itself, which was at the time a marvelous and divine thing. And now, although humdrum, perhaps nearly forgotten, the pinging of mobile phones and computers and tablets does the same work of establishing connection in the condition of regular disconnection.

Attention to infrastructure illuminates the critical work of signaling as a particular form of communication in the absence of representation and reference. Carey, drawing on Norbert Wiener, the inventor of cybernetics, credits the telegraph with the critical shift to the economy of signals.[101] Wiener himself specifically notes that signals received the "first reasonably scientific treatment at the hands of Lord Kelvin, after the failure of the first transatlantic cable."[102] Wiener's treatise on computing declares that it was the effort to reproduce *signals* that defines the contemporary age of cybernetics.[103] Wiener's signals are diverse: "the tap of a key to be reproduced as the tap of a telegraph receiver at the other end; or it may be a sound transmitted and received through the apparatus of a telephone; or it may be the turn of a ship's wheel, received as the angular position of the rudder."[104] Wiener's signals are a mode of communication that has less to do with representing ideas or referring to words and more to do with the demands and management of machines. The agents that determine the form of the signals are as much the telegraph keys as their so-called operators, as much the faulty wires that disconnect as often as they connect, as much the arbitrary Vs that mark reestablished connection or repeat and repeat and repeat without response. Here, if meaning comes into view, it insists without consisting of anything in particular. Di-di-di-dah.

An infrastructural approach refuses the stark separation of medium and meaning and—contra Saussure—between articulation and the logic of the sign. This infrastructuralism is oriented by Karen Barad's materialist feminism, which urges us to reject "the ontological distinction between representations and that which they purport to represent; in particular, that which is represented is held to be independent of all practices of representing."[105] Barad's rejection of representationalism is not an argument that we have perfect access to the world itself through our representations of it. Rather, she rejects the supposition that haunts Saussure and later diverse iterations of representational logic: that while we don't have perfect access to the world (we can't fully know the world), we somehow have perfect access to our representations of it (we can know what we think about the world and certainly what we mean when we say something about the world).[106]

It is quite a shift to refuse priority to symbolic structures, which make the systems of meaning in which we live, since those structures are where human agency often seems to matter most. An infrastructural approach insists that running alongside and against our attempts to communicate meaning is matter, recognized as "an active participant in the world's becoming."[107] Turning from representationalism to infrastructuralism facilitates attention to both the ways US Americans made the telegraph mean something important *and* the ways telegraph networks shifted how meaning could (and could not) be made in the first place. The best way to see what happened in 1858 through the murky depths of history, failed promises, ocean water, and a nation fervently fantasizing about progress and prominence is not to look back and forth between words and referents, between medium and message, or to insist that these elements are simply one and the same but to lift the infrastructure into view to examine the emerging relationships of religiously charged connection and disconnection *among* these elements.

Infrastructuralism restructures what Saussure posits as the foundation of communication. We are not looking at signs, in which we find a representational logic that exempts the sign from the impact of its articulation. Nor can we understand language as a system barred on all sides from the real; semantics are already charged by and bound up in the real. Barad puts it this way: "The primary semantic units are not 'words' but material-discursive practices through which (ontic and semantic) boundaries are constituted."[108] Language is not signs but practices—an assemblage of meaning and speech, affect and electricity, code and the fingers tapping it out, the lines of connection and the ruptures that run through them. Telegraphy played in a communicative territory with broad nineteenth-century boundaries that included linguistic exchange, transportation, and more intimate relationship (the *Oxford English Dictionary* demonstrates the overlaps: sex was then referred to as communication, and intercourse was what we now call discussion). It behooves us to think about the telegraph in these material-discursive terms; only thus can we make sense of the deep relationship forged between meaningless electrical pulses and the investment of transcendent significance.

In other words, the original communication networks were expansive in scale *and scope*, reaching deep into the ocean and up to the heavens and involving elements ranging from an electron to a world made whole. A great number of the questions asked by people sorting through the failure of the 1858 cable reached into the wide territory of material and cultural practice. While much of the Joint Committee's investigation focused on the cable and its faulty wire and failed insulation, figuring out what happened took the discussion through detailed examinations of wire composition, gutta-percha, the effect of temperature on cable transmissions, and testing apparatus to topics that, at first glance, appear to exceed the mandate of the investigation. Those who provided evidence to the committee discussed weather, financial management, the navigability of rockbound bays, diplomatic relations, and the reach of arctic ice. Detailed reports were given on the quality of ocean sand and microscopic marine life. The Joint Committee's assessment of the failure of the Red Sea cable was that it was largely a failure in taking the expansive context into account: "We consider that the failure of this line is attributable to the cable having been designed without regard to the conditions of the climate or the character of the bottom of the sea over which it had to be laid."[109] Environments mattered to why cables failed and if others were feasible.

Environments were not simply geographic or biological. Colonel Shaffner, in answer to a question about the effects of a marine current on his boat, offered a short analysis of the religious life of the Inuit Greenlanders he encountered: "I may state that the inhabitants of Greenland are nearly all Esquimaux excepting the Government officials at Julianshaab. . . . The Esquimaux are civilized and under religious cultivation. They attend church, and many of them I saw reading their psalms and hymns in church, and we heard some preaching from the Esquimaux."[110] Shaffner, and presumably the Joint Committee that heard his testimony, understood this colonial Christianity to be among the Atlantic Telegraph Cable's requirements—part of the environment necessary to guarantee its safety and success. The wide-ranging evidence in the report signals that material, cultural, and linguistic practices were all integral to attempts to lay and maintain telegraph lines and that such expansiveness was obvious to the people involved in the venture. Shaffner's testimony, which went on to include his broad characterization of the people of Iceland as well, illustrates this point clearly: "Everybody knows, of course, the state of intelligence of the people of Iceland, as being rather superior than otherwise. They are very good people. . . . I have taken all the precautions that I possibly could to investigate the character of the people, their habits, the cost of labour, and the probability of maintaining the line after it is down."[111] The factors involved in oceanic telegraphic communication were myriad, from grains of sand to Christian colonization of Inuits (Kalaallit) in Greenland.

Thus the *V, V, V* was indeed a stutter, in the sense offered by rhetoricians Joshua Gunn and Jenny Edbauer Rice: "The stutter can be heard as an over-exposure of speech. It is an entanglement between body and language."[112] In this case, the entanglement reached beyond the body of a speaker into bodies of telegraphers and engineers, bodies of water, rocky shores, floating ice, charges of electricity, one very fragile cable, and the religions that people lived out among these elements. These stuttering signals across the ocean were required for telegraphic speech and reflected a wide set of material-linguistic-cultural practices. In the *V*s, we see the agency of infrastructural media to restructure language, redefine what could be said and how, and inaugurate a particular necessity for the letter as meaningful speech in the absence of referentiality. That is, telegraphic speech demanded *this* articulation of the entanglement of media and meaning. While the link between the *V* in Morse code and Beethoven's Fifth has been often pondered but never proved, here their coincidence is quite close: the di-di-di-dah begins in silence and inaugurates a symphony of sound that insists on, but does not consist of, meaning.

* * *

It was the religious affiliations between the cable and a divine connected world that brought tears to the eyes of sea-hardy sailors, called for prayer after technological achievement, provoked Captain Hudson's emotive paean, and motivated his public Christian declaration to be projected on the Mechanics Bank in New York City *before any message could be sent on the cable.*[113] The cable had not yet technically succeeded (it was, in fact, probably broken and held together only by its insulation), nor would it ultimately last; but the power of religious affects and imaginaries was already calling into being a powerful (if largely fictional) world of pure connection, united community, and frictionless communication.

For the people involved in the venture directly, and for most US Americans expectantly waiting for word of the venture's outcome, simple signaling fell far short of the success of the cable. As the wait for the queen's message endured, the telegraph operators at the Newfoundland landing sent daily messages to New York, assuring the cable's perfection and citing the signals that successfully shuttled across its length. Signals alone, however, were not enough to assuage mounting anxiety that the cable could not transmit messages. This concern illustrates the significant difference between signals and messages and that the public standard of the success of the cable truly rested on the latter:

> These assurances aroused a new suspicion in the public mind. The Cable, men said, might have been safely laid, signals might be received hourly through its entire length, the operation of the electric current might remain unimpeded,—but could messages be sent through it? The question was one that no one answered: nor did the electricians in charge at Trinity Bay vouchsafe the explanation that would have set doubts at rest. Days passed, and yet the promised Message from Her Majesty did not appear. Intense anxiety began to prevail. The doubting part of the public renewed their prophecies of evil. Success was still far from positive certainty,— when suddenly, in the afternoon of Monday, August 16, the tidings reached New York from Newfoundland, that the Queen's Message was received.[114]

The message that came through was partial, and it was not until the following day that the full message was transmitted. Only this could serve as the sign of success: "The wires had ceased to work when the introductory paragraph was dispatched, but the mistake was rectified, the message transmitted entire, and the anxiety of the public was allayed,— for the cable was a working instrument—an accomplished fact."[115]

But even in the context of the cable's precariousness, widespread doubt over its ultimate success, and the inability of the cable to transmit more than mere signals for the first twenty days after its midocean splice, the signals meant a great deal. These signals bore the religiously charged imaginary and all of its powerful attendant sentiment; because of religion's power to forge meanings through affectively charged affiliations, these signals were both meaningless and profoundly meaningful.

The telegraph cable that would unite the world produced very little conversation. Pulses of electricity opened Beethoven's Fifth again and again without ever playing much more than that. But the insistent *Vs* of this infrastructural signaling established protocols for communication outside the terms of representation; the infrastructural medium, not the meaning of content, was what mattered. It mattered in religious terms to the idea of the United States and the idea of the world: the medium was the mission. Infrastructure's capacious scope of scale—from global network to dots and dashes—and vital mix of matter and discourse open room to consider the cultural techniques of religion that undergird networks and their logistical power. Missionaries and their media, public protestantism, cables, code, and utopian imaginaries wove a web that organized space and time to produce a nation, a world, a present, and a future that we would come to know as a network.

Even as networks have taken more intangible (but nevertheless persistently material) forms, the rituals of signaling to negotiate connection and disconnection have remained integral. Networks have come to embody religiously fueled imaginaries of global connection by making use of and obscuring the disconnections that compose them. As we look to more contemporary forms of networks, signals of disconnection persist. Nearly fifty years after the *Vs* stuttered across the first Atlantic cable, Guglielmo Marconi sent the first long-distance wireless telegraph message from Poldhu, England, to the steamship *Philadelphia* as it traveled west, successfully transmitting messages up to 1,551.5 miles. The last message received before the signal failed was, "All in order. S. S. S. S. S. S. S. Do you understand?"[116] The *Vs*, the *Ss*, and all the many disconnections that constituted the first communication networks were not overcome; they were more deeply woven into how networks worked and thus became more fundamental and more invisible.

The telegraph offers a unique site at the nineteenth-century origins of networks to examine network culture as it came into being. At this originary moment, the telegraph, itself a potent illusion of coherence and singularity, helped produce the now widely held imaginary of networks as primarily connective media. Fueled by religious affect, shaped by religious tropes, undergirded by religious logic, and built for religious ends, the original networks were imagined to connect in *Christian* terms. Now understood in terms largely devoid of religion, networks still bear the imaginary that religion—especially US public protestantism—produced: the proximate utopia of a world connected by friction-free, speedy, ubiquitous communication technology. The novel form of globalization that the first networks helped create through the deep influence of religion celebrated connection while disavowing the disconnections that sustained it. We are still living in this condition of globalization, organized around network logic and its narratives of progress, utopia, US national identity, and global unity. And the fractures and failures foundational to this form of globalization and its media still regularly appear as if they somehow contradict the networks that undergird it all.

Epilogue

Network Resonance

This is, in the end, a book written *about* a time when public celebrations of communication technology were underwritten by a fervent belief that more communication would lead to better living—specifically, more unity, more peace, more (and more fully realized) Christianity. It is also a book written *at* a time when more communication has appeared to have the opposite effect, when the deluge of tweets from our forty-fifth president has led to exclusion in its most vicious forms, nationalism in its most fascist expression, profound ruptures in global relationships, and waves and waves of violence. The techno-utopianism that greeted the advents of the telegraph and the internet have given way to a much more cynical view of our deep entanglements with technology: apocalyptic destruction rather than apocalyptic salvation.

The imaginaries of salvific networks in the nineteenth century and of destructive networks in the twenty-first, however, are not separate. In many ways the telegraph system is the foundation of the internet: the cable technology is strikingly similar, the submarine telegraph pathways largely became the pathways of submarine internet cables, and the imaginaries of network connection as salvation never quite fizzled out, nor have they entirely lost their religious charge. And yet there are important disconnections to consider that prevent any illusion of identicalness or neat linear causality. The telegraph is one of the few communication systems to be formally obsolete, it never truly served as communication for the masses, its net was woven more loosely than the internet would be, and religion's explicit empowerment of the telegraph gave way to far more implicit forms in the internet.[1] Just as the matter, sociality, imagination, and communication of networks are all constituted by the entanglement of connection and disconnection, so are the resonances between then and now. Some aspects of US protestant network imaginaries persist, and some have slipped away, buried under new extensive networks of fiber-optic cables.

This brief epilogue cannot fully address the relationship between the original and contemporary networks; doing that well would require its own book. Yet I aim here to sketch out a possible characterization of that relationship that will make the relevance of this historical study for contemporary critical cultural scholarship clear and invite further inquiry into this particular genealogy.

Noting the important continuities between the telegraph network and the internet foregrounds some of the defining (although often obscured) elements of internet technology. In the early life of the internet, coaxial cables and the fiber-optic cables that followed were built on top of the telegraph network, using its marine and terrestrial routes and landing at the same points.[2] Digital media scholar Nicole Starosielski's compelling correction of popular understandings of internet infrastructure echoes the salient elements of networks at their nineteenth-century origins: "It is wired rather than wireless; semicentralized rather than distributed; territorially entrenched rather than deterritorialized; precarious rather than resilient; and rural and aquatic rather than urban."[3] Which is to say, both the telegraph and the internet are networks hailed through imaginaries that deny some of the most basic elements of their functioning. The telegraph network, like its contemporary counterpart, was imagined to be global, ubiquitous, permanent, and connective of the primary power centers of Europe and the emerging United States. And while the telegraph network was not imagined to be wireless until the tail end of the nineteenth century, it certainly was imagined through immaterial, even ethereal, forms.

Today, these imaginaries of networks give power and purchase to the ideas that media are speedy, ubiquitous, and immediate and that they are these things especially now. As this book has demonstrated, however, these are rather old ideas about networks that originally appeared through protestant discourses, affects, and practices of global connection. Then and now, these imaginaries of the universality and friction-free nature of network media mask how networks participate in irregular configurations of space that trade in forms of localism to produce the very globalism they appear to create. This was true of the telegraph and the telephone, and it remains true of the internet.[4]

The production of localism in the internet often surprises, particularly in an era in which we increasingly imagine digital media through their most disembodied forms: satellites, Wi-Fi, cell signals, and cloud computing. But the turns to wireless and satellite technologies have actually necessitated more wires; cabled networks have a greater capacity for traffic than their wireless counterparts, and wireless technologies cannot function without cabled support.[5] Wires bear particular geographies and necessitate protocols with very material geopolitics. As of 2014, the undersea network of the internet that extends from the United States takes shape as only forty-five cables that emerge from fewer than twenty small areas.[6] As of 2020, the root servers that translate the text of website names to IP addresses are operated by twelve corporations, nine of which are headquartered in the United States.[7] The highly localized, material form of the internet belies the fizzling imaginaries of expansive, disembodied, ubiquitous global connection.

As Starosielski cautions, "Analyses of twenty-first-century media culture have been characterized by a cultural imagination of dematerialization: immaterial information flows appear to make the environments they extend through fluid and matter less."[8] But these environments do matter, of course; they matter for the geopolitics they enforce, for the localities they produce and disrupt, and, of most interest to this study, for the precariousness they create as part of networks.[9] It is because of the fragility of network media—often stemming from their materiality and embeddedness in very material environments—that they require constant monitoring and survive only through regular upkeep and repair.

Which is to say, just like the telegraph that formed the origins of cabled networks, the internet is constituted through various forms of disconnection, and its narratives of connection are, as Starosielski so incisively names it, "speculative fiction."[10] Only once we begin to pay attention to the activity of disconnection in networks can we recognize how much failure and the resulting labor of repair are integral to their functioning. Stephen Graham and Nigel Thrift identify this as an "entropic tendency" of modern systems.[11] For them, "the problem with contemporary social theory is that it has predominantly theorized connection and assembly. But, as we have seen, there are good reasons to think that, in the overall scheme of things, disconnection and disassembly are just as important in that they resist entities' means of enacting themselves: failure is key."[12] This book has taken up their call to analyze failure, while arguing something slightly different with respect to network infrastructure: that failure is key not because it resists networks' self-enactment but because failure is integral to networks coming into being. *Failure is part of how networks work.* The legacy of religion at stake here is a durable imaginary of connection that has obscured the important activity of disconnection in constituting network media and the cultures they participate in.

The refusal to acknowledge disconnection as part of networks leads to technological and social practices that feed the omnivorous appetite of connection as such: every element that falls outside the purview of the network must be integrated into the broader structure. Network theorist Ulises A. Mejias terms this "nodocentrism," in which only nodes already suited to the logic of the network are visible and legible. The consequence of nodocentrism is the exclusion of whatever does not register as a node, effectively excluding from recognizable existence anything that breaks from network logic.[13] Our reliance on networks not only as a metaphor but also as a model for social organization makes it especially difficult to articulate critical positions against this logic, trapping us in a fundamental paradox of network culture: "Networks are designed to attract participation, but the more we participate in them, the more inequality and disparity they produce."[14] Looking to the continuities between the origins of network culture—when the deep ties between network technology and specific forms of cultural dominance and exclusion were clear—and its present-day manifestations can aid in opening possibilities for a critical outside to the hegemony of network logic, particularly the unquestioned celebration of connection as inherently good.

However, there is no uninterrupted continuity between contemporary manifestations of network culture in the internet and its origins in the telegraph. Nor should the telegraph be considered a "Victorian internet" that provided mass access to a multinodal communication infrastructure—unlike the internet, the telegraph was mediated by human operators, its nodes were centers for transmission (not users' homes, places of work, or handheld devices), and it did not come close to providing popular service until 1910.[15] Despite the similarities in cable and infrastructure design, new developments in internet network layout and landing spots shifted in the 1990s away from routes that had persisted since the telegraph.[16] Which is all to say that the lineage from then until now is also a story of disconnection and should not be read as one propelled by the momentum of success. It would not do to forget that the cable at the heart of this book—the Atlantic cable of 1858—still lies broken at the bottom of the sea: "Attempts [were] made to repair the cable, but the decay from rust of the outer covering, which . . . consists of strands of very fine wires, has prevented the cable being raised without breaking."[17]

Nor is the lineage from the original cabled networks of the telegraph to the internet one of smooth lines of easy temporal translation. To put it mildly, much has changed. Most important, the role of public protestantism has shifted significantly, from a convention of public life in the nineteenth century to a contemporary source of rather heated contestation. This is not to say that protestantism, in all its lower-case pervasiveness, is not still powerful—not only are US evangelicals significant determinants of mainstream culture, but the United States continues to prioritize modes of subjectivity that affirm protestant commitments to individual authority, voluntarism, textuality, and belief.[18] Rather, it is to say that the powerful ways protestantism shaped networks in the nineteenth century still act on the imaginaries, inhabitations, and uses of networks today, but not so overtly and not without disjuncture, resistance, and creative reinterpretation.

How, then, might we productively name the relationship between network imaginaries then and now in a way that rigorously considers the interplay of continuity and discontinuity? How might we frame the durable influence of religiously empowered attention to connection as networks' defining characteristic? It is not that religion persists on its own or that it bears some sort of permanent original power. Rather, certain aspects of religion at the origins of networks seem to be amplified today without obvious cause. The relationship is not a straight line, not a clear echo, not unbroken influence, but something more like vibrational agreement.

Resonance is the principle in physics that describes when the external force or vibrations of one system cause another system to oscillate, such as striking a bell so that it rings. Resonance occurs when the first system causes the second system to oscillate at a relative maximum. The singer hits a note just so and thus breaks a glass. Sometimes, however, the oscillation in the second system diminishes or decays, such as the dissatisfying effect of pushing a kid in a swing out of rhythm with the swing. Rather than amplify the second system (the swing), the first system (the pusher) dampens the movement (to the kid's inevitable dismay).

Resonance offers a strategy to name the elements of network imaginaries that were birthed in powerful forms in the nineteenth century and are amplified in network culture today. These would include the "authentic" self-expression that was a mainstay of the emotive performances of revival Protestantism and has become a conventional mode of social media posts. The amplification of such emotive individualism has led to a valuing of singular experience such that ardently expressed personal commitments take precedence over collective action.[19] Likewise, the fervent if paradoxical attention to media as a form of immediacy has profoundly characterized the Bible for Protestants as a "direct link" to God and now resonates in the imaginaries of immediacy that characterize the plethora of media that constitute contemporary digital culture.

These amplifications are entangled with the damping of key elements of networks. While the nineteenth century was rife with new religious movements, they largely identified with Protestantism in its alignment with the establishment of hegemonic US public culture. The contemporary religious scene in the United States is marked by a significant decrease in institutional affiliations in religious identities and the growth of populations who identify with no religion or as "spiritual but not religious." Moreover, the rhetorical convention of Protestant tropes in public discourse now is shifting significantly. For example, the early 2020 Democratic primary race included two candidates whose religious lives have been deeply shaped by new religious movements in the United States, neither one of which is Christian. Tulsi Gabbard long identified with the Science of Identity Foundation, an offshoot of the Hare Krishna movement, before identifying as Hindu. Maryanne Williamson made her fame with a series of self-help books and courses based on a key New Age text, *A Course in Miracles*. One of the leading candidates, Bernie Sanders, was Jewish. None of these candidates faced the kind of religious scrutiny that was commonplace just eight years prior, in 2012, for Mitt Romney (a member of the Church of Jesus Christ of Latter-day Saints) or Barack Obama (a member of a Christian church that professed Black liberation theology and a target of islamophobic criticism based on spurious claims that he was Muslim).

In addition, key elements of prevailing network imaginaries have lost their salience, particularly the promise of global unity. As nativist populism rises around the world and as the exact cost such "unity" would entail becomes explicit, this imaginary feels both less believable to a wide range of political positions and less desirable to many of them. Wrestling with diversity, accountability for historical and contemporary demands of assimilation, and new efforts to protect difference against increasingly violent procedures in the United States (e.g., mass incarceration of black US Americans and mass detention of especially Latinx immigrants) have shifted into a place of priority as models of similitude and connection are met with increased cynicism.

Last, widespread public celebrations of infrastructure as a public spectacle have not just fallen by the wayside; it is now commonplace to think of large-scale infrastructure through its *invisibility*. Gone are the days of massive parades for a telegraph line; now fiber-optic lines are built without fanfare, and, in fact, the prevailing popular sense that the internet runs in the ether obscures the existence of an actual cabled network.

Resonance offers a framework for considering the interplay of these continuities and discontinuities. Doing so highlights some important elements of contemporary digital imaginaries that can easily be obscured without a strong sense of the critical involvement of religion in what so often appears to be an inherently secular technological form. Attention to the religion at the origins of networks demonstrates that many of the defining elements of "the digital age" are old and thus that the attributes it emphasizes (such as connection, speed, ubiquity, and immediacy) are not contemporary technological affordances but the effects of a habituated set of cultural practices. Through these practices we use network technology riddled with disconnections, textured by diverse temporalities, productive of uneven, localized geographies, and marked by all sorts of intense mediation, and we *experience* networks as connective, fast, widespread, and friction-free. That is, our experience of the network is determined by imaginative action, cultivated through religious techniques, and constituted by practices that are, in fact, quite divergent from the reality they appear to produce. Contemporary pairings of connective network imaginaries with disconnective network configurations resonate with their historical, religiously empowered predecessors, which shows that these habits of imagining networks have been amplified by religiously charged affective investment, still fizzling away.

These resonances demand that we become accountable for contemporary network imaginaries and their lived effects, particularly by highlighting the way digital imaginaries remain shaped by their modern roots. Examining the old roots of new imaginaries can remind us of many things—that the desired universality of networks was built through the specificity of protestantism, that claims of ubiquity entail their own exclusions, that declarations of instantaneity are constructed through uneven refigurations of time, and that celebrations of immediacy mask the geopolitics of material infrastructure. And, significantly, they remind us that our singular attention to connection obscures the gaps that constitute any network. The gaps—the sites of failure, breakdown, and disconnection—are not just vital to network functioning; they are key resources for creative politics that seek new possibilities for social and material life outside the hegemonic demands of network logic.

ACKNOWLEDGMENTS

This may be a book about disconnection, but the writing of it has been a study in the generativity of connections in their most enduring and meaningful forms. First and foremost, I offer fullhearted gratitude to Randall Styers, who has mentored me for nearly twenty years and whose guidance, challenge, deep care, and astoundingly thoughtful scholarship opened the possibility of this work in the first place. Any good in these pages stems from his unfathomable generosity. Randall has given me a capacious sense of what I can do, modeled the best ways to do it, and let me in on the magical secret of enjoying it all. I very simply would not be here without him.

Much of this book is indebted to the extraordinary graduate education I received at the University of North Carolina at Chapel Hill, particularly the insights offered by Jason Bivins, Jonathan Boyarin, Gregory Flaxman, Lawrence Grossberg, Richard Langston, Christian Lundberg, Laurie Maffly-Kipp, Todd Ochoa, Sarah Sharma (whose seminar birthed this project and led to my love of media beyond content), and Grant Wacker. I remain profoundly thankful to have studied with such smart and generous scholars who, in their work and their being, represent the very best of scholarship. Swarthmore College taught me the true joy of throwing oneself into writing, with special thanks for the enduring patience of Steven Hopkins, Tamsin Lorraine, Ellen Ross, Donald Swearer, and Mark Wallace.

Every page here has passed through more hands than I can count. Its earliest iteration was shaped by the UNC American Religions Colloquium and the UNC Religious Studies Writing Group. I am grateful for the incisive feedback and kind companionship of many at UNC, including Andrew Aghapour, Brandon Bayne, Kate Bowler, Brandi Denison, John-Charles Duffy, Carrie Duncan, Kathleen Foody, Stephanie Gaskill, Megan Goodwin, Annie Hardison-Moody, Shannon Harvey, Matthew Hotham, Ilyse Morgenstein Fuerst, Jill Peterfeso, Shannon Schorey, Tehseen Thaver, Stanley Thayne, and Alia Wegner.

Among the many delights of working at the University of Iowa has been the staggering generosity of my colleagues here. The Departments of Religious Studies and Communication Studies have faithfully cheered me on, and I am grateful to count myself among such esteemed scholars. The Project on the Rhetoric of Inquiry is a model of what a workshop should be, and the Department of Religious Studies Colloquium gave new life to chapter 1. The true camaraderie of the Friday-morning writing group, whose members' steady practice has made my own writing seem possible, has been an invaluable gift. I thank Prairie Lights, beloved bookstore, whose café allows us to push tables together so that we all have room to write. I am especially thankful for the keen insights and welcome friendship of Anna Blaedel, Diana Cates, E Cram, Melissa Curley, Brian Ekdale, Ahmed Elkhaldy, Natalie Fixmer-Oraiz, Robert Gerstmeyer, Naomi Greyser, Jiyeon Kang, John Kennedy, Rachel McLaren, Sylvia Mikucki-Enyart, Thomas Oates, Morten Schlütter, Tyler Snelling, David Supp-Montgomerie, Melissa Tully, Travis Vogel, and Tyler Williams. Raymond Mentzer deserves special thanks for reading much of this text—far more than was right to ask of him—and offering a formal response. I owe a tremendous debt to Joy Hayes, my compatriot in media history, who reminded me of this book's deep roots in Canadian media theory. I am deeply grateful to Kembrew McLeod and Kristy Nabhan-Warren, who not only read the entire manuscript but were able to see where it could go before I could.

My thinking has been deeply shaped by my work with wonderful graduate students at the University of Iowa, particularly the doctoral students I have had the honor of advising: Gavin Feller, Lin Sun, and Emma Rifai. This book has benefited from the vast talents of four exceptional research assistants: Michelle Flood, Kaitlyn Lindgren-Hansen, Marija Pritchard, and Emma Rifai.

The work on failure in these pages is indebted to a pop-up virtual reading group, which comprised Melissa Curley, M. Gail Hamner, Randall Johnson, Jiyeon Kang, and Iva Patel and was itself a success despite its topic.

John Durham Peters and Jeremy Stolow are cherished colleagues who have created the scholarship that inspires my approach to religion as media and have read this work with unparalleled clarity and kindness. Lisa Gitelman read the manuscript with astounding compassion and gave me the gift of exactly the feedback I needed in exactly the way I could hear it. Her scholarship provides the orientation for my approach to *the* telegraph and has been an extraordinarily generative model for work that is both deeply historical and meaningfully theoretical.

My research has been generously supported by the University of Iowa and my two departmental homes in Religious Studies and Communication Studies; the Iowa Center for Research by Undergraduates; the Digital Bridges Summer Institute and the Andrew W. Mellon Foundation; Get Digital with Your Scholarship and the Digital Humanities Studio at the University of Iowa; and the Caroline H. and Thomas S. Royster Fellowship at UNC–Chapel Hill. The Perry Family Research Award from the Department of Religious Studies at UNC–Chapel Hill and International Programs and the Stanley-UI Foundation Support Organization at the University of Iowa made presenting chapters of this work possible.

I have been extremely fortunate to receive support from organizations that offered funding alongside the indispensable help of astute readers. Members of the Social Science Research Council Religion and International Affairs Dissertation Workshop shaped an early version of this project, particularly Scott Appleby, Letitia Campbell, Ebrahim Moosa, and Danilyn Rutherford. For true pleasure in the academic life, one should write for an afternoon at the Obermann Center for Advanced Studies. To have the honor of being a fellow-in-residence provided the additional gift of an interdisciplinary community made up of Mariola Espinosa, Lisa Heineman, Jason Radley, Catherine Stewart, and the inimitable Teresa Mangum. I am deeply grateful to the Obermann Center staff, who have created the ideal space to think and write in slippers: Erin Hackathorn, Jenna Hammerich, and Jennifer New.

The Public Religion and Public Scholarship in the Digital Age Working Group, generously funded by the Henry Luce Foundation and hosted by the Center for Media, Religion, and Culture at the University of Colorado Boulder, has afforded me the inestimable gift of being in true intellectual community for over five years with a singular group of scholars of religion and media. My deep thanks to Sarah Banet-Weiser, Anthea Butler, Nabil Echchaibi (who also generously helped with names in Arabic), Christopher Helland, Stewart M. Hoover, Marwan Kraidy, Mirca Madianou, Peter Manseau, Nathan Schneider, Sarah McFarland Taylor, and Deborah Whitehead, all of whom have profoundly shaped this book and supported me through the twists and turns of my early career. Stewart Hoover has cultivated the field of religion and media to have the rare gift of plenty of room for all approaches, and I treasure his generous mentoring of me.

This manuscript is marked by the expertise and guidance of a number of curators and librarians, including Amy Chen and Ericka Raber at the University of Iowa; Ali Houissa at Cornell University; Pauline Caputi of the Oneida Community Mansion House; Abigail Lawton and Tony Wonderley, curators at the Oneida Community Mansion House; the librarians of the Oneida Community Collection at the Syracuse University Library; and Robert Dalton, librarian at the University of North Carolina. Special thanks to Aron Aji, who not only provided help with Turkish transliteration but generously walked me through the politics of such a venture. This project is indebted to Bill Burns, who not only has created an exceptionally rich collection of materials and artifacts related to the Atlantic cables and has made many of these materials available online but also graciously opened his home to me and spent hours guiding me through his impressive archive. He has shared a wealth of information, images, and insight.

I have had the unparalleled fortune of working with Jennifer Hammer at NYU Press, who has been unstinting in her responses to requests for guidance and feedback, including reading multiple versions of various parts of this manuscript. I am honored to be included in the North American Religions series and to have the support of three of the scholars I admire most in the field: Tracy Fessenden, Laura Levitt, and David Harrington Watt. Veronica Knutson of NYU Press provided answers to questions of minutiae with incredible speed and was kind enough to encourage me when I needed it most. May we all have the good fortune of working with a copy editor as meticulous as Andrew Katz. I am grateful beyond measure for the gracious, discerning, and thorough feedback of the two anonymous reviewers who offered the incomparable gift of impeccable advice.

Annie Alvarez, Jane Haxby (whose writerly talents saved me from panic and who also indexed this book), MC Hyland, Kate Leslie, Rachel McLaren, and Stacey Whitmire have made the academic life sweet. Mary-Jane Rubenstein's ability to see the heart of the matter made sense out of jumbled prose and gave this book a title that reflected its topic.

It has also anchored a sustaining and inspiring friendship for which I will always be grateful. It is impossibly dreamy to have left North Carolina only to find two of our closest friends from there—Natalie and V Fixmer-Oraiz—here. To Natalie I give my heartfelt thanks for a daily life happily shaped by bighearted support, sage advice, a strong moral compass, and unfathomable compassion.

I had the fortune of a childhood shaped by intellectual women: Bertha Supp Kister, Cara Kister, Deborah McKoy, Elizabeth McKoy, Judith McKoy, and Carol Roach. Josephine Ives earned her PhD in 1954 and is, as that might make clear, fearlessly true to herself. She was my mother's doctoral mentor and is, in a family forged by love, my grandmother. I have been buoyed the big embrace of the fabulous Montgomerie clan, who have been a constant source of love and humor. Above all, I thank my mother, Katrin Tiitsman, a true intellect, who read every word of more versions of this than I can count, encouraged every interest I ever developed, and equipped me with courage, fortitude, and love every step of the way.

My deepest source of joy is David Supp-Montgomerie and our children, Jonah and Siimo, both of whom were born while I wrote this and whose irrepressible wonder and creativity are what it is all about. David and I wrote side by side when the first draft of this book came into being, and words really and truly fail before the task of expressing the depth of my gratitude for who he is and everything he has done to make this book appear, to bolster me in its creation, and to make *this* astoundingly wonderful life a reality.

NOTES

PREFACE

1. G.W.N., "The World's Holiday," *Circular* 7, no. 29 (August 12, 1858): 114.
2. Peters, "Mormonism and Media," 1.

INTRODUCTION

1. John, *Network Nation*, 24.
2. Jones, "MCI TV Ad 1997." My thanks to Brian Ekdale for this reference.
3. Friedman, *World Is Flat*, 10.
4. Tsotsis, "RIAA Goes Offline."
5. "The medium was the mission" is, of course, a nod at McLuhan's aphorism "the medium is the message." McLuhan, *Understanding Media*, 7. The title of this book is also indebted to Carolyn Marvin's extraordinary book, *When Old Technologies Were New: Thinking about Electric Communication in the Late Nineteenth Century*, which inspired this project and served as a formidable model of media history.
6. This study takes up religion as a broad category. However, most of this book is about the alignments between US Protestantism, specifically, and telegraph technology. The establishment of Protestantism's cultural dominance in the United States emerged through the relationship it bore to network technology and social life, and its reigning power over public life at the time continues to matter to what networks have become.
7. Board of Trade and the Atlantic Telegraph Company, *Report of the Joint Committee*, ix.
8. "James Buchanan to Victoria," telegram, August 19, 1858, in Board of Trade and the Atlantic Telegraph Company, *Report of the Joint Committee*, 232.
9. Clark, "Our Great Trust," xiv.
10. G.W.N., "The World's Holiday," *Circular* 7, no. 29 (August 12, 1858): 114.
11. Kelley, *Oration Delivered by Hon. William D. Kelley*, 2.
12. Kelley, 8–11.
13. The violence riddling this "peaceful" world included the wars between the US Army and Native Americans in the 1850s—such as the Navajo War (1846–64), Cayuse War (1847–55), Apache Wars (1849–1924), California Indian Wars (1850–56), Battle of Ash Hollow (1855), Rogue River Wars (1855–56), Puget Sound War (1855–56), Third Seminole War (1855–58), Yakima War (1855–58), 1857 Cheyenne Expedition, Utah War (1857–58), Coeur d'Alene War (1858), and Fraser Canyon

War (1858)—and colonial conflicts such as the Xhosa War between the Xhosa and Europeans (1779–1879), Taiping Rebellion (1850–64), Second Anglo-Burmese War (1852), Crimean War (1853–56), French conquest of Senegal (1854–60), Anglo-Persian War (1856–57), Campaign of 1856–57 in Nicaragua and Costa Rica, Second Opium War (1856–60), Indian Rebellion of 1857, and Cochinchina Campaign (1858–62).

14. Gitelman, *Always Already New*, 10.
15. Starosielski, *Undersea Network*, 1–2.
16. Hoover, *Religion in the Media Age*, 9.
17. Stolow, "Religion and/as Media," 125.
18. Stolow, 125.
19. Barad, *Meeting the Universe Halfway*, esp. 23–33.
20. Sullivan, *Impossibility of Religious Freedom*, 8.
21. The small *p* emphasizes how this perspective has become a "set of political ideas and cultural practices" that exceed the bounds of church life. Sullivan, 8.
22. Lacan, *Triumph of Religion*, 66.
23. "James Buchanan to Victoria."
24. Leonard Bacon quoted in Anderson, *Memorial Volume*, 385.
25. For this definition of tactical, see Certeau, *Practice of Everyday Life*.
26. This list refers in part to Weiner, *Religion Out Loud*.
27. Latour, *Pandora's Hope*, 266–92.
28. Anderson, *Imagined Communities*; Eisenstein, "Emergence of Print Culture in the West."
29. Fessenden, *Culture and Redemption*.
30. Moore, "Religion, Secularization, and the Shaping of the Culture Industry in Antebellum America," 227; see also Modern, *Secularism in Antebellum America*; Morgan, *Lure of Images*.
31. Fessenden, *Culture and Redemption*.
32. Mahmood, "Can Secularism Be Other-Wise?"
33. Jakobsen and Pellegrini, "Introduction: Times Like These."
34. Kelley, *Oration Delivered by Hon. William D. Kelley*, 1–2.
35. Creighton, *Harold Adams Innis*; Marchand, *Marshall McLuhan*; Miller, *Lewis Mumford*; Soukup, "Contexts of Faith"; Carey, *Communication as Culture*, 13–36; Kittler, *Gramophone, Film, Typewriter*; Peters, *Speaking into the Air*, 268.
36. James Gamble, "Wiring a Continent," *Californian*, June 1881, 561.
37. For an excellent study of the westward expansion of the telegraph system, see Schwoch, *Wired into Nature*. A helpful discussion of the relationship of railroads to the reservation system can be found in Adas, *Dominance by Design*, 67–127.
38. Bowker and Star, *Sorting Things Out*, 16.
39. Bowker and Star, esp. 16–17.
40. Levine, *Forms*.
41. Otis, *Networking*.

42. See Lacan's theory of metaphor in Lacan, "Instance of the Letter," esp. 421–23, 429–31.

43. Annelise Riles identifies networks as an "aesthetic of information" particular to modernity. Here, to bring the social work of networks beyond transmission of information, I shift her term slightly. Riles, *Network Inside Out*, 2.

44. J.S.W., "A Quarter of the Century in Chicago," *Chicago Daily Press*, October 27, 1857, reprinted in *Lake Superior Miner* (Ontonagon, MI), January 16, 1858.

45. See Marvin, *When Old Technologies Were New*.

46. "An Aid to Nervousness," *Atlanta Constitution*, August 16, 1899.

47. Beard, *American Nervousness*. See also Longworth-Dunbar, *Increasing a Hundred-Fold the Distresses*, 37–40.

48. Longworth-Dunbar offers a rigorous cataloguing of such anxieties around telegraphy in *Increasing a Hundred-Fold the Distresses*.

49. A Non-Believer in the Telegraphic Millennium, letter to the editor, *New York Times*, August 24, 1858.

50. This book is rooted in a theory of language that contends that meaning is not made by words pointing to objects; meaning is made through the complex of contingent, fluxing, social affiliations that haunt any given word as it moves among contexts. According to Jacques Derrida, Jacques Lacan, and Paul Ricoeur, all language works through the mechanisms of metaphor, that is, through affiliation, not identity. This allows us to trace the emergence of the metaphor, "network," according to the multiple meanings that adhered to it in the nineteenth century before it was a word in popular use. These meanings—from religion-fueled dreams of global Christian conversion to the coherence of a young and fractured nation to the perfection of communication itself—accumulate and conglomerate around "network," coloring any use of the term. This approach to language also refuses us the fantasy that language works with precision. Network means different things to different groups in different moments, and different words come to stand in for it: "web," "chain," "girdle," "cable," "internet." Thus, this book tends toward expansive attention to salient themes as they emerge in context.

51. "Humors of the Day," *Harper's Weekly*, August 18, 1866.

52. J. D. Davis, "Our Present Responsibility," *Missionary Herald* 70, no. 4 (April 1874): 106–8; Samuel Morse "Letter from S. F. B. Morse to the Hon. F. O. J. Smith"; "James Buchanan to Victoria"; "Hymn," *Circular* 7, no. 32 (September 2, 1858): 127; Hardinge, *Modern American Spiritualism*.

53. Latour, *Reassembling the Social*, 5. While networks are defined by an associative principle throughout Latour's work, he draws attention to discontinuity at the end of *Reassembling the Social* (245). He claims discontinuities are inherent to any system in his later text *An Inquiry into Modes of Existence*, esp. 41–42.

54. Peter Gould goes so far as to say that geography itself relies on the principle of connection: "You cannot have a geography of anything that is unconnected. No connection, no geography. No connections means mere checklists without any relations between the items. . . . As human geographers, we have at the forefront of

our concern the way connections are made between peoples and places in all sorts of different spaces, and how these spaces are being constantly restructured and reshaped by the human presence." Gould, "Dynamic Structures of Geographic Space," 4.

55. In *The Network Inside Out*, Annelise Riles raises this important critique of the network as a dominant metaphor for communication and social organization: it forecloses an account of the fragmentation that is also always present in social relationships, which are riddled with enmity, gossip, jealousies, and miscommunications. Riles, *Network Inside Out*, 175–78.

56. Castells, *Rise of the Network Society*, 24.

57. Castells, 135, 161.

58. Graham and Thrift, "Out of Order," 5.

59. Graham and Thrift, 7.

60. Board of Trade and the Atlantic Telegraph Company, *Report of the Joint Committee*, v.

61. With particular thanks to members of the failure reading group, Melissa Curley, M. Gail Hamner, Randall Johnson, and Jiyeon Kang, for this framing.

62. Picker, "Atlantic Cable," 35.

63. Obach, *Cantor Lectures on Gutta Percha*, 102.

64. Peters, *Marvelous Clouds*, 37–38.

65. Edwards, "Infrastructure and Modernity," 189.

66. Edwards, 186.

67. McMillan, "Sharks Want to Bite Google's Undersea Cables."

68. Edwards, "Infrastructure and Modernity."

69. Wilson, "Infrastructure of Intimacy."

70. There is no quintessential or original version of the global network imaginary. As a lived enactment, the imaginary of a global telegraph network was never performed the same way twice. Yet many of the imaginaries produced around the Atlantic telegraph share key elements: communication technology would unify the world, this unified world would be Christian, unity would entail agreement and peace, and this unified world would culminate a progressive history ordained by God. These elements repeat like motifs in the diverse renditions of this imaginary. To identify this as an imaginary in the singular rather than imaginaries in the plural is a slight misnomer. The intention is only to indicate the important ways that distinct imaginaries of the world at the advent of the Atlantic telegraph held certain elements, commitments, and effects in common. These imaginaries bore a family resemblance and contributed to each other by substantiating and strengthening a diverse body of practices aimed toward a similar global whole. Each rendition that appears in this study is one aspect of a widespread and heterogeneous cultural habit.

71. This term comes from a body of literature in the field of public culture. See Anderson, *Imagined Communities*; Castoriadis, *Imaginary Institution of Society*; Gaonkar, "Toward New Imaginaries"; Taylor, *Modern Social Imaginaries*.

72. Gaonkar, "Toward New Imaginaries," 1.

73. Lawrence Grossberg offers the concept of a "mattering map," which is "a socially determined structure of affect which defines the things that do and can matter to those living within the map"; Grossberg, *We Gotta Get Out*, 398. The notion of affective investment is from Lundberg, *Lacan in Public*.
74. Peters, *Speaking into the Air*, 1.
75. Peters, 5.
76. For a rich discussion of cultural techniques, see Winthrop-Young, Iurascu, and Parikka, "Cultural Techniques."
77. Parks, *Cultures in Orbit*; Parks, "Technostruggles"; Parks and Starosielski, *Signal Traffic*; Peters, *Marvelous Clouds*; Starosielski, *Undersea Network*; Bowker and Star, *Sorting Things Out*; Edwards, "Infrastructure and Modernity"; Edwards et al., "Introduction."
78. Williams, *Keywords*; Williams, *Marxism and Literature*; Williams, *Technology*.
79. Leo Marx in his ominously titled article "Technology: The Emergence of a Hazardous Concept," suggests that US Americans in the late nineteenth century were struggling to understand the sweeping changes they were experiencing, from the ability to travel with unprecedented speed by rail to the ability to send messages that flew even faster by telegraph, the illumination of homes and streets by electricity, the amalgamation of science and industry, and the very prevalence and increasing dependency on all sorts of machines. US Americans got to a sort of breathless moment and asked how they had arrived at this strange new way of life. "Technology" appeared as a viable answer. In other words, for Marx, technology in its present sense did not actually have its own positive meaning; it didn't point to a thing in the world. Technology, rather, emerged out of a void, a vast and gaping question of how a culture arrived at itself. As an answer to that question, technology was necessarily vague (really, how does one answer that with just one word?) and acquisitive. Marx, "Technology."
80. The concept of intra-action is taken from Barad, "Posthumanist Performativity," 801–31.
81. Tyrrell, *Reforming the World*.
82. For example, President Buchanan's telegram to Queen Victoria on the Atlantic cable reveals his concerns that the telegraph cable itself would become a pawn in the ripe tensions that still sat between these recently separated nations: "that [the transatlantic cable] shall be forever neutral, and that its communications shall be held sacred in passing to the place of their destination." "James Buchanan to Victoria."
83. Board of Trade and the Atlantic Telegraph Company, *Report of the Joint Committee*, 230–37.
84. This concept of pedagogy is modeled on Sarah Ahmed's study of happiness. While this study does not focus on happiness per se, the allure of a universal happy future certainly grounds much of how we value globalization. Ahmed's work highlights the close relationships between promise, pedagogy, and demand. She argues that the promise of happiness teaches us what we should want and how we

should want it and directs us to a set of objects already deemed to be happy ones. Thus, the promise of happiness works by demanding that we be a certain kind of subject who wants certain objects in certain ways. This is a helpful model for understanding the demands this network imaginary makes on us. We must become the kinds of subjects who can live and thrive in the world we are imagining. Ahmed, *Promise of Happiness*.

85. Glover, "Atlantic Cables: 1856–2012."

CHAPTER 1. WHAT'S THE MATTER WITH NETWORKS?

1. Hamlin, *Among the Turks*, 185–94.
2. Emily Conroy-Krutz's study of the term "civilization" in US missionary literature from the nineteenth century includes agriculture, technology, patriarchal monogamy, literacy, and a gendered division of labor. Conroy-Krutz, *Christian Imperialism*, 14; see also Adas, *Dominance by Design*.
3. A robust account of the everyday in the "civilizing" efforts of missionaries can be found in Comaroff and Comaroff, *Of Revelation and Revolution*.
4. Mr. Hume quoted in Strong, *Story of the American Board*, 166.
5. Hamlin, *Among the Turks*, 354.
6. Veer, introduction to *Conversion to Modernities*, 4.
7. Adas, *Dominance by Design*, esp. 33–127.
8. Excellent and field-defining examples of scholarship on religion and colonialism include Asad, *Formations of the Secular*; Chidester, *Savage Systems*; King, *Orientalism and Religion*; Masuzawa, *Invention of World Religions*; Said, *Orientalism*; Styers, *Making Magic*. This work joins other recent texts that attend to media's place in the relationship of religion and empire, such as Klassen, *Story of Radio Mind*; Müller, *Wiring the World*.
9. Morse, "Bound Volume—18 May 1847–28 January 1848," 324–26; Bektas, "American Genius," 219.
10. Conroy-Krutz, *Christian Imperialism*, 3.
11. Davison, *Essays in Ottoman and Turkish History*, 133–65.
12. Strong, *Story of the American Board*, 80 (spelling as in original).
13. Curtis, "Charity Begins Abroad."
14. For a thorough account of the kinds of trouble that met US missionaries, see Salt, "Trouble Wherever They Went."
15. Phillips, *Protestant America*, 32.
16. Conroy-Krutz, *Christian Imperialism*, 3.
17. Conroy-Krutz, 5.
18. Hamlin, "Reasons for Prosecuting Missions in Turkey," *Missionary Herald* 76, no. 8 (August 1880): 295.
19. Presbyterian Church in the U.S.A., "Missions in the Levant: A General Survey," *Church at Home and Abroad* 6 (1889): 490–91.
20. The London Missionary Society commended US efforts in the Levant and noted the uniqueness of the US presence there. See "Missions in the Levant,"

Chronicle of the London Missionary Society, February 1890, 56; "The Field Is the World," *Chronicle of the London Missionary Society* 1, no. 2 (February 1892): 39.

21. Becker, *Revival and Awakening*, 29.
22. Hamlin, "Reasons for Prosecuting Missions in Turkey," 295.
23. Deringil, "The Invention of Tradition as Public Image in the Late Ottoman Empire," 21.
24. Deringil, "They Live in a State of Nomadism and Savagery," 311–12.
25. Deringil, "The Invention of Tradition as Public Image in the Late Ottoman Empire."
26. Hurewitz, *Middle East and North Africa*, 269.
27. Abu-Manneh, "Islamic Roots of the Gulhane Rescript."
28. Shahvar, "Tribes and Telegraphs in Lower Iraq."
29. Deringil, *Well-Protected Domains*, 39–42; Deringil, "They Live in a State of Nomadism and Savagery," 317.
30. Deringil, "They Live in a State of Nomadism and Savagery"; Shahvar, "Tribes and Telegraphs in Lower Iraq."
31. Low, "Ottoman Infrastructures of the Saudi Hydro-State."
32. Shahvar, "Tribes and Telegraphs in Lower Iraq," esp. 95–96.
33. Minawi, "Beyond Rhetoric."
34. Shahvar, "Iron Poles, Wooden Poles."
35. Strong, *Story of the American Board*, 326; Phillips, *Protestant America*, 63. This model was used in early missions to the Choctaw and Cherokee, based on a Moravian station in the Cherokee Nation. It was, however, ultimately rejected for international mission when it became clear that blacksmiths were less motivated than preachers to go abroad to win souls for Christ.
36. Strong, *Story of the American Board*, 327 (emphasis mine). Many members of the ABCFM considered preaching to be less successful in certain contexts than approaches that integrated direct evangelization with other kinds of cultural interactions and services. For example, by the early 1830s, the board's official policy for missions in the Mediterranean was to use education and conversational approaches over formal preaching. Phillips, *Protestant America*, 43.
37. Anderson, *Foreign Missions*, 96–98. For a discussion of Anderson's influence on the ABCFM, see Becker, *Revival and Awakening*, 16–18.
38. Nadis, *Wonder Shows*; Morus, *Frankenstein's Children*.
39. Delbourgo, *Most Amazing Scene of Wonders*.
40. "Constantinople: Extracts from the Journal of the Mission," *Missionary Herald* 33, no. 11 (November 1837): 447.
41. Additional examples of missionaries using demonstrations of electricity to spark Christian conversion are "Siam: Letter from Mr. Caswell, Bangkok, 1st July 1841," *Missionary Herald* 38, no. 4 (April 1842): 147–48; "Letter from Mr. Pohlman, December 18, 1847," *Missionary Herald* 44, no. 5 (June 1848): 205–10.

42. "South Seas: Extracts from the Journal of the 'John Williams' on Her Last Visit to the Islands of Western Polynesia," *Missionary Magazine and Chronicle* 28, no. 49 (January 1864): 7.

43. Samuel Ella, "The Pacific in 1795 and Now: Third Paper," *Chronicle of the London Missionary Society*, no. 33 (September 1894): 212.

44. Hamlin, *Among the Turks*, 199.

45. Bektas, "American Genius," 200.

46. Hamlin details these efforts in both of his monographs. Hamlin, *Among the Turks*; Hamlin, *My Life and Times*.

47. Hamlin, *Among the Turks*, 77.

48. Strong, *Story of the American Board*, 328.

49. Hamlin, *Among the Turks*, 58; Hamlin, *My Life and Times*, 212.

50. Hamlin, *My Life and Times*, 212.

51. Hamlin, *Among the Turks*, 354; Phillips, *Protestant America*, 303–4; Perkins, *Residence of Eight Years*, 295–96.

52. For more on performances of technology and their inspiration of awe and wonder, see Morus, *Frankenstein's Children*; Nadis, *Wonder Shows*.

53. Crain, "Children of Media, Children as Media," 66.

54. Wozniak, *Mind and Body*, 9–30.

55. The concept of intra-action is taken from Barad, "Posthumanist Performativity."

56. Marx, "Technology."

57. Hamlin, *Among the Turks*, 188.

58. Peters, "Religious Attitudes towards Modernization," 93.

59. Peters, 94.

60. Carey describes the transmission view in *Communication as Culture*, 13–36.

61. Wosh, *Spreading the Word*, 228–56; see also Nord, *Faith in Reading*.

62. Brown, *Word in the World*, 17.

63. Carey, *Communication as Culture*, 13–36.

64. Peters, *Marvelous Clouds*, 5.

65. Peters, 14.

66. Jessup, *Fifty Three Years in Syria*, 1:360–61.

67. Perkins, *Residence of Eight Years*, 296.

68. Carey, *Communication as Culture*, 201–30.

69. Barad, *Meeting the Universe Halfway*; Bennett, *Vibrant Matter*; Latour, *Reassembling the Social*; Latour, *Pandora's Hope*; see also Chen, *Animacies*; Deleuze and Guattari, *Thousand Plateaus*; Greyser, *On Sympathetic Grounds*; TallBear, *Native American DNA*; Tompkins, *Racial Indigestion*.

70. Judson Smith, "China and Christian Missions," *Missionary Herald* 77, no. 12 (December 1881): 490–91.

71. J. D. Davis, "The Early Difficulties and Present Opportunities in Mission Work in Japan," *Missionary Herald* 88, no. 4 (April 1892): 150.

72. Latour, *Reassembling the Social*, 71.

73. Bennett, *Vibrant Matter*, 23.

74. Marx, "Technology," 575–76.

75. Bennett, *Vibrant Matter*.

76. Davison, *Essays in Ottoman and Turkish History*, 133–65; Hamlin, *Among the Turks*, 185–94.

77. Frank E. Bailey, *British Policy and the Turkish Reform Movement: A Study in Anglo-Turkish Relations, 1826–1853* (Cambridge, 1942), 85 and 256, table 7, cited in Davison, *Essays in Ottoman and Turkish History*, 135.

78. Bektas, "Telegraph," 557; Davison, *Essays in Ottoman and Turkish History*, 133.

79. Hamlin, *Among the Turks*, 186.

80. Hamlin, 185–94.

81. Hamlin, 194.

82. Aksan, "Ottoman Military and Social Transformations," 74.

83. Bektas, "Sultan's Messenger," 673.

84. Bektas, 673.

85. Bright, *Submarine Telegraphs*, 21; see also Davison, *Essays in Ottoman and Turkish History*, 134.

86. Davison, *Essays in Ottoman and Turkish History*, 135. These lines were built by both the British and the French to protect interests in Crimea; Bektas, "Sultan's Messenger," 673.

87. Hamlin, *Among the Turks*, 194.

88. Bektas, "Sultan's Messenger," 675.

89. Bektas, 694; Davison, *Essays in Ottoman and Turkish History*, 147.

90. Jessup, *Fifty Three Years in Syria*, 2:438.

91. See, for example, Peters, "Religious Attitudes towards Modernization."

92. Bektas, "Sultan's Messenger," 694.

93. Echchaibi, "Islam, Mediation, and Technology," 441.

94. Bektas, "Sultan's Messenger," 696.

95. Bektas, 694; Minawi, "Beyond Rhetoric"; Shahvar, "Tribes and Telegraphs in Lower Iraq."

96. Davison, *Essays in Ottoman and Turkish History*, 145.

97. "Foreign," *London Examiner*, February 27, 1864.

98. A similar disjunction between imperial hopes for a binding network and telegraphic fragmentation occurred for the British Empire in India. See Headrick, "A Double-Edged Sword."

99. Davison, *Essays in Ottoman and Turkish History*, 156.

100. Bektas, "Telegraph," 558.

101. Louis Edgar Browne, "Coup by Allies Pens Up Turks in Dardanelles: Bold Stroke Cuts Off Line of Communication and Blocks Retreat of 100,000," *Chicago Tribune*, August 22, 1915.

102. Davison, *Essays in Ottoman and Turkish History*, 157.

103. Louis Edgar Browne, "Bloodless Revolution in Turkey Based on Demand for American Mandate and Enmity to British: Correspondent Who Was on Scene

Describes Dramatic Dispatch of Ultimatum to Sultan by Nationalist Leaders,"
St. Louis Post-Dispatch, October 19, 1919.

104. Kemal Atatürk, *Nutuk*, 13th printing (Istanbul, 1973), 1:399, quoted in Davison, *Essays in Ottoman and Turkish History*, 157.

105. Şapolyo, *Kemal Atatürk ve Milli Mücadele Tarihi*, 349.

106. Bektas, "Sultan's Messenger," 695–96; see also Davison, *Essays in Ottoman and Turkish History*, 156–59.

107. Latour, *Pandora's Hope*, 281.

108. Versions of such fragmentary causality include the mutual constitution of "intra-action" (Barad, *Meeting the Universe Halfway*, 33); "emergent" and "fractal" causality replacing "efficient" and "linear" causality (Bennett, *Vibrant Matter*, 33); and the revision of causal action to translation by mediators (Latour, *Pandora's Hope*, 178; Latour, *Reassembling the Social*, 46, 39, 58).

109. "Anniversary of the London Missionary Society: Seventy-Second General Meeting," *Missionary Magazine and Chronicle* 30, no. 78 (June 1866): 176.

110. Josiah Tyler, "Civilizing Alone Inadequate to Elevate Barbarians," *Missionary Herald* 79, no. 9 (September 1883): 334.

111. Judson Smith, "The Historical Argument for Christian Missions," *Missionary Herald* 80, no. 12 (December 1884): 488.

112. Parikka, "New Materialism as Media Theory," 98.

113. Parikka, 96.

114. Bennett, *Vibrant Matter*, 20.

115. George T. Washburn, "The Pasumalai Institutions, Southern India," *Missionary Herald* 80, no. 6 (June 1884): 215.

116. Hamlin's full account of the introduction of the telegraph to the Ottoman Empire can be found in Hamlin, *Among the Turks*.

117. Gitelman, "Modes and Codes," 123–24.

118. *Telegraphic Journal and Electrical Review* 5 (15 October 1877): 246–47, cited in Bektas, "Sultan's Messenger," 669.

119. Geyer and Bright, "World History in a Global Age," 1047.

120. One of the Secretaries of the American Tract Society, *Home Evangelization*, 142–43.

121. Appadurai, *Modernity at Large*, 1.

122. Hopkins, "Semi-centennial Discourse," 34.

123. American Board of Commissioners for Foreign Missions, "Annual Meeting of the Board," *Missionary Herald* 32, no. 11 (November 1836): 439.

124. "Annual Survey of the Missions of the Board," *Missionary Herald* 47, no. 1 (January 1851): 1.

125. Hopkins, "Semi-centennial Discourse," 16.

126. Hopkins, 34.

127. For excellent studies of the globalism of US Protestant mission in the nineteenth century, see Conroy-Krutz, *Christian Imperialism*; Tyrrell, *Reforming the World*.

128. American Board of Commissioners for Foreign Missions, "Annual Meeting of the Board," *Missionary Herald* 32, no. 11 (November 1836): 442.

129. Phillips, *Protestant America*, 266.
130. American Board of Commissioners for Foreign Missions, "Annual Meeting of the Board," *Missionary Herald* 32, no. 11 (November 1836): 439; American Board of Commissioners for Foreign Missions, "Annual Meeting," *Missionary Herald* 55, no. 11 (November 1859): 32; American Board of Commissioners for Foreign Missions, "Annual Meeting of the Board, Part 1," *Missionary Herald* 74, no. 11 (November 1878): 353; American Board of Commissioners for Foreign Missions, "Reports of Committees at the Annual Meeting," *Missionary Herald* 91, no. 12 (December 1895): 537. This was not true just for US missionaries; the powerful idea of the whole world on the brink of universal evangelization was significant for British missionaries as well. In his remarks to celebrate the fifty-year anniversary of the ABCFM, Mark Hopkins quoted the founding constitution of the London Missionary Society, which described the new missionary enterprise as the "greatest of all schemes—the evangelizing of the world." *The Founding Documents of the London Missionary Society* (1795), quoted in Hopkins, "Semi-centennial Discourse," 23. This shared goal provided an important common ground between the British and US missionary societies. When reporting on the forty-second anniversary of the British Church Missionary Society, the *Missionary Herald* assured its readership that the English missionaries and their patrons all bear "hearts . . . enlisted in the great work of converting the world to Christ." "Proceedings of Other Societies," *Missionary Herald* 38, no. 8 (August 1842): 343.
131. Within the context of the goal of universal Christianity, the ABCFM valued particular sites of mission as steps toward this expansive goal. In a paper read at the 1881 Annual Meeting of the Board, Judson Smith called for the conversion of China as "one of the most significant and decisive steps toward the evangelization of the whole world." He closed his remarks with a prayer in a similar vein: "And God grant to the young men . . . with a noble ambition to press forward to this work in such numbers and with such importunity that the majestic movements of God's providence and Spirit may only surpass the resistless march of the Christian host that arm themselves for the world's conquest to Christ." Smith, "China and Christian Missions," 486.
132. A. N. Hitchcock, "Congregationalism in Foreign Missions," *Missionary Herald* 93, no. 1 (January 1897): 13.
133. Simonson, "Assembly, Rhetoric, and Widespread Community."
134. For example, see "Go ye into all the world, and preach the Gospel to every creature" (Mark 16:15), quoted in American Board of Commissioners for Foreign Missions, "Annual Meeting," 321; Hitchcock, "Congregationalism in Foreign Missions," 13; "The earth shall be full of the knowledge of the Lord, as the waters cover the sea" (Habakkuk 2:14), quoted in Condit, "The Monthly Concert," *Missionary Herald* 65, no. 11 (November 1868): 373; American Board of Commissioners for Foreign Missions, "Annual Meeting of the Board, Part 1," 337; E. K. Alden, "Foreign Missions the Test of Christian Character," *Missionary Herald* 80, no. 11 (November 1884): 80.

135. Hopkins, "Semi-centennial Discourse," 23.
136. Founding documents of the London Missionary Society, quoted in Hopkins, 22–23.
137. Hamlin, *My Life and Times*, 97. Much of the Christian unity that Cyrus Hamlin celebrated in his writing can be traced to the revival culture that surrounded him at Bowdoin College. While at Bowdoin, Hamlin described occasions when the unity of various Christians in revivals and societies impacted his own religious formation and contributed to his path toward international mission. Hamlin, 97–116. Similarly, he described the ecumenical revival that took hold of prayer meetings in his junior year at Bowdoin and which he attributed in part to the influence of revivals that students had encountered when home. Hamlin, 103–16. Revival enthusiasm swept through US colleges and divinity schools in the first half of the nineteenth century and motivated many to commit their lives to missionary work. A secret fraternity called the Brethren developed at Andover from which more than two hundred candidates applied to the ABCFM. Phillips, *Protestant America*, 23. Among the Brethren's members was John Humphrey Noyes. He withdrew from the Andover Brethren in 1834, claiming that he had "embraced such doctrines as he thinks the Board would not wish to diffuse among the heathen." "Record Book of the Andover Brethren," 72, quoted in Phillips, 25. Noyes went to Yale, where he unsuccessfully attempted to start another chapter of the Brethren. Phillips, 25. The mark of Noyes's membership in the Brethren can be seen in elements he borrowed from their practice and instituted as part of the Oneida Community, such as the practice of "mutual criticism." Phillips, 28. For further discussion of the origins of mutual criticism, see John Humphrey Noyes, "Mutual Criticism," *Congregational Quarterly* 17, no. 2 (April 1875): 272–81. The ecumenical temperance movement, in which Hamlin played an enthusiastic role, also provides evidence for a theme of pan-Christian unity that he located on the righteous side of religious development. The transatlantic nature of these revivals helped to forge an improbable alliance between England and the United States. The revivals, which had roots in England, fueled missionary interest in the United States and a shared international evangelical project between the two nations. Phillips, *Protestant America*, 4–20.
138. Anderson, *Imagined Communities*.
139. Müller-Pohl, "Working the Nation State."
140. For an excellent study of the complicated relationship between imperialism and moral reform, see Tyrrell, *Reforming the World*.
141. Strong, *Story of the American Board*, 227.
142. Strong, *Story of the American Board*, esp. 168–72, 320–21, 430–33.
143. American Board of Commissioners for Foreign Missions, "Address to the Christian Public," 48.
144. A. N. Andrus, "The Missing Link," *Missionary Herald* 73, no. 3 (March 1877): 72.
145. Judson Smith, "The Crisis in Turkey," *Missionary Herald* 92, no. 11 (November 1896): 444.

146. M. A. Sherring, "Protestant Missions in India," quoted in "Providence in Missions: Number Two," *Missionary Herald* 73, no. 3 (March 1877): 67.
147. Smith, "The Missionary Outlook," xliv.
148. Smith, xlv.
149. "Extracts from Late Speeches," *Missionary Herald* 22, no. 8 (August 1826): 249.
150. Lev. 19:18 (NRSV). The account in Matthew depicts Jesus's elevation of this commandment thus: "When the Pharisees heard that he had silenced the Sadducees, they gathered together, and one of them, a lawyer, asked him a question to test him. 'Teacher, which commandment in the law is the greatest?' He said to him, "'You shall love the Lord your God with all your heart, and with all your soul, and with all your mind.' This is the greatest and first commandment. And a second is like it: "You shall love your neighbor as yourself." On these two commandments hang all the law and the prophets."' Matt. 22:34-40 (NRSV). Similar passages are found in Mark 12:28-43 (NRSV) and Luke 10:25-28 (NRSV).
151. Luke 10:25-37 (NRSV).
152. Dow, *History of Cosmopolite*, 463.
153. Finney, "Reproof a Christian Duty," 45 (emphasis mine). The text on which the sermon was based was "you shall reprove your neighbor, or you will incur guilt yourself." Lev. 19:17 (NRSV).
154. Taylor, *Sermon Preached at Northampton*, 12.
155. "Western Turkey Mission: The Distressing Famine," *Missionary Herald* 71, no. 3 (March 1875): 79.
156. Davis, "Our Present Responsibility."
157. Halttunen, "Humanitarianism and the Pornography of Pain in Anglo-American Culture."
158. Marvin, *When Old Technologies Were New*, 193.
159. Castelli, *Imitating Paul*, 15.
160. Castelli, 119.
161. American Board of Commissioners for Foreign Missions, *Report of the American Board*, 221.
162. Mr. Trowbridge quoted in "Albert Barnes and the Native Ministry," *Missionary Herald* 67, no. 6 (June 1871): 168.
163. Harris and Harris, *Letter from the Scene of the Recent Massacres in Armenia*, quoted in "Miscellany: Bibliographical," *Missionary Herald* 93, no. 7 (July 1897): 286.
164. Rufus Anderson to John Van Nest Talmage, March 7, 1850, American Board of Commissioners for Foreign Missions Archives, 8.1, vol. 2, p. 273, Houghton Library, Harvard University, quoted in Phillips, *Protestant America*, 261.
165. "Report of the Prudential Committee," 14.
166. Fessenden, *Culture and Redemption*, esp. "Protestant Expansion, Indian Violence, and Childhood Death: The New England Primer," 34-59.
167. Phillips, *Protestant America*, 23-33.

168. Cyrus Hamlin himself made significant contributions to US-British relations. When Hamlin saw that British soldiers were living and often dying in vermin-infested clothes and blankets during the Crimean War, he organized a laundry service for them. He even invented a makeshift washing machine to retain the washerwomen who initially fled when asked to touch the infested blankets. Hamlin also used the Bebek Seminary bakery to supply their hospitals and military stations with bread. Hamlin, *Among the Turks*, 228–39. According to Phillips, Hamlin's actions were the primary catalyst for the formation of the Turkish Mission Aid Society in London in 1854 to provide British aid to the efforts of the ABCFM in the Ottoman Empire. After the initial refusal by the British to support US missionary efforts, they contributed £2,000 to £2,500 annually for churches and schools in Turkey. Phillips, *Protestant America*, 163.

169. For an excellent study of the complicated, religiously informed relationship between the United States and Britain in the nineteenth century, see Carwardine, *Transatlantic Revivalism*.

170. Tyrrell, *Reforming the World*.

CHAPTER 2. THE GREAT FIZZLE

1. Kelley, *Oration Delivered by Hon. William D. Kelley*, 2.
2. See Otis, *Networking*.
3. Gitelman, *Always Already New*; Gitelman, *Scripts, Grooves, and Writing Machines*.
4. Crain, "Children of Media, Children as Media"; Lancaster, *Lancasterian System of Education*.
5. See Corrigan, "Habits from the Heart."
6. "Atlantic Telegraph: Absolute Success of the Enterprise," *New York Times*, August 9, 1858.
7. There is ample evidence that religious discourse and logics helped constitute these very publics in the United States. See Anderson, *Imagined Communities*; Fessenden, *Culture and Redemption*; Jakobsen and Pellegrini, *Secularisms*.
8. Kelley, *Oration Delivered by Hon. William D. Kelley*.
9. Savage to Cass; African Slave Trade; Howard, "Appendix H: Some American Slavers from Cuban Ports, 1857–1860," in *American Slavers and the Federal Law*, 246.
10. African Slave Trade.
11. "The Atlantic Telegraph: Probable Failure of the Enterprise," *New York Times*, August 10, 1865.
12. "Atlantic Telegraph: Absolute Success of the Enterprise."
13. "Atlantic Telegraph: Absolute Success of the Enterprise"; see also Briggs and Maverick, *Story of the Telegraph*, 193.
14. Briggs and Maverick, *Story of the Telegraph*, 193.
15. Briggs and Maverick, 245–50.
16. "Editorial Correspondence," *Weekly Wisconsin Patriot*, August 14, 1858.

17. Consideration of telegraphy as inherently public was particular to the US context. The French optical telegraph, for example, was a largely military venture and thus did not engage ideas of global or national publics in the same way. McCloy, *French Inventions of the Eighteenth Century*, 41–49.

18. "The public confidence, therefore, was great that the experiment would have a satisfactory termination, and that a triumph would be achieved unparalleled in the history of the world." "The Atlantic Telegraph," *San Antonio Ledger*, April 3, 1858.

19. Morse, Telegraphs for the United States (emphasis mine).

20. This definition is particularly influenced by Anderson, *Imagined Communities*; Laclau, *On Populist Reason*; Lundberg, *Lacan in Public*; Warner, *Publics and Counterpublics*.

21. Choi, *Gender and Mission Encounters in Korea*; Spigel, *Welcome to the Dreamhouse*; Kelly, "Personal Is Political"; Murphy, "Family Values."

22. Habermas, *Structural Transformation*, 30.

23. Anderson, *Imagined Communities*, 35.

24. Arendt, *The Human Condition*; Habermas, *Structural Transformation*; Anderson, *Imagined Communities*; Warner, *Publics and Counterpublics*.

25. Barad, *Meeting the Universe Halfway*, 3.

26. This particular description of the salient elements of protestantism and the lower-case term itself come from Sullivan, *Impossibility of Religious Freedom*, 8.

27. Laclau, *On Populist Reason*; Laclau, "Why Do Empty Signifiers Matter for Politics?"

28. "The Atlantic Telegraph: Probable Failure of the Enterprise."

29. For example, see descriptions of the 2010–11 labor strikes and acts of disobedience in Egypt in the effort to unseat President Hosni Mubarak as the "Facebook Revolution" such as that in Ghonim, *Revolution 2.0*; see also the mission statement of One Laptop per Child: "We aim to provide each child with a rugged, low-cost, low-power, connected laptop. . . . With access to this type of tool, children are engaged in their own education, learn, share, and create together. They become connected to each other, to the world and to a brighter future." "Mission of One Laptop per Child."

30. Jakobsen and Pellegrini, *Love the Sin*, esp. 45–73.

31. Laclau, *On Populist Reason*, 224.

32. Warner, *Publics and Counterpublics*, 8.

33. Lundberg, *Lacan in Public*, 3.

34. Lundberg, 2–3.

35. Supp-Montgomerie, "Affect and the Study of Religion," 336. This definition of affect draws on the following sources: Ahmed, *Promise of Happiness*; Brennan, *Transmission of Affect*; Grossberg, *We Gotta Get Out*; Lundberg, *Lacan in Public*. While often used interchangeably with "emotion," "affect" as used here is different from emotion in three critical ways. First, unlike emotion, affect does not well up from within an individual. Affect is social, moves among bodies, and helps

determine what subjectivities can emerge. Second, unlike emotion, affect does not signify something beyond itself, nor is it successfully represented in language, whereas "sadness," "anger," and "joy" appear to name emotions relatively well. Third, unlike emotion, affect gives critical texture to our social lives in ways that fundamentally determine who we are, how we live, and how we imagine the world we inhabit. Affect is addressed more directly later in this chapter.

36. Kelley, *Oration Delivered by Hon. William D. Kelley*, 2.
37. Kelley, 1.
38. Kelley, 2–3.
39. Kelley, 6.
40. Kelley, 11.
41. Kelley, 12.
42. The controversy over these forms of US imperialism demonstrates that none were sources of nationalist consensus. Howe, *What Hath God Wrought*, esp. 701–43. A rich account of the coining of "manifest destiny" and the erroneous attribution of the phrase to John O'Sullivan can be found in Hudson, *Mistress of Manifest Destiny*, 59–90.
43. Müller, *Wiring the World*.
44. Quoted in Prescott, *History, Theory, and Practice of the Electric Telegraph*, 189.
45. Morse, Telegraphs for the United States.
46. Morse, *Foreign Conspiracy against the Liberties*, 118.
47. Morse, *Imminent Dangers to the Free Institutions*.
48. "The Progress of Crime and Prejudice," *Israelite*, September 1, 1865.
49. Brigham Young and the First Presidency of the Church, "A Circular Letter of Instruction," November 9, 1865, quoted in Arrington, "Deseret Telegraph," 122.
50. Arrington, 117.
51. Arrington, 133.
52. Lussana, "Enslaved Men, the Grapevine Telegraph, and the Underground Railroad," chap. 5 in *My Brother Slaves*.
53. "Tubman: Conductor on the Greatest Railroad," *New York Age*, June 15, 1911.
54. George P. Rawick, Jan Hillegas, and Ken Lawrence, *American Slave: A Composite Autobiography*, supp. ser. 1, vol. 6, pt. 1, p. 11, quoted in Lussana, *My Brother Slaves*, 133.
55. Washington, *Up from Slavery*, 8. For additional examples, see "Hospitality," *Christian Recorder*, August 12, 1875; "A Banks County Row," *Constitution*, June 13, 1876; "Army Secret Service," *Boston Daily Globe*, January 25, 1885.
56. Du Bois, *Economic Co-operation among Negro Americans*, 32.
57. Loughran, *Republic in Print*, xvii.
58. Gilroy, *Black Atlantic*, 2.
59. Kelley, *Remarks of Hon. William D. Kelley*.
60. "Ships were the living means by which the points within that Atlantic world were joined. They were mobile elements that stood for the shifting spaces in between the fixed places that they connected. Accordingly they need to be thought of as

cultural and political units rather than abstract embodiments of the triangular trade. They were something more—a means to conduct political dissent and possibly a distinct mode of cultural production. The ship provides a chance to explore the articulations between the discontinuous histories of England's ports, its interfaces with the wider world. Ships also refer us back to the middle passage, to the half-remembered micro-politics of the slave trade and its relationship to both industrialisation and modernisation. As it were, getting on board promises a means to reconceptualise the orthodox relationship between modernity and what passes for its prehistory." Gilroy, *Black Atlantic*, 16–17.

61. "The Frigate Niagara and Her New Mission," *New York Times*, September 8, 1858; "Salting of the United States Frigate Niagara," *New York Times*, September 13, 1858; "The Voyage of the Frigate Niagara," *New York Times*, December 13, 1858.

62. Gilroy, *Black Atlantic*, 29.

63. Schwoch, *Wired into Nature*, 25.

64. Schwoch, 72–74.

65. Stolow, "Wired Religion."

66. The full text of President Buchanan's telegram to Queen Victoria: "The President cordially reciprocates the congratulations of her Majesty the Queen on the success of the great international enterprise, accomplished by the skill, science, and indomitable energy of the two countries. It is a triumph more glorious, because far more useful to mankind, than was ever won by conqueror on the field of battle. May the Atlantic Telegraph, under the blessing of Heaven, prove to be a bond of perpetual peace and friendship between the kindred nations, and an instrument destined by Divine Providence to diffuse religion, civilization, liberty, and law throughout the world. In this view will not all nations of Christendom spontaneously unite in the declaration that it shall be for ever neutral, and that its communications shall be held sacred in passing to the places of their destination, even in the midst of hostilities." "James Buchanan to Victoria."

67. "Our Foreign Correspondence," *New York Times*, October 1, 1858.

68. John, *Network Nation*, 98.

69. Morse, "Letter from S. F. B. Morse to the Hon. F. O. J. Smith," 81.

70. William Ellery Channing, "The Union," *Christian Examiner* 6, no. 2 (May 1829): 160. Richard John provides a particularly helpful genealogy of this term. John, *Network Nation*, 10.

71. For a full discussion of the political economy behind the establishment of telegraphy in the United States, see Blondheim, *News over the Wires*; John, *Network Nation*.

72. Blondheim, *News over the Wires*, 35.

73. Downey, *Telegraph Messenger Boys*, 22.

74. Bulletin of the Unites States Bureau of Labor, at 668.

75. Schwartz and Hayes, "A History of Transatlantic Cables," 44.

76. John, *Network Nation*, 6–7.

77. Benjamin Peters makes the compelling case that "whatever else the Internet is (interoperable, generative, nonproprietary, a platforms for other platforms), it is not public." Peters, *How Not to Network a Nation*, 201.
78. Styers, *Making Magic*, 17.
79. Styers, 18.
80. Styers, esp. chap. 4.
81. Lubar, "The Transformation of Antebellum Patent Law," 939.
82. Smith, "Electro-Magnetic Telegraphs," 2 (emphasis mine).
83. John, *Network Nation*, 11.
84. Hardinge, *Modern American Spiritualism*, 32.
85. Hardinge, 32.
86. Hardinge, 29.
87. Geoghegan, "Mind the Gap"; Noakes, "Telegraphy Is an Occult Art"; Sconce, *Haunted Media*; Sollors, "Dr. Benjamin Franklin's Celestial Telegraph"; Stolow, "Salvation by Electricity"; Stolow, "Wired Religion."
88. Stolow, "Wired Religion," 84.
89. Moore, "Spiritualism and Science," 476.
90. Geoghegan, "Mind the Gap," 906.
91. Geoghegan, 907.
92. Sollors, "Dr. Benjamin Franklin's Celestial Telegraph," 470.
93. Albanese, *Republic of Mind and Spirit*, 220–21.
94. Stolow, "Salvation by Electricity," 672.
95. Stolow, "Wired Religion," 82.
96. Hardinge, *Modern American Spiritualism*, 54.
97. Sollors, "Dr. Benjamin Franklin's Celestial Telegraph," esp. 477; Hardinge, *Modern American Spiritualism*, 532–36.
98. Sollors, "Dr. Benjamin Franklin's Celestial Telegraph," 463.
99. Davis, *Philosophy of Spiritual Intercourse*, 130.
100. Hardinge, *Modern American Spiritualism*, 22.
101. Stolow, "Salvation by Electricity," 683; Walker, "Humbug in American Religion," 37; see also Fowler, *New Testament "Miracles"*; Moore, "Spiritualism and Science."
102. Moore, "Spiritualism and Science," 497.
103. Davis, *Philosophy of Spiritual Intercourse*, 43.
104. Walker, "Humbug in American Religion," 38–39.
105. Walker, 38.
106. Walker, 38.
107. Walker, 36.
108. Walker, 30–31.
109. Walker.
110. Stolow, "Salvation by Electricity"; Stolow, "Wired Religion."
111. Fara, *Entertainment for Angels*, 116–22.
112. Morse, "Letter from S. F. B. Morse to the Hon. F. O. J. Smith."

113. Kelley, *Oration Delivered by Hon. William D. Kelley.*

114. For these and other names for electricity, see "Constantinople: Extracts from the Journal of the Mission," *Missionary Herald* 33, no. 11 (November 1837): 447; Kelley, *Oration Delivered by Hon. William D. Kelley*, 2.

115. *Congressional Globe*, 27th Cong., 3rd Sess., 323 (1843).

116. John, *Network Nation*, 48.

117. Smith, "Ben Franklin with a Key and a Kite?"

118. "The Atlantic Telegraph: Probable Failure of the Enterprise."

119. Downey, *Telegraph Messenger Boys*, 11.

120. John, *Network Nation*, 14.

121. McLuhan, *Understanding Media*, 8.

122. Downey, *Telegraph Messenger Boys*, 16.

123. Downey, 7.

124. Glover, "Cabot Straight Cable and 1857–58 Atlantic Cables."

125. Downey, *Telegraph Messenger Boys*, 23.

126. Downey, 23.

127. *Boston Atlas* reprinted in "Atlantic Telegraph: Absolute Success of the Enterprise."

128. Communication studies scholar William Keith locates the rise of discussion as the model for deliberation in the early twentieth century. This movement entailed three significant changes: a shift away from casual conversation, a shift toward populist participation, and the development of a site in which such formal, populist discussion could take place. Keith, *Democracy as Discussion*, 7.

129. "James Buchanan to Victoria"; Weingärtner, *Torchlight Procession*; Kelley, *Oration Delivered by Hon. William D. Kelley.*

130. Annelise Riles makes a similar point in her study of the network: "The effectiveness of the Network is generated by the Network's self-description. As we have seen, the naming of a Network is the existence of a Network, and the existence of a Network is synonymous with Action on its behalf . . . in other words, one need not show a link once one pronounces the existence of a network." Riles, *Network Inside Out*, 172.

131. Morse, Telegraphs for the United States.

132. Pred, *Urban Growth*, 38. Pred also notes that there is "extensive evidence . . . that by the mid-1840's news items were being transmitted between the cities in less than twenty-four hours by means of regular and special express" (11n3).

133. Blondheim, *News over the Wires*, 12n5.

134. Pred, *Urban Growth*, map 2.5, p. 41; map 2.6, p. 44; map 2.9, p. 51; table 2.4, p. 56.

135. Downey, *Telegraph Messenger Boys*, 21.

136. Otis, *Networking*, 25–29.

137. Unattributed quotation, "The Atlantic Telegraph," April 3, 1858.

138. John, *Network Nation*, 42.

139. Grossberg, *We Gotta Get Out*, 82–83.

140. Grossberg, 84.

141. "Our Foreign Correspondence."

142. Part of the European surprise at US enthusiasm was the understanding in England that this was not a US endeavor: "The contrast in the manner in which the news of the event was received in England and in America, was also very striking, and has been, as you will see, the occasion of comment in most of the London papers. The Times is quite indignant at the attempt of the Americans to monopolize the credit of the whole affair." "Our Foreign Correspondence."

143. Brian Massumi defines intensity, which he equates to affect, as "a nonconscious, never-to-be-conscious autonomic remainder." Massumi, *Parables for the Virtual*, 25.

144. "The Atlantic Cable Successfully Laid!!," *Farmer's Cabinet* 57, no. 2 (August 11, 1858): 2.

145. "Atlantic Telegraph: Absolute Success of the Enterprise" (emphasis mine).

146. "Atlantic Telegraph: Absolute Success of the Enterprise."

147. *Boston Atlas* quoted in "Atlantic Telegraph: Absolute Success of the Enterprise."

148. For example, the *New York Times* described the reaction of some as an ultimate explosion of suppressed celebration: "When, therefore, towards night the rumor was confirmed, no excitement followed. All were too eager in digesting the important fact itself to be excited. The subject was the all-absorbing topic of conversation everywhere during Friday and Saturday; and it was not until the confirmatory telegraphs of Saturday afternoon that the people dared give vent to their heretofore suppressed emotions—fearing, after all, that the news 'was too good to be true.' By Saturday evening the most sceptical were convinced and great was the rejoicing." "Atlantic Telegraph: Absolute Success of the Enterprise."

149. The idea of affect as pedagogical comes from Ahmed, *Promise of Happiness*; see also Berlant, *Cruel Optimism*.

150. "The Atlantic Telegraph," April 3, 1858.

151. "The Atlantic Telegraph: The Failure of the First Effort in Eighteen Hundred and Fifty-Eight," *New York Times*, August 7, 1858.

152. McLuhan understood the electric age to cause unifying mutual involvement: "The immediate prospect for literate, fragmented Western man encountering the electric implosion within his own culture is his steady and rapid transformation into a complex and depth-structured person emotionally aware of his total interdependence with the rest of human society." Or, more famously, "As electrically contracted, the globe is no more than a village." McLuhan, *Understanding Media*, 50–51, 5.

153. Blondheim, *News over the Wires*.

CHAPTER 3. THE END OF DISTANCE AND THE END OF WAR

1. The original edition of More's *Utopia* was prefixed by a letter from Peter Giles to Jerome de Busleyden in which Giles joins More in pretending the island is a real place. The letter includes the following: "More seems embarrassed not to be able to report the location of the island. Raphael made no attempt to conceal it, but he did mention it only briefly and incidentally, as if he was saving it for another time. And then unfortunately neither of us took in what he did say. For while Raphael

was talking about it one of More's servants came over and whispered something or other in his ear. Of course I listened all the more carefully, but one of the people present, who had, I think, caught a chill while at sea, coughed so loudly that he prevented me from hearing some of what Raphael was saying." Peter Giles to Jerome de Busleyden, 1516, in More, *Utopia*.

2. "'No-Place' (Utopia) I once was named, by reason of my solitude; / But now I rival Plato's state, perhaps exceed her, for / What he sketched out in words, that I alone exemplify / In men and skills, and the most excellent laws: / By the name of 'Happy Place' (Eutopia) / I do deserve to be called." More, 48.

3. For an excellent discussion of the relationship of the Erie Canal and revival Protestantism, see Rodriguez-Plate, "The Erie Canal and the Birth of American Religion."

4. "Extravagant excitement" comes from Charles Finney's description of a revival in *Charles G. Finney*, 78.

5. Rodriguez-Plate.

6. "Ocean Telegraph," *N.Y. Observer*, reprinted in "Ocean Telegraph," *Circular* 2, no. 2 (November 20, 1852): 1, 6. I arrived at the figure of 570 articles through keyword searches of the digital archive of the *Circular* available through the American Periodical Series accessed through ProQuest. I read each article to verify pertinent content.

7. G.W.N., "The World's Holiday," *Circular* 7, no. 29 (August 12, 1858): 114.

8. Smith, "The Missionary Outlook," 465.

9. "Hymn," *Circular* 7, no. 32 (September 2, 1858): 127.

10. I am referring here to Deleuze and Guattari's reading of utopia in Samuel Butler's Erewhon as now-here and not no-where. Deleuze and Guattari, *What Is Philosophy?*, 100; Butler, *Erewhon*.

11. G.W.N., "The World's Holiday."

12. "An Oneida Journal," *Circular* 7, no. 33 (September 9, 1858): 131.

13. Oneida Community, *Handbook of the Oneida Community*, 40.

14. Noyes describes his realization thus: "This view was altogether new and surprising to me; but accumulating proof was stronger than the fright of novelty, and at the end of the examination, my mind was clear. I no longer *conjectured* or *believed*, in the inferior sense of that word; but I knew that the time appointed for the Second Advent [coming of Christ] was within one generation from the time of Christ's personal ministry." Noyes, *Confessions of John H. Noyes*, 8. See also Noyes, *Religious Experience of John Humphrey Noyes*, 69–99; Thomas, *Man Who Would Be Perfect*, 27–28.

15. Noyes, *Berean*, 160–61.

16. "Advertisement 1—No Title," *Circular* 2, no. 89 (September 21, 1853): 1.

17. Kern, *Ordered Love*; Mandelker, *Religion, Society, and Utopia*; Robertson, *Oneida Community: The Breakup*; Oneida Community, *Handbook of the Oneida Community*.

18. Dieter, *Holiness Revival*, 15–16. In a sermon delivered on January 1, 1733, and later printed in his landmark text on perfectionism, Wesley defines holiness as

follows: "That habitual disposition of the soul which, in the sacred writings, is termed holiness, and which directly implies being cleansed from sin, from all filthiness both of flesh and spirit, and, by consequence, being endued with those virtues which were in Christ Jesus, being so renewed in the image of our mind, as to be perfect as our Father in heaven is perfect." Wesley, *Plain Account of Christian Perfection*, 4.

19. See Mandelker, *Religion, Society, and Utopia*; Pitzer, *America's Communal Utopias*.
20. Guarneri, *Utopian Alternative*, 81.
21. Fourier, *Design for Utopia*.
22. Fourier ultimately thought that "humankind would evolve through no less than thirty-two phases covering the 80,000-year life span of the globe." Guarneri, *Utopian Alternative*, 17.
23. Robertson, *Oneida Community: An Autobiography*, 23.
24. Our Special Correspondent, "The Oneida Community," *New-York Tribune*, May 1, 1867.
25. Nord, *Faith in Reading*, 5.
26. Wayland-Smith, *Oneida*, 4.
27. Noyes, *Free Love in Utopia*, 242.
28. Van de Warker, "Gynecological Study."
29. Hawley, *Special Love/Special Sex*; Herrick, *Desire and Duty at Oneida*; Noyes, *Free Love in Utopia*.
30. For reports on the telegraph as a mechanism of global unity, see "The Age of Unity." This article was printed in the *Circular* originally on July 11, 1852 (vol. 1, no. 35), and then reprinted on May 15, 1856 (vol. 5, no. 17), August 19, 1858 (vol. 7, no. 30; the day the newspaper reported on the success of the Atlantic Telegraph Cable), and November 27, 1862 (vol. 11, no. 42). See also "A Universal Language," *Home Journal*, reprinted in the *Circular* 2, no. 54 (May 21, 1853): 215; "Unity, the Measure of Power," *Circular* 2, no. 100 (October 29, 1853): 398; E. L. Blanchard, "Song of the Electric Telegraph," *Reynolds' Newspaper*, reprinted in the *Circular* 3, no. 96 (July 15, 1854): 384; T.L.P., "The Future of Commerce," *Circular* 7, no. 51 (January 13, 1859): 202; "Andrew Crosse, Electrician," *Circular* 1, no. 7 (May 2, 1864): 50; "The Good Time," *Circular* 6, no. 25 (September 6, 1869): 193–94. For uses of the telegraph as a metaphor for ideal communication with the heavens, see "About the Convention," *Circular* 1, no. 15 (February 15, 1852): 58; John Humphrey Noyes, "Table-Talk," *Circular* 1, no. 28 (May 23, 1852): 111; W., "Progress," *Circular* 2, no. 8 (December 11, 1852): 29–30; H.J.S., "Communications," *Circular* 3, no. 124 (September 19, 1854): 496; H.N.L., "Morning Thoughts," *Circular* 3, no. 141 (October 28, 1854): 564; J.R.M., "Lesson in a Telegraph Office," *Circular* 3, no. 22 (January 24, 1854): 87; E.G.H., "Community Paragraphs," *Circular* 7, no. 35 (September 23, 1858): 140; John Humphrey Noyes, "Noon Discourses," *Circular* 4, no. 11 (May 27, 1867): 81–82; John Humphrey Noyes, "Noon Discourses," *Circular* 4, no. 12 (June 3, 1867): 89–90; "The Good Time." For examples of the telegraph understood as a gift from God, see W., "Talk about the Press," *Circular* 2, no. 37 (March 23, 1853):

147; H.J.S., "A Look at Society," *Circular* 6, no. 47 (December 10, 1857): 186–87; "Our Relations to Inspiration," *Circular* 1, no. 2 (March 28, 1864): 10–12; "Ice-Treatment," *Circular* 1, no. 50 (March 6, 1865): 405; Z., "Broad Piety," *Circular* 2, no. 38 (December 4, 1865): 298; "The Second Coming of Christ: Its Significance as the Closing Event of the Apostolic Age," *Circular* 3, no. 37 (November 26, 1866): 291–92.

31. "An Oneida Journal," September 9, 1858.

32. "Hymn."

33. Oneida Community, *Handbook of the Oneida Community*, 46.

34. "An Oneida Journal," September 9, 1858.

35. For additional examples of the telegraph paralleled to the Oneidans' confrontation with impossibility, see "The Resurrection Change," *Circular* 3, no. 96 (July 15, 1854): 382; D., "Communism Illustrated in Nature," *Circular* 3, no. 99 (July 22, 1854): 395; A.W.C., "Preparation for the Kingdom of God," *Circular* 4, no. 14 (April 26, 1855): 53–54; "A Long Look Ahead," *Circular* 5, no. 25 (July 10, 1856): 100; C.S.J., "Give Communism a Chance," *Circular* 1, no. 43 (January 9, 1865): 337–38; G., "Malthus on Equality," *Circular* 3, no. 21 (August 6, 1866): 161–62; L., "'Twin Relics' Again," *Circular* 4, no. 33 (October 28, 1867): 263; G., "Signs of the Times," *Circular* 5, no. 52 (March 15, 1869): 411; H.J.S., "Providential Stirpiculture," *Circular* 7, no. 6 (April 25, 1870): 41–42.

36. "The Oneida Community," *Chicago Tribune*, May 1, 1870; "Going to Bed," *Chicago Tribune*, June 18, 1870; "Plurality or What?," *Minneapolis Daily Tribune*, May 29, 1873; "Communities in America," *New York Times*, June 7, 1876. A rare exception is an account by John Humphrey Noyes on the nomination of Rutherford B. Hayes for president. "The New Administration," *St. Louis Dispatch*, March 12, 1877.

37. "Financial Romance: How the O.C. Got Its Capital," *Circular* 2, no. 43 (January 8, 1866): 337–38; "The Oneida Community," *New York Herald*, June 6, 1869; "The Oneida Communists," *Chicago Tribune*, January 17, 1870; "Oneida's Queer People," *New York Times*, August 8, 1878; "The Oneida Community," *New York Times*, February 15, 1879; "Oneida Community," *New York Herald*, February 15, 1879.

38. Noyes, *Berean*, 150.

39. John Humphrey Noyes, "Without Impediment: Home-Talk by J.H.N., W.C. May 8, 1865," *Circular* 5, no. 48 (February 15, 1869): 377.

40. S.C.H., "Our Model of Association," *Circular* 7, no. 21 (June 17, 1858): 81.

41. "Harmonies of Science," *Circular* 4, no. 19 (May 31, 1855): 75.

42. "Headway of Civilization," *Circular* 4, no. 18 (May 24, 1855): 69–70 (emphasis mine).

43. H., "Moral Painting," *Circular* 2, no. 56 (May 28, 1853): 222; "A New Microscope of Astonishing Power," *Circular* 2, no. 5 (April 17, 1865): 39; "Photographic Printing and Engraving," *Circular* 12, no. 36 (November 5, 1863): 144; "Watchmaking by Machinery," *Circular* 8, no. 2 (February 3, 1859): 8.

44. "Perfection of the Atlantic Cables," *Circular* 3, no. 37 (November 26, 1866): 295.

45. "It was found by reference to the telegraph instrument that the current did not pass through the whole cable, and on stopping to discover the cause it was found that a nail in the shoe of one of the workmen had penetrated through the wire covering of the cable and the gutta-percha [a form of latex produced in Asia] coating of the conductor. Through the small opening produced in this way the electrical fluid had been dissipated and thus failed to make the circuit of the whole wire." Notably, the article continued in the very next sentence to hail the perfection of the device that caught the error: "The unerring certainty with which the telegraph indicator works in such cases is one of the most remarkable and interesting features of the science of telegraphing." "The Great Ocean Telegraph," *New York Herald*, April 20, 1858.

46. Board of Trade and the Atlantic Telegraph Company, *Report of the Joint Committee*, ix.

47. "The Atlantic Telegraph," *London Times*, March 11, 1858, reprinted in *New York Herald*, March 29, 1858, morning edition.

48. "The Atlantic Telegraph."

49. "General News," *Columbus Tri-Weekly Enquirer*, May 15, 1858.

50. "The Atlantic Telegraph," *New York Herald*, May 11, 1858. A similar incorporation of failure into success can be seen elsewhere in this article's discussion of splicing: "There is in fact no department of the work in which there is more skill and ingenuity displayed than in that of splicing; and it is particularly deserving of remark here that only in one instance during the last expedition was the cable known to part at a splicing. This, however, requires an explanation, from which it will be seen that the case was an extraordinary one, and such as under the new arrangement will not be likely to occur again. The splice had been made at the junction of the shore end of the cable with the deep sea line, and was not as perfect as could be desired, on account of the difference in size between the two portions, so that when subject to a strain it parted while in the act of passing over the wheels or sheaves of the paying out machine. The second attempt to join the two parts was, however, most successful, and by the aid of a hawser to relieve the spliced portion from any undue strain, it was lowered safely into the water. The continuity was found to have been unimpaired by the fracture, and the cable worked as well as if it had never been parted."

51. "The Age of Unity," *Circular* 1, no. 35 (July 11, 1852): 188; and reprinted in *Circular* 5, no. 17 (May 15, 1856): 66; *Circular* 7, no. 30 (August 19, 1858): 120 (this reprint occurred on the day the newspaper reported on the success of the Atlantic Telegraph Cable and included this note: "The following, which we reprint from the *Circular* of 1853, receives a new emphasis from the recent event."); and *Circular* 11 no. 42 (November 27, 1862): 166–67.

52. Noyes, *Berean*, 153.

53. Noyes, 157.

54. Noyes, 148–49.

55. Noyes, vii.

56. Noyes, 443.
57. Noyes, 446.
58. Noyes, 461.
59. Noyes, 461.
60. Noyes, 462.
61. Noyes, 444.
62. Noyes, 444, 446.
63. Fourier, *Design for Utopia*. For an example of the way the Oneida Community universalized its project, see A.W.C., "Preparation for the Kingdom of God." The only exceptions to this are some references to the telegraph enabling the kind of communication necessary for global democracy, as in "Democratic Theocracy," *Circular* 8, no. 50 (January 5, 1860): 167–68.
64. G.W.N., "The World's Holiday." This sentiment was affirmed by Edward Inslee, an Oneida Community member, who expressed his support for the meaning of the cable as unity in a letter then printed in the paper. E.R. Inslee, "Correspondence," *Circular* 7, no. 31 (August 26, 1858): 123.
65. "An Oneida Journal," *Circular* 7, no. 29 (August 12, 1858): 115; "The Age of Unity."
66. See G.W.N., "Future Telegraph Lines," *Circular* 7, no. 27 (July 29, 1858): 106; "A Universal Language."
67. "Andrew Crosse, Electrician."
68. Noyes, *Berean*, 341.
69. "An Oneida Journal," September 9, 1858.
70. J.L.S., "Article 1—No Title," *Circular* 6, no. 33 (September 3, 1857): 130.
71. "The Ocean Telegraph," *Circular* 5, no. 36 (September 25, 1856): 144.
72. "The Good Time."
73. Noyes, *Berean*, 143.
74. Blanchard, "Song of the Electric Telegraph."
75. Noyes, *Berean*, 27.
76. The Oneida Community, ultimately successful in its own commercial endeavors, did not see commerce as opposed to the kind of communism its members lived and advocated. Rather, they asserted: "It is an undoubted fact that the commercial intercourse of nations and individuals, is bringing men into new and closer relations of dependence and harmony; that it is bringing the wide world under the influence of civilization; that it is a mighty agency in the providence of God in preparing the way for the reign of human brotherhood and unity." T.L.P., "The Future of Commerce." Commerce was useful precisely by promoting another means for global unity. This early form of globalization, while particular to the Oneida Community, reflects a powerful and persistent enthusiasm for global commercial systems as a practice of global community implying unity where indeed there may be none.
77. T.L.P.
78. "Generalizing Faith," *Circular* 3, no. 117 (September 2, 1854): 467.
79. "About the Convention" (emphasis mine).

80. "Hymn."
81. "The Ocean Telegraph."
82. "The Atlantic Cable—The World Revolution Begun," *New York Herald*, August 6, 1858.
83. "An Oneida Journal," *Circular* 7, no. 30 (August 19, 1858): 119.
84. "An Oneida Journal," August 19, 1858.
85. "An Oneida Journal," August 19, 1858.
86. For other modern utopias that position the good place out of reach, see Butler, *Erewhon*; Voltaire, *Candide*.
87. Jameson, *Archaeologies of the Future*, xiii.
88. Jameson, "Politics of Utopia," 40.
89. Jameson, "Progress versus Utopia," 153.
90. Jameson, 153.
91. Jameson, *Archaeologies of the Future*, xiii.
92. Jameson, "Politics of Utopia," 36.
93. Jameson, *Archaeologies of the Future*, xv—xvin12.
94. Deleuze and Guattari, *What Is Philosophy?*, 108.
95. Deleuze and Guattari, "Geophilosophy," 112.
96. Jameson, *Archaeologies of the Future*, 228.
97. Noyes, *Berean*, 276.
98. Noyes does not specify exactly when this third coming will take place. See Noyes, 275–300; Noyes, *Putney Community*, 236.
99. Noyes, *Berean*, 335.
100. Boyer, *When Time Shall Be No More*, 82.
101. "Future Operations," *Advent Herald and Signs of the Times Reporter*, April 10, 1844.
102. William Miller, "Letter from WM. Miller," *Midnight Cry!*, December 5, 1844; see also Judd, "William Miller."
103. Butler, "Making of a New Order," 198.
104. Hamlin, *Among the Turks*, 22–23.
105. Hamlin, 308. Hamlin provides a lengthy description of his recommended treatment for cholera (305–12).
106. Hamlin, 313.
107. Hamlin, 19.
108. For example, see B. B. Wisner, "Proposed Enlargement of the Missions of the Board during the Present Year," *Missionary Herald* 29, no. 3 (March 1833): 108; "Northern Baptist Education Society," *Missionary Herald* 29, no. 7 (July 1833): 255; American Board of Commissioners for Foreign Missions, "Forty-Fourth Annual Meeting, Part 1," *Missionary Herald* 49, no. 11 (November 1853): 321.
109. American Board of Commissioners for Foreign Missions, "Thirty-Fifth Annual Meeting, Part 1," *Missionary Herald* 40, no. 10 (October 1844): 325.
110. William Kincaid, "National Beneficence the Safeguard of National Life," *Missionary Herald* 82, no. 12 (December 1886): 490.

111. Deferral famously serves as an important component of Jacques Derrida's *dif-férance,* a combination of the deferral and difference through which language functions. Unlike Derrida's usage of deferral to point to language's infinite postponement of the culmination of meaning, however, nineteenth-century US Protestants deferred a fixed and predictable end and understood that end to be on the cusp of arrival. Derrida, *Margins of Philosophy,* 1–27.

112. Otis, *Networking.*

113. "The Method of Progress," *Circular* 4, no. 15 (May 3, 1855): 58.

114. Smith, "China and Christian Missions," 490–91.

115. Hamlin, *Among the Turks,* 194.

116. Hamlin, 90.

117. Hamlin, 26–27.

118. Hamlin, 22 (emphasis mine).

119. "The Atlantic Telegraph," *London Times,* March 11, 1858, reprinted in *New York Herald,* March 29, 1858 (emphasis mine).

120. "The Atlantic Telegraph," *San Antonio Ledger,* April 3, 1858.

CHAPTER 4. "RECEIVED BUT NOT INTELLIGIBLE"

1. Mullaly, *Laying of the Cable,* 264.

2. Mullaly, 251 (emphasis mine).

3. Board of Trade and the Atlantic Telegraph Company, *Report of the Joint Committee,* 71.

4. Mullaly, *Laying of the Cable,* 274.

5. Mullaly, 254.

6. For metacommunication, see Ruesch and Bateson, *Communication*; for phatic communication, see Jakobson, "Closing Statement"; for a helpful discussion of the later definitions of "signal," see Mills, "On Disability and Cybernetics," 81–82.

7. The final words sent on the telegraph cable were sent from Valentia to Newfoundland and were received as: "C.W. Field, New York, please inform . . . government we are now in position to do best to forward . . ." Board of Trade and the Atlantic Telegraph Company, *Report of the Joint Committee,* 237.

8. Board of Trade and the Atlantic Telegraph Company, 231. While this is the most complete transcript of the telegrams available, it should be noted that it was provided to the committee by Colonel Tagliaferro Preston Shaffner, who was attempting to run a competing line between Europe and North America through Greenland. His attempt ultimately failed.

9. Board of Trade and the Atlantic Telegraph Company, 286–87.

10. Many have wondered if the Morse code for V is arranged to refer to the iconic opening notes of Beethoven's Fifth Symphony. While the link to Morse code is unproved, it is a helpful theme to the chapter both for its play between fate and victory and because, notably, of the notoriously difficult eighth rest that precedes the first notes. If that starting silence can echo here too, the tenuous

connection seems well worth it. Guerrieri, *First Four Notes*, 5, 212–13; see also Peters, *Speaking into the Air*, 6.

11. Peters, "Gaps of Which Communication Is Made," 130.
12. Board of Trade and the Atlantic Telegraph Company, *Report of the Joint Committee*, 220. Notably, he estimates that "the very best working lines" require at least 5 percent of messages for clarifications and management of the signal.
13. Engelder, "Three Principles of the Reformation"; Anderson, *Imagined Communities*; Eisenstein, "Emergence of Print Culture in the West."
14. Board of Trade and the Atlantic Telegraph Company, *Report of the Joint Committee*, 232.
15. Mullaly, *Laying of the Cable*, 277.
16. "Atlantic Telegraph: Absolute Success of the Enterprise."
17. Peters, *Marvelous Clouds*, 33.
18. Saussure, *Course in General Linguistics*, 66–67.
19. Saussure, 67–70, 120.
20. Saussure, 65–66, 111–12.
21. Saussure, 66.
22. Saussure, 9.
23. Saussure, 8–9.
24. Saussure, 10.
25. Saussure, 77.
26. Saussure, 15.
27. Saussure, 12, 15.
28. Saussure, 14.
29. Saussure, 9.
30. Cyrus Field, "Second Dispatch to the President," August 7, 1858, quoted in Briggs and Maverick, *Story of the Telegraph*.
31. Board of Trade and the Atlantic Telegraph Company, *Report of the Joint Committee*, 121, 232.
32. Peters, "Technology and Ideology," 146.
33. Saussure, *Course in General Linguistics*, 18.
34. Board of Trade and the Atlantic Telegraph Company, *Report of the Joint Committee*, 120.
35. Lacan, *Triumph of Religion*, 64.
36. Lacan, 64.
37. Lacan, 64–65.
38. Fink attributes this to Shelly Silver. Fink, "Knowledge and Jouissance," 34.
39. Lacan, *Television*, 3. Language's indebtedness to failure also forms a central point of Jacques Derrida's writings. See especially Derrida, *Margins of Philosophy*, 1–27, 207–71.
40. Fink, *Lacanian Subject*, 25.
41. Fink, *Clinical Introduction to Lacanian Psychoanalysis*, 42n3.
42. Lacan, *Seminar XX*, 19.

43. Fink, "Reading 'The Instance of the Letter in the Unconscious,'" 85.
44. Lacan, *Seminar XX*, 19–20.
45. Lacan, 20.
46. In *Seminar XX*, Lacan addresses the barring function of the signifier with respect to the signifier of the Other. While the Other holds a particular place in Lacanian thought, the barring action of the signifier can be read more broadly to constitute the symbolic register in general. Lacan, 28.
47. Lundberg, *Lacan in Public*, 99. The same principle applies to the imaginary register as well.
48. Board of Trade and the Atlantic Telegraph Company, *Report of the Joint Committee*, ix.
49. Lundberg provides a helpful discussion on how signs mediate the real, producing "reality," which one can experience as more real than the real itself. Lundberg, *Lacan in Public*, 100.
50. Lundberg, *Lacan in Public*, esp. 98–123.
51. Saussure, *Course in General Linguistics*, 66.
52. Saussure, 114.
53. Lacan's discussion of this can be found in Lacan, *Seminar XX*, 18–21.
54. Lacan, 19–21.
55. Lacan, "Instance of the Letters," 418.
56. Lacan, 419.
57. In a public lecture delivered to the Catholic Faculté Universitaire Saint-Louis in Brussels in 1960, Lacan suggests that "the purest example of signifiers are letters, typographical letters." Lacan, *Triumph of Religion*, 13. As his evidence, however, he mentions the ideograms of Chinese letters, which he parallels not to letters in the Latinate alphabet but to words: "Strictly speaking, meaning is born from a set of letters or words only insofar as it presents itself as a modification of their already received usage." The *V*s did not bear a legacy of usage; they were newly isolated as pulsing code. This echoes the bait and switch he appears to make in "The Instance of the Letter in the Unconscious," in which he insists that "letter" designates "the material medium that concrete discourse borrows from language." Lacan, "Instance of the Letter," 413. However, the simplicity he promises is elusive. The letter seems to stand in for the signifier or the "localized structure of the signifier." Lacan, 418; see also Fink, "Reading 'The Instance of the Letter in the Unconscious,'" 75–79. The letter and its materiality only matter insofar as they help to structure the unconscious, but not as a letter per se.
58. Lundberg, "Enjoying God's Death," 389.
59. Lacan, *Triumph of Religion*, 66.
60. Lacan, 66.
61. Lacan, 64. Here, he also states, "It's absolutely fabulous."
62. Mullaly, *Laying of the Cable*, 274.
63. Mullaly, 278.
64. Carey, *Communication as Culture*, 19.

65. Carey, 15.
66. Carey, 18.
67. Carey, 14.
68. Carey, 16.
69. Carey, 16.
70. Soderlund, "Communication Scholarship as Ritual."
71. Carey, *Communication as Culture*, 19.
72. Mullaly, *Laying of the Cable*, 248.
73. Mullaly, 150.
74. Carey, *Communication as Culture*, 28.
75. Carey, 19. Many thanks to E Cram for their reminder of Carey's use of architecture in the essay.
76. This reading also subjects ritual communication to Catherine Bell's critique of ritual in religious studies and anthropology as a form of social action that is distinct from thought but always based on a blueprint of conceptual activity. Bell, *Ritual Theory, Ritual Practice*, 19.
77. Carey, *Communication as Culture*, 18, 29. For his discussion of constructivism, see pp. 23–29.
78. Jakobson, "Closing Statement," 355. Jakobson credits Bronislaw Malinowski with the concept of "phatic communication."
79. Mullaly, *Laying of the Cable*, 277.
80. Carey, *Communication as Culture*, 17.
81. Carey, 16; see also p. 19.
82. Carey, 206.
83. Carey, 207–9, 204.
84. This phrasing is a play on Barad's attention to "the entanglement of matter and meaning" and reflects the indebtedness of my work to Barad, *Meeting the Universe Halfway*.
85. Edwards, "Infrastructure and Modernity," 186.
86. Peters, *Marvelous Clouds*, 38.
87. For the social processes involved with infrastructure, see Edwards, "Infrastructure and Modernity"; for materialist analysis as a consideration of the "slight surprise of action," see Latour, *Pandora's Hope*, 266–92; for the negotiation of environment through infrastructure, see Starosielski, *Undersea Network*.
88. Cram, *Violent Inheritance*.
89. Board of Trade and the Atlantic Telegraph Company, *Report of the Joint Committee*, xxxvii–xliv.
90. Board of Trade and the Atlantic Telegraph Company, 228.
91. Carey, *Communication as Culture*, 210.
92. Board of Trade and the Atlantic Telegraph Company, *Report of the Joint Committee*, 232.
93. Carey, *Communication as Culture*, 204.
94. Carey, 202.

95. Carey, 215.

96. Carey, 203.

97. Sterne, "Transportation and Communication," 118.

98. Carey, *Communication as Culture*, 15.

99. Marx, *Machine in the Garden*; Sterne, "Transportation and Communication," 125.

100. Sterne, "Transportation and Communication," 120.

101. Carey, *Communication as Culture*, 202.

102. Wiener, *Cybernetics*, 50.

103. Wiener, 50.

104. Wiener, 50.

105. Barad, "Posthumanist Performativity," 804.

106. Rouse, *Engaging Science*, 209, cited in Barad, "Posthumanist Performativity," 806.

107. Barad, "Posthumanist Performativity," 803.

108. Barad, *Meeting the Universe Halfway*, 141.

109. Board of Trade and the Atlantic Telegraph Company, *Report of the Joint Committee*, x.

110. Board of Trade and the Atlantic Telegraph Company, 228.

111. Board of Trade and the Atlantic Telegraph Company, 228.

112. Gunn and Rice, "About Face/Stuttering Discipline," 218.

113. "Atlantic Telegraph: Absolute Success of the Enterprise."

114. Briggs and Maverick, *Story of the Telegraph*, 186.

115. Briggs and Maverick, 187.

116. "Marconi's New Triumph," *Great Round World* 19, no. 278 (March 8, 1902): 242. With many thanks to Lisa Gitelman for this apt detail.

EPILOGUE

1. John, *Network Nation*, 2; Müller, *Wiring the World*.

2. Starosielski, *Undersea Network*, 40, 45.

3. Starosielski, 10.

4. "Despite the steady stream of corporate public relations advertising that trumpeted the possibilities of regional, interregional, and even transcontinental telephone service, the most relevant spatial unit for telephone service long remained neither the nation, nor even the region, but the locality." John, *Network Nation*, 11; Starosielski, *Undersea Network*.

5. Starosielski, *Undersea Network*, 8–9, 38.

6. Root-Servers.org, "FAQ," accessed August 3, 2020, https://root-servers.org; for a helpful discussion of the geopolitics of root servers, see Terranova, *Network Culture*, esp. 42–47.

7. Starosielski, *Undersea Network*, 11.

8. Starosielski, 6.

9. Starosielski, 17.

10. Starosielski, 67.

11. Graham and Thrift, "Out of Order," 5.

12. Graham and Thrift, 7.
13. Mejias, *Off the Network*, 10.
14. Mejias, 3.
15. John, *Network Nation*, 6–7.
16. Starosielski, *Undersea Network*, 50.
17. Board of Trade and the Atlantic Telegraph Company, *Report of the Joint Committee*, ix.
18. Sullivan, *Impossibility of Religious Freedom*, 8.
19. For a striking example of this, see Banet-Weiser, *Empowered*.

BIBLIOGRAPHY

HISTORICAL NEWSPAPERS CONSULTED
Citations for individual articles are given in the endnotes.
Advent Herald and Signs of the Times Reporter
Atlanta Constitution
Boston Daily Globe
Californian
Chicago Tribune
Christian Examiner
Christian Recorder
Chronicle of the London Missionary Society
Church at Home and Abroad
Circular
Columbus Tri-Weekly Enquirer
Congregational Quarterly
Constitution
Farmer's Cabinet
Great Round World
Harper's Weekly
Home Evangelization
Israelite
Lake Superior Miner
London Examiner
London Times
Midnight Cry!
Minneapolis Daily Tribune
Missionary Herald
Missionary Magazine and Chronicle
New York Age
New York Herald
New York Times
New-York Tribune
San Antonio Ledger
St. Louis Dispatch

St. Louis Post-Dispatch
Weekly Wisconsin Patriot

OTHER SOURCES

Abu-Manneh, Butrus. "The Islamic Roots of the Gulhane Rescript." *Die Welt Des Islams* 34, no. 2 (November 1994): 173–203.

Adas, Michael. *Dominance by Design: Technological Imperatives and America's Civilizing Mission*. Cambridge, MA: Harvard University Press, 2006.

African Slave Trade. H.R. Exec. Doc. 36–7. December 5, 1860.

Ahmed, Sara. *The Promise of Happiness*. Durham, NC: Duke University Press, 2010.

Aksan, Virginia H. "Ottoman Military and Social Transformations, 1826–28: Engagement and Resistance in a Moment of Global Imperialism." In *Empires and Autonomy: Moments in the History of Globalization*, edited by Stephen M. Streeter, John C. Weaver, and William D. Coleman, 61–78. Vancouver: University of British Columbia Press, 2010.

Albanese, Catherine L. *A Republic of Mind and Spirit: A Cultural History of American Metaphysical Religion*. New Haven, CT: Yale University Press, 2007.

American Board of Commissioners for Foreign Missions. "Address to the Christian Public." In *Minutes of the Third Annual Meeting (1812), in First Ten Annual Reports of the American Board of Commissioners for Foreign Missions, with Other Documents of the Board*. Boston: Crocker and Brewster, 1834.

———. *Report of the American Board of Commissioners for Foreign Missions Presented at the Thirty-Seventh Annual Meeting Held in New Haven, Connecticut, Sept. 8–11, 1846*. Boston: T. R. Marvin, 1846.

Anderson, Benedict. *Imagined Communities: Reflections on the Origin and Spread of Nationalism*. New York: Verso, 2006.

Anderson, Rufus. *Foreign Missions: Their Relations and Claims*. New York: Charles Scribner, 1869.

———. *Memorial Volume of the First Fifty Years of the American Board of Commissioners for Foreign Missions*. Boston: American Board of Commissioners for Foreign Missions, 1862.

Appadurai, Arjun. *Modernity at Large: Cultural Dimensions of Globalization*. Minneapolis: University of Minnesota Press, 1996.

Arendt, Hannah. *The Human Condition*. Chicago: University of Chicago Press, 1998.

Arrington, Leonard J. "The Deseret Telegraph—A Church-Owned Public Utility." *Journal of Economic History* 11, no. 2 (1951): 117–39.

Asad, Talal. *Formations of the Secular: Christianity, Islam, Modernity*. Stanford, CA: Stanford University Press, 2003.

Banet-Weiser, Sarah. *Empowered: Popular Feminism and Popular Misogyny*. Durham, NC: Duke University Press, 2018.

Barad, Karen. *Meeting the Universe Halfway: Quantum Physics and the Entanglement of Matter and Meaning*. Durham, NC: Duke University Press, 2007.

———. "Posthumanist Performativity: Toward an Understanding of How Matter Comes to Matter." *Signs: Journal of Women in Culture and Society* 28, no. 3 (March 2003): 801–31.

Beard, George M. *American Nervousness: Its Causes and Consequences; A Supplement to Nervous Exhaustion (Neurasthenia)*. New York: G. P. Putnam's Sons, 1881.

Becker, Adam H. *Revival and Awakening: American Evangelical Missionaries in Iran and the Origins of Assyrian Nationalism*. Chicago: University of Chicago Press, 2015.

Bektas, Yakup. "Displaying the American Genius: The Electromagnetic Telegraph in the Wider World." *British Journal for the History of Science* 34, no. 2 (June 2001): 199–232.

———. "The Sultan's Messenger: Cultural Constructions of Ottoman Telegraphy, 1847–1880." *Technology and Culture* 41, no. 4 (2000): 669–96.

———. "Telegraph." In *Encyclopedia of the Ottoman Empire*, edited by Gábor Ágoston and Bruce Alan Masters, 557–58. New York: Facts on File, 2009.

Bell, Catherine. *Ritual Theory, Ritual Practice*. New York: Oxford University Press, 2009.

Bennett, Jane. *Vibrant Matter: A Political Ecology of Things*. Durham, NC: Duke University Press, 2010.

Berlant, Lauren Gail. *Cruel Optimism*. Durham, NC: Duke University Press, 2011.

Blondheim, Menahem. *News over the Wires: The Telegraph and the Flow of Public Information in America, 1844–1897*. Cambridge, MA: Harvard University Press, 1994.

Board of Trade and the Atlantic Telegraph Company. *Report of the Joint Committee Appointed by the Lords of the Committee of Privy Council for Trade and the Atlantic Telegraph Company to Inquire into the Construction of Submarine Telegraph Cables; Together with the Minutes of Evidence and Appendix*. London: G. E. Eyre and W. Spottiswoode for Her Majesty's Stationery Office, 1861.

Bowker, Geoffrey C., and Susan Leigh Star. *Sorting Things Out: Classification and Its Consequences*. Cambridge, MA: MIT Press, 2000.

Boyer, Paul. *When Time Shall Be No More: Prophecy Belief in Modern American Culture*. Cambridge, MA: Harvard University Press, 1994.

Brennan, Teresa. *The Transmission of Affect*. Ithaca, NY: Cornell University Press, 2004.

Briggs, Charles F., and Augustus Maverick. *The Story of the Telegraph, and a History of the Great Atlantic Cable; A Complete Record of the Inception, Progress, and Final Success of That Undertaking. A General History of Land and Ocean Telegraphs. Descriptions of Telegraphic Apparatus, and Biographical Sketches of the Principal Persons Connected With the Great Work*. New York: Rudd and Carleton, 1858.

Bright, Charles. *Submarine Telegraphs: Their History, Construction, and Working. Founded in Part on Wünschendorff's "Traité de Télegraphie Sous-Marine" and Compiled from Authoritative and Exclusive Sources*. London: Crosby Lockwood and Son, 1898.

Brown, Candy Gunther. *The Word in the World: Evangelical Writing, Publishing, and Reading in America, 1789–1880*. Chapel Hill: University of North Carolina Press, 2004.

Bulletin of the United States Bureau of Labor 3, no. 18. H.R. Doc 55–206, pt. 5. September 1898.

Butler, Jonathan M. "The Making of a New Order: Millerism and the Origins of Seventh-Day Adventism." In *The Disappointed: Millerism and Millenarianism in the Nineteenth Century*, edited by Ronald L. Numbers and Jonathan M. Butler, 189–208. Knoxville: University of Tennessee Press, 1993.

Butler, Samuel. *Erewhon or, Over the Range*. Northridge, CA: Aegypan, 2009.

Carey, James W. *Communication as Culture: Essays on Media and Society*. New York: Routledge, 1992.

Carwardine, Richard. *Transatlantic Revivalism: Popular Evangelicalism in Britain and America, 1790–1865*. Waynesboro, GA: Paternoster, 2006.

Castelli, Elizabeth A. *Imitating Paul: A Discourse of Power*. Louisville, KY: John Knox, 1991.

Castells, Manuel. *The Rise of the Network Society*. 2nd ed. Malden, MA: Blackwell, 2000.

Castoriadis, Cornelius. *The Imaginary Institution of Society*. Translated by Kathleen Blamey. Cambridge, MA: MIT Press, 1998.

Certeau, Michel de. *The Practice of Everyday Life*. Translated by Steven Rendall. Berkeley: University of California Press, 1984.

Chen, Mel Y. *Animacies: Biopolitics, Racial Mattering, and Queer Affect*. Durham, NC: Duke University Press, 2012.

Chidester, David. *Savage Systems: Colonialism and Comparative Religion in Southern Africa*. Charlottesville: University of Virginia Press, 1996.

Choi, Hyaeweol. *Gender and Mission Encounters in Korea: New Women, Old Ways*. Berkeley: University of California Press, 2009.

Clark, N. G. "Our Great Trust." In *Seventy-First Annual Report of the American Board of Commissioners for Foreign Missions*, xii–xviii. Boston: Riverside, 1881.

Comaroff, Jean, and John L. Comaroff. *Of Revelation and Revolution*. Vol. 2, *The Dialectics of Modernity on a South African Frontier*. Chicago: University of Chicago Press, 1997.

Congressional Globe, 27th Cong., 3rd Sess., 1843.

Conroy-Krutz, Emily. *Christian Imperialism: Converting the World in the Early American Republic*. Ithaca, NY: Cornell University Press, 2015.

Corrigan, John. "'Habits from the Heart': The American Enlightenment and Religious Ideas about Emotion and Habit." *Journal of Religion* 73, no. 2 (April 1, 1993): 183–99.

Crain, Patricia. "Children of Media, Children as Media: Optical Telegraphs, Indian Pupils, and Joseph Lancaster's System for Cultural Replication." In *New Media, 1740–1915*, edited by Lisa Gitelman and Geoffrey Pingree, 61–89. Cambridge, MA: MIT Press, 2003.

Cram, E. *Violent Inheritance: Sexuality, Land, and the Making of the North American West*. Oakland: University of California Press, forthcoming.

Creighton, Donald. *Harold Adams Innis: Portrait of a Scholar*. Toronto: University of Toronto Press, 1957.

Curtis, Sarah A. "Charity Begins Abroad: The Filles de La Charité in the Ottoman Empire." In *In God's Empire: French Missionaries and the Modern World*, edited by Owen White and J. P. Daughton, 89–108. New York: Oxford University Press, 2012.

Davis, Andrew Jackson. *The Philosophy of Spiritual Intercourse: Being an Explanation of Modern Mysteries*. Boston: Colby and Rich, 1880.

Davison, Roderic H. *Essays in Ottoman and Turkish History, 1774–1923: The Impact of the West*. Austin: University of Texas Press, 1990.

Delbourgo, James. *A Most Amazing Scene of Wonders: Electricity and Enlightenment in Early America*. Cambridge, MA: Harvard University Press, 2006.

Deleuze, Gilles, and Félix Guattari. "Geophilosophy." In *What Is Philosophy?*, 85–113. Translated by Hugh Tomlinson and Graham Burchell. New York: Columbia University Press, 1994.

———. *A Thousand Plateaus: Capitalism and Schizophrenia*. Translated by Brian Massumi. Minneapolis: University of Minnesota Press, 2003.

———. *What Is Philosophy?* Translated by Hugh Tomlinson and Graham Burchell. New York: Columbia University Press, 1994.

Deringil, Selim. "The Invention of Tradition as Public Image in the Late Ottoman Empire, 1808 to 1908." *Comparative Studies in Society and History* 35, no. 1 (1993): 3–29.

———. "'They Live in a State of Nomadism and Savagery': The Late Ottoman Empire and the Post-colonial Debate." *Comparative Studies in Society and History* 45, no. 2 (April 2003): 311–42.

———. *The Well-Protected Domains: Ideology and the Legitimation of Power in the Ottoman Empire, 1876–1909*. New York: I. B. Tauris, 1999.

Derrida, Jacques. *Margins of Philosophy*. Translated by Alan Bass. Chicago: University of Chicago Press, 1982.

Dieter, Melvin E. *The Holiness Revival of the Nineteenth Century*. 2nd ed. Lanham, MD: Scarecrow, 1996.

Dow, Lorenzo. *History of Cosmopolite; or Journal of Lorenzo Dow, Containing His Experience and Travels from Childhood to 1814, Being Upwards of Thirty-Six Years*. Pittsburgh: Israel Rees, 1849.

Downey, Gregory J. *Telegraph Messenger Boys: Labor, Communication and Technology, 1850–1950*. New York: Routledge, 2002.

Du Bois, William Edward Burghardt, ed. *Economic Co-operation among Negro Americans: Report of a Social Study Made by Atlanta University under the Patronage of the Carnegie Institution of Washington, D.C.: Together with the Proceedings of the 12th Congress for the Study of the Negro Problems, Held at Atlanta University on Tuesday, May the 28th, 1907*. Atlanta: Atlanta University Press, 1907.

Echchaibi, Nabil. "Islam, Mediation, and Technology." In *The Handbook of Communication History*, edited by Peter Simonson, Janice Peck, Robert T. Craig, and John Jackson, 441–52. New York: Routledge, 2013.

Edwards, Paul. "Infrastructure and Modernity: Force, Time, and Social Organization in the History of Sociotechnical Systems." In *Modernity and Technology*, edited by

Thomas J. Misa, Philip Brey, and Andrew Feenberg, 185–225. Cambridge, MA: MIT Press, 2004.

Edwards, Paul N., Geoffrey C. Bowker, Steven J. Jackson, and Robin Williams. "Introduction: An Agenda for Infrastructure Studies." *Journal of the Association for Information Systems* 10, no. 5 (2009): 364–74.

Eisenstein, Elizabeth. "The Emergence of Print Culture in the West." *Journal of Communication* 30, no. 1 (1980): 99–106.

Engelder, Theodore. "The Three Principles of the Reformation: Sola Scriptura, Sola Gratia, Sola Fides." In *Four Hundred Years; Commemorative Essays on the Reformation of Dr. Martin Luther and Its Blessed Results, in the Year of the Four-hundredth Anniversary of the Reformation*, edited by William Herman Theodore Dau, 97–109. St. Louis: Concordia, 1916.

Fara, Patricia. *An Entertainment for Angels: Electricity in the Enlightenment.* New York: Columbia University Press, 2002.

Fessenden, Tracy. *Culture and Redemption: Religion, the Secular, and American Literature.* Princeton, NJ: Princeton University Press, 2007.

Fink, Bruce. *A Clinical Introduction to Lacanian Psychoanalysis: Theory and Technique.* Cambridge, MA: Harvard University Press, 1999.

———. "Knowledge and Jouissance." In *Reading Seminar XX: Lacan's Major Work on Love, Knowledge, and Feminine Sexuality*, edited by Bruce Fink and Suzanne Barnard, 21–45. Albany: State University of New York Press, 2002.

———. *The Lacanian Subject: Between Language and Jouissance.* Princeton, NJ: Princeton University Press, 1995.

———. "Reading 'The Instance of the Letter in the Unconscious.'" In *Lacan to the Letter: Reading Ecrits Closely*, 63–105. Minneapolis: University of Minnesota Press, 2004.

Finney, Charles Grandison. *Charles G. Finney: An Autobiography.* Westwood, NJ: Fleming H. Revell, 1876.

———. "Reproof a Christian Duty." In *Lectures to Professing Christians: Delivered in the City of New York in the Years 1836 and 1837*, 44–56. New York: John S. Taylor, 1837.

Fourier, Charles. *Design for Utopia: Selected Writings of Charles Fourier.* Translated by Julia Franklin. New York: Schocken Books, 1971.

Fowler, J. H. *New Testament "Miracles," and Modern "Miracles": The Comparative Amount of Evidence for Each, the Nature of Both, Testimony of a Hundred Witnesses.* 2nd ed. Boston, 1856.

Friedman, Thomas L. *The World Is Flat: A Brief History of the Twenty-First Century.* New York: Farrar, Straus and Giroux, 2005.

Gaonkar, Dilip Parameshwar. "Toward New Imaginaries: An Introduction." *Public Culture* 14, no. 1 (January 2002): 1–19.

Geoghegan, Bernard Dionysius. "Mind the Gap: Spiritualism and the Infrastructural Uncanny." *Critical Inquiry* 42, no. 4 (June 2016): 899–922.

Geyer, Michael, and Charles Bright. "World History in a Global Age." *American Historical Review* 100, no. 4 (October 1995): 1034–60.

Ghonim, Wael. *Revolution 2.0: The Power of the People Is Greater Than the People in Power: A Memoir*. New York: Houghton, Mifflin, Harcourt, 2012.

Gilroy, Paul. *The Black Atlantic: Modernity and Double-Consciousness*. Cambridge, MA: Harvard University Press, 1993.

Gitelman, Lisa. *Always Already New: Media, History, and the Data of Culture*. Cambridge, MA: MIT Press, 2008.

———. "Modes and Codes: Samuel F. B. Morse and the Question of Electronic Writing." In *This Is Enlightenment*, edited by Clifford Siskin and William Warner. Chicago: University of Chicago Press, 2010.

———. *Scripts, Grooves, and Writing Machines: Representing Technology in the Edison Era*. Stanford, CA: Stanford University Press, 2000.

Glover, Bill. "Atlantic Cables: 1856–2012." History of the Atlantic Cable and Undersea Communications from the First Submarine Cable of 1850 to the Worldwide Fiber Optic Network. Last modified June 15, 2020. http://atlantic-cable.com.

———. "Cabot Straight Cable and 1857–58 Atlantic Cables." History of the Atlantic Cable and Undersea Communications from the First Submarine Cable of 1850 to the Worldwide Fiber Optic Network. Last modified May 27, 2019. http://atlantic-cable.com.

Gould, Peter. "Dynamic Structures of Geographic Space." In *Collapsing Space and Time: Geographic Aspects of Communications and Information*, edited by Stanley D. Brunn and Thomas R. Leinbach, 3–30. London: HarperCollinsAcademic, 1991.

Graham, Stephen, and Nigel Thrift. "Out of Order: Understanding Repair and Maintenance." *Theory, Culture and Society* 24, no. 3 (May 2007): 1–25.

Greyser, Naomi. *On Sympathetic Grounds: Race, Gender, and Affective Geographies in Nineteenth-Century North America*. New York: Oxford University Press, 2017.

Grossberg, Lawrence. *We Gotta Get Out of This Place: Popular Conservatism and Postmodern Culture*. New York: Routledge, 1992.

Guarneri, Carl J. *The Utopian Alternative: Fourierism in Nineteenth-Century America*. Ithaca, NY: Cornell University Press, 1991.

Guerrieri, Matthew. *The First Four Notes: Beethoven's Fifth and the Human Imagination*. New York: Knopf, 2012.

Gunn, Joshua, and Jenny Edbauer Rice. "About Face/Stuttering Discipline." *Communication and Critical/Cultural Studies* 6, no. 2 (June 2009): 215–19.

Habermas, Jürgen. *Structural Transformation of the Public Sphere: An Inquiry into a Category of Bourgeois Society*. Translated by Thomas Burger and Frederick Lawrence. Cambridge, MA: MIT Press, 1991.

Halttunen, Karen. "Humanitarianism and the Pornography of Pain in Anglo-American Culture." *American Historical Review* 100, no. 2 (April 1995): 303–34.

Hamlin, Cyrus. *Among the Turks*. New York: Robert Carter and Brothers, 1878.

———. *My Life and Times*. 2nd ed. Boston: Congregational Sunday-School and Publishing Society, 1893.

Hardinge, Emma. *Modern American Spiritualism: A Twenty Years' Record of the Communion between Earth and the World of Spirits*. 3rd ed. New York: The author, 1870.

Harris, J. Rendel, and Helen B. Harris. *Letter from the Scene of the Recent Massacres in Armenia*. New York: Fleming H. Revell, 1897.

Hawley, Victor. *Special Love/Special Sex: An Oneida Community Diary*. Edited by Robert S. Fogarty. Syracuse, NY: Syracuse University Press, 1994.

Headrick, Daniel. "A Double-Edged Sword: Communications and Imperial Control in British India." *Historical Social Research/Historische Sozialforschung* 35, no. 1 (2010): 51–65.

Herrick, Tirzah Miller. *Desire and Duty at Oneida: Tirzah Miller's Intimate Memoir*. Edited by Robert S. Fogarty. Bloomington: Indiana University Press, 2000.

Hoover, Stewart M. *Religion in the Media Age*. New York: Routledge, 2006.

Hopkins, Mark. "Semi-centennial Discourse." In *Memorial Volume of the First Fifty Years of the American Board of Commissioners for Foreign Missions*, edited by Rufus Anderson, 9–36. 5th ed. Boston: The Board, 1862.

Howard, Warren. *American Slavers and the Federal Law: 1837–1862*. Berkeley: University of California Press, 1963.

Howe, Daniel Walker. *What Hath God Wrought: The Transformation of America, 1815–1848*. Oxford: Oxford University Press, 2009.

Hudson, Linda S. *Mistress of Manifest Destiny: A Biography of Jane McManus Storm Cazneau, 1807–1878*. Austin: Texas State Historical Association, 2001.

Hurewitz, J. C. *The Middle East and North Africa in World Politics: A Documentary Record*. 2nd ed. New Haven, CT: Yale University Press, 1975.

Jakobsen, Janet R., and Ann Pellegrini. "Introduction: Times Like These." In *Secularisms*, edited by Janet R. Jakobsen and Ann Pellegrini, 1–38. Durham, NC: Duke University Press, 2008.

———. *Love the Sin: Sexual Regulation and the Limits of Religious Tolerance*. New York: NYU Press, 2003.

———, eds. *Secularisms*. Durham, NC: Duke University Press, 2008.

Jakobson, Roman. "Closing Statement: Linguistics and Poetics." In *Style in Language*, edited by Thomas A. Sebeok, 350–77. Cambridge, MA: MIT Press, 1960.

Jameson, Fredric. *Archaeologies of the Future: The Desire Called Utopia and Other Science Fictions*. New York: Verso, 2005.

———. "The Politics of Utopia." *New Left Review* 25 (2004): 35–54.

———. "Progress versus Utopia; Or, Can We Imagine the Future?" *Science Fiction Studies* 9, no. 2 (1982): 147–58.

Jessup, Henry Harris. *Fifty Three Years in Syria*. Vol. 1. New York: Fleming H. Revell, 1910.

———. *Fifty Three Years in Syria*. Vol. 2. New York: Fleming H. Revell, 1910.

John, Richard R. *Network Nation: Inventing American Telecommunications*. Cambridge, MA: Harvard University Press, 2010.

Jones, Steven. "MCI TV Ad 1997." Accessed November 22, 2017. https://www.youtube.com/watch?v=ioVMoeCbrig.

Judd, Wayne R. "William Miller: Disappointed Prophet." In *The Disappointed: Millerism and Millenarianism in the Nineteenth Century*, edited by Ronald L. Numbers and Jonathan M. Butler, 17–35. Knoxville: University of Tennessee Press, 1993.

Keith, William M. *Democracy as Discussion: Civic Education and the American Forum Movement*. New York: Lexington Books, 2007.

Kelley, William D. *Oration Delivered by Hon. William D. Kelley at the Celebration of the Laying of the Atlantic Cable, Held at Philadelphia, September 1, 1858*. N.p., 1858.

———. *Remarks of Hon. William D. Kelley, of Pennsylvania, in Opposition to the Employment of Slaves in Navy-Yards, Arsenals, Dock-Yards, Etc., and in Favor of the Pacific Railroad, Delivered to the House of Representatives May 9, 1862*. Washington, DC: Scammell, 1862.

Kelly, Christopher J. "'Personal Is Political.'" In *Encyclopedia of Gender and Society*, edited by Jodi O'Brien, 635–36. Thousand Oaks, CA: Sage, 2009.

Kern, Louis J. *An Ordered Love: Sex Roles and Sexuality in Victorian Utopias: The Shakers, the Mormons, and the Oneida Community*. Chapel Hill: University of North Carolina Press, 1981.

King, Richard. *Orientalism and Religion: Postcolonial Theory, India, and "The Mythic East."* New York: Routledge, 2007.

Kittler, Friedrich A. *Gramophone, Film, Typewriter*. Stanford, CA: Stanford University Press, 1999.

Klassen, Pamela E. *The Story of Radio Mind: A Missionary's Journey on Indigenous Land*. Chicago: University of Chicago Press, 2018.

Lacan, Jacques. "The Instance of the Letter in the Unconscious, or Reason since Freud." In *Écrits: The First Complete Edition in English*, translated by Bruce Fink, 412–41. New York: Norton, 2006.

———. *The Seminar, Book XX, Encore: On Feminine Sexuality: The Limits of Love and Knowledge*. Edited by Jacques-Alain Miller. Translated by Bruce Fink. New York: Norton, 1999.

———. *Television: A Challenge to the Psychoanalytic Establishment*. New York: Norton, 1980.

———. *The Triumph of Religion, Preceded by Discourse to Catholics*. Translated by Bruce Fink. Cambridge: Polity, 2013.

Laclau, Ernesto. *On Populist Reason*. New York: Verso, 2005.

———. "Why Do Empty Signifiers Matter to Politics?" In *Emancipation(s)*, 36–46. New York: Verso, 2007.

Lancaster, Joseph. *The Lancasterian System of Education, with Improvements*. Baltimore: Published for the author, and sold only at the Lancasterian Institute, 1821.

Latour, Bruno. *An Inquiry into Modes of Existence: An Anthropology of the Moderns*. Translated by Catherine Porter. Cambridge, MA: Harvard University Press, 2013.

———. *Pandora's Hope: Essays on the Reality of Science Studies*. Cambridge, MA: Harvard University Press, 1999.

———. *Reassembling the Social: An Introduction to Actor-Network-Theory*. New York: Oxford University Press, 2005.

Levine, Caroline. *Forms: Whole, Rhythm, Hierarchy, Network*. Oxford: Oxford University Press, 2015.

Longworth-Dunbar, Alex. "'Increasing a Hundred-Fold the Distresses of Humanity': A History of Negative Representations of the Telegraph, 1837–1914." Master's thesis, University of Manchester, 2018.

Loughran, Trish. *The Republic in Print: Print Culture in the Age of U.S. Nation Building, 1770–1870.* New York: Columbia University Press, 2007.

Low, Michael Christopher. "Ottoman Infrastructures of the Saudi Hydro-State: The Technopolitics of Pilgrimage and Potable Water in the Hijaz." *Comparative Studies in Society and History* 57, no. 4 (October 2015): 942–74.

Lubar, Steven. "The Transformation of Antebellum Patent Law." *Technology and Culture* 32, no. 4 (1991): 932–59.

Lundberg, Christian. "Enjoying God's Death: The Passion of the Christ and the Practices of an Evangelical Public." *Quarterly Journal of Speech* 95, no. 4 (November 2009): 387–411.

———. *Lacan in Public: Psychoanalysis and the Science of Rhetoric.* Tuscaloosa: University of Alabama Press, 2012.

Lussana, Sergio A. *My Brother Slaves: Friendship, Masculinity, and Resistance in the Antebellum South.* Lexington: University Press of Kentucky, 2016.

Mahmood, Saba. "Can Secularism Be Other-wise?" In *Varieties of Secularism in a Secular Age,* edited by Michael Warner, Jonathan VanAntwerpen, and Craig Calhoun, 282–99. Reprint, Cambridge, MA: Harvard University Press, 2013.

Mandelker, Ira L. *Religion, Society, and Utopia in Nineteenth-Century America.* Amherst: University of Massachusetts Press, 1984.

Marchand, Philip. *Marshall McLuhan: The Medium and the Messenger.* Revised, subsequent edition. Cambridge, MA: MIT Press, 1998.

Marvin, Carolyn. *When Old Technologies Were New: Thinking about Electric Communication in the Late Nineteenth Century.* New York: Oxford University Press, 1988.

Marx, Leo. *The Machine in the Garden: Technology and the Pastoral Ideal in America.* New York: Oxford University Press, 1964.

———. "Technology: The Emergence of a Hazardous Concept." *Technology and Culture* 51, no. 3 (2010): 561–77.

Massumi, Brian. *Parables for the Virtual: Movement, Affect, Sensation.* Durham, NC: Duke University Press Books, 2002.

Masuzawa, Tomoko. *The Invention of World Religions, or, How European Universalism Was Preserved in the Language of Pluralism.* Chicago: University of Chicago Press, 2005.

McCloy, Shelby T. *French Inventions of the Eighteenth Century.* Lexington: University Press of Kentucky, 2014.

McLuhan, Marshall. *Understanding Media: The Extensions of Man.* New York: Signet, 1964.

McMillan, Robert. "Sharks Want to Bite Google's Undersea Cables." *Wired,* August 15, 2014. Accessed August 23, 2017. www.wired.com.

Mejias, Ulises Ali. *Off the Network: Disrupting the Digital World.* Minneapolis: University of Minnesota Press, 2013.

Miller, Donald L. *Lewis Mumford: A Life.* New York: Grove Press, 2002.

Mills, Mara. "On Disability and Cybernetics: Helen Keller, Norbert Wiener, and the Hearing Glove." *Differences* 22, no. 2–3 (January 2011): 74–111.

Minawi, Mostafa. "Beyond Rhetoric: Reassessing Bedouin-Ottoman Relations along the Route of the Hijaz Telegraph Line at the End of the Nineteenth Century." *Journal of the Economic and Social History of the Orient* 58, no. 1–2 (2015): 75–104.

"Mission of One Laptop per Child." Accessed March 5, 2013. http://one.laptop.org.

Modern, John Lardas. *Secularism in Antebellum America.* Chicago: University of Chicago Press, 2015.

Moore, R. Laurence. "Religion, Secularization, and the Shaping of the Culture Industry in Antebellum America." *American Quarterly* 41, no. 2 (June 1989): 216–42.

———. "Spiritualism and Science: Reflections on the First Decade of the Spirit Rappings." *American Quarterly* 24, no. 4 (1972): 474–500.

More, Thomas. *Utopia.* Edited and translated by David Wooten. Indianapolis: Hackett, 1999.

Morgan, David. *The Lure of Images: A History of Religion and Visual Media in America.* New York: Routledge, 2007.

Morse, Samuel Finley Breese. "Bound Volume—18 May 1847–28 January 1848." 1848. Samuel Finley Breese Morse Papers, 1793–1944. Library of Congress.

———. *Foreign Conspiracy against the Liberties of the United States. The Numbers of Brutus, Originally Published in the New-York Observer, Revised and Corrected with Notes, by the Author.* New York: Leavitt, Lord, 1835.

———. *Imminent Dangers to the Free Institutions of the United States through Foreign Immigration, and the Present State of the Naturalization Laws: A Series of Numbers, Originally Published in the New-York Journal of Commerce.* New York: E. B. Clayton, 1835.

———. "Letter from S. F. B. Morse to the Hon. F. O. J. Smith, February 15, 1838." In *The American Electro Magnetic Telegraph: With the Reports of Congress, and a Description of All Telegraphs Known, Employing Electricity or Galvanism,* by Alfred Vail, 80–82. Philadelphia: Lea and Blanchard, 1845.

———. *Telegraphs for the United States.* H.R. Doc. 25–15. 1837.

Morus, Iwan Rhys. *Frankenstein's Children: Electricity, Exhibition, and Experiment in Early-Nineteenth-Century London.* Princeton, NJ: Princeton University Press, 2016.

Mullaly, John. *The Laying of the Cable, or the Ocean Telegraph; Being a Complete and Authentic Narrative of the Attempt to Lay the Cable across the Entrance to the Gulf of St. Lawrence in 1855, and of the Three Atlantic Telegraph Expeditions of 1857 and 1858: With a Detailed Account of the Mechanical and Scientific Part of the Work, as Well as Biographical Sketches of Messrs. Cyrus W. Field, William E. Everett, and Other Prominent Persons Connected with the Enterprise.* New York: D. Appleton, 1858.

Müller, Simone M. *Wiring the World: The Social and Cultural Creation of Global Telegraph Networks.* New York: Columbia University Press, 2016.

Müller-Pohl, Simone. "*Working* the Nation State: Submarine Cable Actors, Cable Transnationalism and the Governance of the Global Media System, 1858–1914." In

The Nation State and Beyond: Governing Globalization Processes in the Nineteenth and Early Twentieth Centuries, edited by Isabella Löhr and Roland Wenzlhuemer, 101–23. New York: Springer, 2013.

Murphy, Andrew. "Family Values." In *The Encyclopedia of Political Science*, edited by George Thomas Kurian, 559. Washington, DC: CQ Press, 2011.

Nadis, Fred. *Wonder Shows: Performing Science, Magic, and Religion in America*. New Brunswick, NJ: Rutgers University Press, 2005.

Noakes, Richard J. "Telegraphy Is an Occult Art: Cromwell Fleetwood Varley and the Diffusion of Electricity to the Other World." *British Journal for the History of Science* 32, no. 4 (1999): 421–59.

Nord, David Paul. *Faith in Reading: Religious Publishing and the Birth of Mass Media in America*. New York: Oxford University Press, 2004.

Noyes, George. *Free Love in Utopia: John Humphrey Noyes and the Origin of the Oneida Community*. Edited by Lawrence Foster. Urbana: University of Illinois Press, 2001.

Noyes, George Wallingford, ed. *John Humphrey Noyes: The Putney Community*. Oneida, NY: 1931.

———, ed. *Religious Experience of John Humphrey Noyes, Founder of the Oneida Community*. Freeport, NY: Books for Libraries Press, 1971.

Noyes, John Humphrey. *The Berean: A Manual for the Help of Those Who Seek the Faith of the Primitive Church*. Putney, VT: Office of the Spiritual Magazine, 1847.

———. *Confessions of John H. Noyes, Part 1: Confession of Religious Experience: Including a History of Modern Perfectionism*. Oneida Reserve, NY: Leonard, 1849.

Obach, Eugene. *Cantor Lectures on Gutta Percha. Delivered November 29, December 6, 13, 1897*. London: William Trounce, 1898.

One of the Secretaries of the American Tract Society. *Home Evangelization: A View of the Wants and Prospects of Our Country, Based on the Facts and Relations of Colportage*. New York: American Tract Society, 1849.

Oneida Community. *Handbook of the Oneida Community, 1867 & 1871 Bound with Mutual Criticism*. New York: AMS Press, 1976.

Otis, Laura. *Networking: Communicating with Bodies and Machines in the Nineteenth Century*. Ann Arbor: University of Michigan Press, 2001.

Parikka, Jussi. "New Materialism as Media Theory: Medianatures and Dirty Matter." *Communication and Critical/Cultural Studies* 9, no. 1 (March 2012): 95–100.

Parks, Lisa. *Cultures in Orbit: Satellites and the Televisual*. Durham, NC: Duke University Press, 2005.

———. "Technostruggles and the Satellite Dish: A Populist Approach to Infrastructure." In *Cultural Technologies: The Shaping of Culture in Media and Society*, edited by Göran Bolin, 64–84. New York: Routledge, 2012.

Parks, Lisa, and Nicole Starosielski, eds. *Signal Traffic: Critical Studies of Media Infrastructures*. Urbana: University of Illinois Press, 2017.

Perkins, Justin. *A Residence of Eight Years in Persia, among the Nestorian Christians; with Notices of the Mohammedans*. Andover, MA: Allen, Morrill and Wardwell, 1843.

Peters, Benjamin. *How Not to Network a Nation: The Uneasy History of the Soviet Internet*. Cambridge, MA: MIT Press, 2017.

Peters, John Durham. "The Gaps of Which Communication Is Made." *Critical Studies in Mass Communication* 11, no. 2 (June 1994): 117–40.

———. *The Marvelous Clouds: Toward a Philosophy of Elemental Media*. Chicago: University of Chicago Press, 2015.

———. "Mormonism and Media." In *The Oxford Handbook of Mormonism*, edited by Terry L. Givens and Philip L. Barlow, 407–20. New York: Oxford University Press, 2015.

———. *Speaking into the Air: A History of the Idea of Communication*. Chicago: University of Chicago Press, 1999.

———. "Technology and Ideology: The Case of the Telegraph Revisited." In *Thinking with James Carey: Essays on Communications, Transportation, History*, edited by Jeremy Packer and Craig Robertson, 137–55. New York: Peter Lang, 2006.

Peters, Rudolph. "Religious Attitudes towards Modernization in the Ottoman Empire: A Nineteenth-Century Pious Text on Steamships, Factories, and the Telegraph." *Die Welt Des Islams* 26, no. 1/4 (1986): 76–105.

Phillips, Clifton. *Protestant America and the Pagan World: The First Half Century of the American Board of Commissioners for Foreign Missions, 1810–1860*. Cambridge, MA: East Asian Research Center at Harvard University, 1969.

Picker, John M. "Atlantic Cable." *Victorian Review* 34, no. 1 (2008): 34–38.

Pitzer, Donald E., ed. *America's Communal Utopias*. Chapel Hill: University of North Carolina Press, 1997.

Pred, Allan. *Urban Growth and the Circulation of Information: The United States System of Cities, 1790–1840*. Cambridge, MA: Harvard University Press, 1973.

Prescott, George. *History, Theory, and Practice of the Electric Telegraph*. Boston: Ticknor and Fields, 1860.

"Report of the Prudential Committee." In *Report of the American Board of Commissioners for Foreign Missions, Presented at the Forty-Fifth Annual Meeting, Held in Hartford, Connecticut, September 12–15, 1854*, 12–25. Boston: T. R. Marvin, 1854.

Riles, Annelise. *The Network Inside Out*. Ann Arbor: University of Michigan Press, 2001.

Robertson, Constance Noyes, ed. *Oneida Community: An Autobiography, 1851–1876*. Syracuse, NY: Syracuse University Press, 1970.

———, ed. *Oneida Community: The Breakup, 1876–1881*. Syracuse, NY: Syracuse University Press, 1972.

Rodriguez-Plate, S. Brent. "The Erie Canal and the Birth of American Religion." *Religion News Service* (blog), June 30, 2017. https://religionnews.com.

Rouse, Joseph. *Engaging Science: How to Understand Its Practices Philosophically*. Ithaca, NY: Cornell University Press, 1996.

Ruesch, Jurgen, and Gregory Bateson. *Communication: The Social Matrix of Psychiatry*. New Brunswick, NJ: Transaction, 2006.

Said, Edward. *Orientalism*. New York: Vintage Books, 1979.

Salt, Jeremy. "Trouble Wherever They Went: American Missionaries in Anatolia and Ottoman Syria in the Nineteenth Century." *Muslim World* 92, no. 3–4 (2002): 287–313.

Şapolyo, Enver Behnan. *Kemal Atatürk ve Milli Mücadele Tarihi.* Istanbul: Rafet Zaim-
ler Yayınevi, 1958.

Saussure, Ferdinand de. *Course in General Linguistics.* Edited by Charles Bally and Albert Sechehaye. Translated by Wade Baskin. New York: Philosophical Society, 1959.

Savage, Thomas. Thomas Savage to Lewis Cass, No. 51, August 7, 1859. In African Slave
Trade. H.R. Exec. Doc. 36–7, at 200. December 5, 1860.

Schwartz, Mischa, and Jeremiah Hayes. "A History of Transatlantic Cables." *IEEE Communications Magazine* 46, no. 9 (September 2008): 42–48.

Schwoch, James. *Wired into Nature: The Telegraph and the North American Frontier.*
Urbana: University of Illinois Press, 2018.

Sconce, Jeffrey. *Haunted Media: Electronic Presence from Telegraphy to Television.* Durham, NC: Duke University Press, 2000.

Shahvar, Soli. "Iron Poles, Wooden Poles: The Electric Telegraph and the Ottoman–
Iranian Boundary Conflict, 1863–1865." *British Journal of Middle Eastern Studies* 34,
no. 1 (April 2007): 23–42.

———. "Tribes and Telegraphs in Lower Iraq: The Muntafiq and the Baghdad–Basrah
Telegraph Line of 1863–65." *Middle Eastern Studies* 39, no. 1 (January 2003): 89–116.

Simonson, Peter. "Assembly, Rhetoric, and Widespread Community: Mass Communication in Paul of Tarsus." *Journal of Media and Religion* 2, no. 3 (August 2003): 165–82.

Smith, Francis Ormand Jonathan. "Electro-Magnetic Telegraphs (To Accompany Bill
H.R. No. 713)." House Report. 25th Cong., 2nd Sess., April 6, 1838. Serial Set Vol.
No. 335, Session Vol. No. 3.

Smith, Judson. "Missionary Outlook." In *Eightieth Annual Report of the American
Board of Commissioners for Foreign Missions. Presented at the Meeting Held at Minneapolis, Minnesota. October 8–11, 1890,* xlii–xlix. Boston: Samuel Usher, 1890.

Smith, Kiona N. "Ben Franklin with a Key and a Kite?" *Forbes,* June 15, 2017. www.
forbes.com.

Soderlund, Gretchen. "Communication Scholarship as Ritual: An Examination of
James Carey's Cultural Model of Communication." In *Thinking with James Carey:
Essays on Communications, Transportation, History,* edited by Jeremy Packer and
Craig Robertson, 101–16. New York: Peter Lang, 2006.

Sollors, Werner. "Dr. Benjamin Franklin's Celestial Telegraph, or Indian Blessings to
Gas-Lit American Drawing Rooms." *American Quarterly* 35, no. 5 (Winter, 1983):
459–80.

Soukup, Paul A. "Contexts of Faith: The Religious Foundation of Walter Ong's Literacy
and Orality." *Journal of Media and Religion* 5, no. 3 (August 2006): 175–88.

Spigel, Lynn. *Welcome to the Dreamhouse: Popular Media and Postwar Suburbs.* Durham, NC: Duke University Press, 2001.

Starosielski, Nicole. *The Undersea Network.* Durham, NC: Duke University Press,
2015.

Sterne, Jonathan. "Transportation and Communication: Together as You've Always Wanted Them." In *Thinking with James Carey: Essays on Communications, Transportation, History*, edited by Jeremy Packer and Craig Robertson, 117–35. New York: Peter Lang, 2006.

Stolow, Jeremy. *Orthodox by Design: Judaism, Print Politics, and the ArtScroll Revolution*. Berkeley: University of California Press, 2010.

———. "Religion and/as Media." *Theory, Culture and Society* 22, no. 4 (August 2005): 119–45.

———. "Salvation by Electricity." In *Religion: Beyond a Concept*, edited by Hent De Vries, 668–86. New York: Fordham University Press, 2008.

———. "Wired Religion: Spiritualism and Telegraphic Globalization in the Nineteenth Century." In *Empires and Autonomy: Moments in the History of Globalization*, edited by Stephen Streeter, John Weaver, and William D. Coleman, 79–92. Vancouver: University of British Columbia Press, 2010.

Strong, William E. *The Story of the American Board: An Account of the First Hundred Years of the American Board of Commissioners for Foreign Missions*. New York: Pilgrim, 1910.

Styers, Randall. *Making Magic: Religion, Magic, and Science in the Modern World*. New York: Oxford University Press, 2004.

Sullivan, Winnifred Fallers. *The Impossibility of Religious Freedom*. Princeton, NJ: Princeton University Press, 2005.

Supp-Montgomerie, Jenna. "Affect and the Study of Religion." *Religion Compass* 9, no. 10 (October 2015): 335–45.

TallBear, Kim. *Native American DNA: Tribal Belonging and the False Promise of Genetic Science*. Minneapolis: University of Minnesota Press, 2013.

Taylor, Charles. *Modern Social Imaginaries*. Durham, NC: Duke University Press, 2004.

Taylor, James. *A Sermon Preached at Northampton before the Hampshire Missionary Society: At Their Annual Meeting, August 20, 1818*. Northampton, MA: Thomas W. Shepard, 1818.

Terranova, Tiziana. *Network Culture: Politics for the Information Age*. London: Pluto, 2004.

Thomas, Robert David. *The Man Who Would Be Perfect: John Humphrey Noyes and the Utopian Impulse*. Philadelphia: University of Pennsylvania Press, 1977.

Tompkins, Kyla Wazana. *Racial Indigestion: Eating Bodies in the 19th Century*. New York: NYU Press, 2012.

Tsotsis, Alexia. "RIAA Goes Offline, Joins MPAA as Latest Victim of Successful DDoS Attacks." *TechCrunch* (blog), September 19, 2010. http://social.techcrunch.com.

Tyrrell, Ian. *Reforming the World: The Creation of America's Moral Empire*. Reprint, Princeton, NJ: Princeton University Press, 2013.

Van de Warker, Ely. "A Gynecological Study of the Oneida Community." *American Journal of Obstetrics and Diseases of Women and Children* 17, no. 8 (August 1884): 785–810.

Veer, Peter van der. Introduction to *Conversion to Modernities: The Globalization of Christianity*, edited by Peter van der Veer, 1–21. New York: Routledge, 1996.

Voltaire. *Candide, or, Optimism*. Translated by Robert M. Adams. New York: Norton, 1991.

Walker, David. "The Humbug in American Religion: Ritual Theories of Nineteenth-Century Spiritualism." *Religion and American Culture: A Journal of Interpretation* 23, no. 1 (March 1, 2013): 30–74.

Warner, Michael. *Publics and Counterpublics*. New York: Zone Books, 2005.

Washington, Booker T. *Up from Slavery: An Autobiography*. New York: A. L. Burt, 1901.

Wayland-Smith, Ellen. *Oneida: From Free Love Utopia to the Well-Set Table*. New York: Picador, 2016.

Weiner, Isaac. *Religion Out Loud: Religious Sound, Public Space, and American Pluralism*. New York: NYU Press, 2013.

Wesley, John. *A Plain Account of Christian Perfection, as Believed and Taught, by the Rev. Mr. John Wesley, from the Year 1725, to the Year 1777*. 7th ed. Dublin: Robert Napper, 1794.

Wiener, Norbert. *Cybernetics*. New York: Wiley, 1948.

Williams, Raymond. *Keywords: A Vocabulary of Culture and Society*. Rev. ed. New York: Oxford University Press, 2015.

———. *Marxism and Literature*. New York: Oxford University Press, 1977.

———. *Television: Technology and Cultural Form*. New York: Schocken Books, 1975.

Wilson, Ara. "The Infrastructure of Intimacy." *Signs: Journal of Women in Culture and Society* 41, no. 2 (December 2015): 247–80.

Winthrop-Young, Geoffrey, Ilinca Iurascu, and Jussi Parikka, eds. "Cultural Techniques." Special issue, *Theory, Culture and Society* 30, no. 6 (November 2013).

Wosh, Peter J. *Spreading the Word: The Bible Business in Nineteenth-Century America*. Ithaca, NY: Cornell University Press, 1994.

Wozniak, Robert H. *Mind and Body: René Descartes to William James*. Exhibition catalog. Bethesda, MD: National Library of Medicine; Washington, DC: American Psychological Association, 1992.

INDEX

Page numbers in *italics* denote illustrations.

ABOUT THE AUTHOR

Jenna Supp-Montgomerie is Assistant Professor of Religion and Media, jointly appointed in the Department of Religious Studies and the Department of Communication Studies at the University of Iowa.